Understanding Your International Students

Understanding Your International Students

An Educational, Cultural, and Linguistic Guide

Jeffra Flaitz, Editor

Leslie Kosel Eckstein

Kimberly S. Kalaydjian

Ariadne Miranda

Deborah A. Mitchell

Amna Mohamed

Barbara Smith-Palinkas

Jerome York, Jr.

L. Elizabeth Zollner

Ann Arbor
THE UNIVERSITY OF MICHIGAN PRESS

To all our students at the English Language Institute
(University of South Florida, Tampa),
who have become our teachers

Copyright © by the University of Michigan 2003
All rights reserved
ISBN 0-472-08866-1
Published in the United States of America by
The University of Michigan Press
Manufactured in the United States of America

2011   2010   2009   2008   6   5   4   3

ISBN 978-0-472-08866-9

Preface

In *The Power of Myth* (New York: Doubleday, 1988), Bill Moyers asks anthropologist Joseph Campbell to explain the striking similarities that exist in the stories, folk tales, and myths that are shared by cultures that are "far, far apart." Campbell responds:

> One explanation is that the human psyche is essentially the same all over the world. The psyche is the inward experience of the human body, which is essentially the same in all human beings, the same organs, the same instincts, the same impulses, the same conflicts, the same fears. Out of this common ground have come what Jung has called the archetypes.... All over the world and at different times of human history, these archetypes ... have appeared in different costumes. The differences in the costumes are the results of environmental and historical conditions. (51–52)

It is helpful to perceive in the behavior and traditions of people from other cultures certain universal strivings. There is no denying, however, that the superficial manifestation of these impulses—or "costumes," to use Joseph Campbell's metaphor—can hoist up formidable obstacles to tapping into those reassuring, resonating universals. Just ask those who have a modicum of cross-cultural experience. They will recount episodes of bewilderment and frustration, hilarity and wonder, brought on by the flawed assumption of sameness or the ignorance of difference. Information appears to help. Even tidbits of information that capture the essence of cultural differences can have a profound effect on our ability to adjust our expectations, emotional reactions, and coping strategies.

One summer when I was feeling particularly exasperated, I assigned my ESL students a role play. I had in my class a smattering of Latin American, East European, Korean, and Taiwanese students and a large cluster of young Japanese women. It was by far the least cohesive and most reticent group I had ever encountered. I believe they dreaded coming to class as much as I did. Attempting to address the growing affective malaise, I divided the group into cultural subsections and asked them to come to class the following day prepared to show us a typical classroom in their home cultures, complete with typical teacher behaviors, typical student behaviors, typical dress, and so on. The exercise transformed us all. Its success lay in the concrete, observable details, while the underlying values were left for us to contemplate or simply assimilate on our own. Readers will find vignettes such as this one in the "Personal Snapshot" segment of each chapter, and the voices heard may come from the authors themselves, from students, or from individuals who were interviewed during the preparation of this book.

Understanding Your International Students will help its readers to give more than a respectful nod to the notion of cultural differences. It cites specific circumstances that may give rise to *culture bumps,* and it will deepen readers' capacity to address the significance of the cross-cultural discrepancies that they encounter. Moreover, it provides strategies for coping with cultural differences in the classroom. Each chapter closes with a "Problem/Solution" segment that provides the reader with classroom-based descriptions of specific problems, brief discussions about the root causes of the problems, and advice on how to address and possibly resolve the problems. Some of the problems presented are introduced in this segment for the first time in the chapter. Others represent a reiteration of a problem highlighted elsewhere in the chapter yet perceived to be sufficiently characteristic, complex, or downright daunting. As insights, questions, other problems, and possible solutions present themselves while reading or during the course of interacting with internationals, readers are encouraged to note them at the end of each chapter in the section called "My Observations."

This book addresses the educational, cultural, and linguistic backgrounds of international students who today, in unprecedented numbers, are living and studying in English-speaking countries. Acknowledging that school, home, and language intersect in every student's life, the authors have treated each area, providing kernels of information that will be of use and interest to teachers, counselors, administrators, and service personnel who interact with students from abroad.

The benefits accruing to the aforementioned professionals will hopefully be transparent even before this book is read. The countless teachers at all levels of the educational system who encounter learners from one or more of the 16 countries described herein can use this volume as a tool to demystify student behaviors that are culture-based; to prepare lessons geared to the unique needs, expectations, or background of a given student; to quickly locate basic information about the educational setting from which a student comes; and to make use of the specific strategies presented in the "Problem/ Solution" segment of each chapter. Even teachers who do not normally have nonnative English speakers in their classes will find this book of use and interest. With diversity virtually the issue of the day in education, teachers will find in this book a broad array of cultural facts, issues, anecdotes, and perceptions to launch an entire series of diversity units over the course of several years. Finally, teachers of teachers will regard this book as a handy reference and training manual in teacher preparation programs in colleges and universities throughout the country.

But the usefulness of *Understanding Your International Students* extends beyond the classroom. How much better could mental health counselors, academic advisors, administrative and clerical staff, and medical and security personnel at all levels of the educational system serve their nonnative English-speaking constituencies if they were equipped with this easily digestible compendium of cross-cultural insights?

No doubt, in-depth study of each culture we encounter would generate a superior, more profound understanding of cultural differences. Indeed, the authors recognized and experienced the difficulty of describing a construct as complex as culture via brief expository paragraphs, and they tried mightily to avoid overgeneralization and underrepresentation as they conducted their research and compared and synthesized their findings. The result is a collection of perceptions and recurrent observations balanced by institutional data from official government sources. Although the book contains significant detail, it does not attempt to attain any other goal than to introduce the reader to the countries selected. It is intended to sensitize the reader to the myriad differences that exist among schools and students around the world, to pique his or her interest in deeper cultural exploration, and to provide encouragement and support for effective cross-cultural problem solving.

The authors began forming this book by consulting a publication called *Open Doors: Report on International Educational Exchange* released annually by the Institute of International Education. *Open Doors* provided data as to the countries of origin of foreign students studying in the United States and, more specifically, the numbers of students enrolled in Intensive English Programs (IEPs) in the United States. Korea, Japan, Taiwan, Saudi Arabia, Colombia, and Brazil, among other countries, figure strongly in the mix. Further research led us to expand our list to include learners of English in elementary, middle, and secondary schools. Haiti and Vietnam are not prominently represented in the university-level IEP rosters, but in such states as Florida and New York, the Haitian and Vietnamese student populations are of considerable size in K–12 settings. We also looked for emerging trends, such as the influx of East European students in the nation's public schools; thus, the chapters on Russia and Poland.

The authors—either in pairs or individually—then assumed responsibility for preparing their chapters by using the same, agreed-on strategy for collecting data. In addition to consulting country-specific books (academic and nonacademic), journal articles, government documents, encyclopedias, and on-line resources, authors conducted hours of interviews with representatives of their assigned countries. Fellow ESL and EFL teachers, both in the United States and abroad, also offered valuable information, insights, and anecdotes about the students, schools, and cultural settings with which they had grown familiar and by which they were fascinated.

Readers may notice that a handful of the chapters in this volume contain quite a bit more detail than the others. Specifically, Japan, Cuba, and Vietnam were targeted for more comprehensive treatment. Because Japan has been one of the largest and most consistent "exporters" of students to U.S. schools and because of the stature of Japan in the international arena, the authors believed that a particularly close look at the country, its schools, and its students would be both warranted and appreciated. Cuba and Vietnam represent a somewhat different perspective: we considered the inaccessibility of these settings to the majority of the book's readers. Unlike Taiwan or Saudi Arabia, Cuba and Vietnam do not receive significant numbers of foreign tourists or delegations of teachers. We hoped to offer information, observations, and insights that those working with international students might otherwise find difficult to obtain. Information about five additional countries—Kuwait, Venezuela, Thailand, Turkey, and United Arab Emirates—has been placed on the University of Michigan Press website rather than in this book. Kuwait's profile is remarkably similar to that of Saudi Arabia, which is included in this volume, and much of what we encountered in researching Venezuela is described in our chapter on Colombia. An abbreviated profile of Thailand gives Web users a glimpse of this fascinating culture. Regardless of the relative accessibility of information, we certainly learned much. We are delighted to share our discoveries with interested readers.

Acknowledgments

The authors wish to thank the following individuals for the cultural and linguistic information and insights they offered as this book was researched.

Brazil: Vera Mello, Jomara Oliveira, Philip Smith, Karen Squillaro, Maria Augusta Vaz

Colombia: Andrés Mejia, Gloria Moreno, Ana Patricia Restrepo, María Díaz Vega

Côte d'Ivoire: Moulaye Kone, Stefane Kone, William Martin, Papa Ahmadou Sarr, Ramatou Traore

Cuba: Norma T. Caltagirone, Roberto Castillero, Amaurys Fernandez, Owen Martinez, Carlos A. Suarez, Iliana Valdez

Egypt: Nader Anis, Mohamed al-Dahoud, Anan Faten, Marshall Mitchell, Dr. Leslie E. Sheldon and students from English Language Teaching Department at the University of Strathclyde (Glasgow, Scotland); Dr. Hoda Zaki

French language: Dr. Carine Feyten, Dr. Lise Lawson, Dr. Christine Probes, Dr. Roberta Tucker

Haiti: Cindy Aldrich, Linda Counts, Marjorie Delli, Paul LeCorde, Steve Medvedeff, Linda Stargel

Japan: Hitomi Furuno, Yuko Hagihara, Hitomi Iramina, Nobaru Iwata, Yuri Nobugaki, Dr. Shirley E. Ostler, Yoshihiro Sakamoto, Midori Toyoshima, Dr. Makoto Yoshii, Ikumi Yoshimoto

Korea: Jae Pil Chong, In Ae Chun, Seosun Lee, Joo Yeon Lee, Yujin Lee, Eunwook Park, Scott Redfern, Sung Wook Yi

Mexico: Robin Gomez, Veronica Hernandez, Ruth Roux-Rodriguez

Morocco: Dr. Merton L. Bland, Fatima Bouiamr, Soundous Cherradi, Mourad Fikri

People's Republic of China: Walter Lu, Liu Xiaomin, Dr. Wei Zhu

Poland: Dr. Jacob Caflisch, Lt. Col. (Ret.) Joyce A. Halstrom, Alvina Jankowski, Dr. Barbara Malinowska-Jolley, Ela Nowicki, I. Pajak, M. Pajak, J. Pieniek, S. Reichfelder

Russia: Natalia Nikolskaia, Dr. Victor Peppard

Saudi Arabia: Ahmad al-Hamrani, Wessam Jamjoom, Ghaida Kaziha, Mansour al-Manea, Kayum McDoom, Laila McDoom, Mosad al-Mehbash, Raeed al-Mohammed, Reem al-Mohammed, Fahad al-Musaibah, Hani al-Rayes, Mansor al-Saraf, Saeed al-Shafa, Fawaz al-Zayer

Taiwan: Bill Algeo, Ying-feng Chen, James Green

Vietnam: Tran Hung A., Hien Bui, Hoang Van Bui, Joseph Castellana, Kim Chi, Kelly Curtwright, Khang Dinh, Charles Eckstein, Alicia Ellison, Dr. Donna Nelson-Beene, Dinh Q. Nguyen, Hahn Nguyen, Cecilia Pham, Phuong Vu, Carolyn Young

Contents

Brazil

 Focus on Brazil

Capital: Brazilia

Population: 172,860,370

Size: 3,286,478 sq. mi. (8,511,965 sq. km.)

Location: South America, bordering the Atlantic Ocean

Climate: mostly tropical, but temperate in the south; average daytime temperatures 60 to 90 degrees Fahrenheit. The Amazon Basin, covering half of the country, receives rain daily.

Monetary Unit: real

Urban/Rural Life: 79% urban; greatest population along the Atlantic coast

Religion: 80% Roman Catholic

Languages: Portuguese (official), Spanish, English, French

Ethnicity: 55% white (Portuguese, German, Italian, Spanish, Polish), 38% mixed black and white, 6% black, 1% other (Amerindian, Japanese, Arab)

Government: federal republic (the Federal District of Brazilia plus 26 states retaining certain powers)

 Personal Snapshot

"Are there snakes on the streets where you live?" One of my ESL students told me that she was very amused by the stereotypical views that her classmates had had of Brazil. She said that some of the other "funny" questions that people from other countries had asked her were: "Do you have telephones and the Internet?" "Is it true that at every corner on the street there's a man from the mafia carrying a gun?" "Are there monkeys where you live?"

"Brazil is not just a rain forest," she exclaimed. "Furthermore, São Paulo is the third largest city in the world!" In fact, she has never been in the rain forest. Because of Brazil's size (it is the fifth largest country in the world), it would be difficult for someone to visit all of the nation's tourist spots. Moreover, most people live along the Atlantic coast, far away from the rain forest.

In addition, Brazil is divided into five distinct regions (the North, the Northeast, the Midwest, the Southeast, and the South), and there are different traditional foods, dialects, music, dance, weather, and economical situations in each region. Some people say that there is more than one Brazil inside Brazil.

⭐ Cultural Closeup

- European, African, and Amerindian cultures have blended over the last 500 years through Portuguese colonization, slavery, and the presence of Roman Catholic missionaries.

- Much of the architecture and literature reflects European patterns, whereas the food, music, art, and folklore have definite influences from Africans and Native Americans.

- Folklore about magical beasts or people is very popular. One story from this genre is about a boylike creature called Curupira whose feet are reversed so that the toes point backward. He protects animals by leading hunters in the wrong direction as they try to follow his footprints.

- Brazilians value being informal, outgoing, pleasant, tolerant, warm, and spontaneous.

- Traditional values and societal norms include machismo and a strong patriarchal family, but today's modern society also supports equality and women's rights. While Brazilians are comfortable with progressive ideas and practices, they are also prudent, and the eldest man in the family will usually be consulted for major decisions.

- Thousands of street children *(meninos de rua)* are the products of poverty and unwanted pregnancies. Some have been abandoned while others are helping their families by working. They make money by shining shoes, selling groceries on the street at traffic lights, washing cars, or stealing.

- Two-thirds of the population live below the poverty line, and illiteracy is estimated at 18 percent overall. It is considerably higher in some rural areas.

- One of the characteristics of Brazil is captured by the word *jeito.* It is very difficult to translate, but it refers to ways of cutting red tape, bending the rules, or looking the other way. Some might call it corruption, while others see it as finding practical solutions without making waves.

- Carnaval is celebrated every year at the end of February or the beginning of March, on the four days before Ash Wednesday and Lent. Businesses close down for these four days, streets are roped off, and thousands of people celebrate by wearing elaborate costumes, dancing to samba music, and playing tambourines and drums.

- Brazil's history has five different periods that have significantly influenced society and culture—the period of trees, the period of sugar, the period of gold, the period of coffee, and, finally, the period of industrialization. Pedro

Alvares Cabral arrived in Brazil in the early 1500s, and colonists from Portugal began to arrive shortly thereafter. The first period included the exploitation of trees as well as people, namely, the natives who were used as slaves to cut and transport the trees to European ships. The second period, from 1530 to 1650, was the sugar era, when Africans were imported to work as slaves in the cane fields. Next, the Portuguese moved into the interior of Brazil during the time of gold and diamond mining, from the 1690s to the 1750s. During that period, the population began to move away from the cities and the ruling authority of the Portuguese crown. The fourth period began in the early 1800s with the cultivation and export of coffee. Brazil soon became the world's largest producer of coffee. In 1822, the country gained identity as an empire separate from Portugal. In 1889, the emperor was overthrown by the military, and Brazil became a federal republic fashioned after the United States. By 1940, Brazil had jumped into the industrial age. Farmers either began moving to the cities for jobs or adopted mechanized methods to increase farming production. In the 1950s, the automobile became popular in Brazil, and roads were built into the Amazon region, where large-scale mining and timber harvesting grew quickly, displacing many indigenous people. Serious deforestation also began in this era, and the cycle of exploitation continues today.

Educational Panorama

- The educational picture in Brazil is complicated, with abundant variations. For example, Brazil's national education policy is compromised by the fact that state and local authorities have autonomy and may thus alter or replace its provisions. There is also a large network of private schools, each with its own agenda for religious or industrial promotion. Moreover, Brazil's size creates vast regional differences.

- December and January are taken as summer vacation, the month of July as winter vacation. Some schools have a one-week break in October for children under 12. When a holiday falls on a Tuesday or Thursday, classes are canceled either Monday or Friday. In other words, the holiday is attached to the weekend.

- English is required in the curriculum, but there are not enough English teachers available. Other languages taught include Spanish, German, and Italian.

- Public universities are considered to be the best universities in Brazil and, consequently, have the most difficult vestibular exams (entrance exams). However, public school students usually do not pass the vestibular exams for the public universities. To many people, this system can seem unfair because students from public schools usually do not have enough money to pay to attend a private university since middle- or upper-class students who attend private schools dominate the free public universities.

BRAZIL

Level/Age	Hours/Calendar	Curriculum	Required	Class Size	Exams	Grades	Classroom Setup	Homework
Preprimary, ages 4–6	Feb.–Nov.	National policy is for physical, emotional, cognitive, linguistic, and social development reflecting group cooperation and respect.	No	12–24	None	None	Tables and chairs with 4 students per table. Greenboards with colored chalk.	None
Fundamental, grades 1–8, ages 7–14	Feb.–Nov., 7:30 A.M.–12:30 P.M. or 1:30 P.M.–6:30 P.M.	Basic arithmetic, communication and expression, social studies, science, physical education, art, health, preparing for work, religious education; also music in private schools	Yes	35 in private schools; larger in public schools	Usually written, but schools can adopt their own system of evaluation. Oral presentations, reports, and group projects are also popular.	0–10, with 10 as the highest and 5 as passing. Some private schools use the codes AA (above), AS (sufficient), AP (partial), AI (insufficient).	Desks and chairs in rows; teacher's table and chair in front of a blackboard. Private schools may vary.	Exercises, written reports about science-lab activities, research, preparation for individual or group presentations
Secondary, grades 9–11, ages 15–17	Feb.–Nov., 7:30 A.M.–12:30 P.M. or 1:30 P.M.–6:30 P.M. Mon.–Fri. in night classes for students who have to work during the daytime	Portuguese and Brazilian literature, social studies (geography/history), sciences (physics, chemistry, biology), math, 1 foreign language (English is required but not always offered due to shortage of qualified teachers), health, physical education. Students who complete the fundamental grades may opt to attend vocational school rather than secondary school.	No	35 in private schools; larger in public schools.	Written vestibular exams must be taken after grade 11 and before entering a university.	Same as above	Same as above	Same as above
University, age 18+	Semesters Feb.–Nov. Hours vary.	As many women as men are studying law, medicine, dentistry, and engineering.	No	Varies	Vary	A, B, C, D, I (insufficient) 1–100. Passing = 55% or 75% depending on university.	Public schools normally have better facilities than do private schools.	Emphasis on reading and research

(👁) A Closer Look

POLICY

- It is very difficult for foreigners and citizens alike to comprehend the educational policy of Brazil. Although it has the eighth largest economy in the world, the government has not done much to improve education. Nowadays, many media campaigns espousing better education are being launched throughout the country. Unfortunately, much of this effort is seen as just a form of government propaganda, because these campaigns have not brought significant, if any, improvement. Furthermore, public schools are very different from private schools. The latter frequently receive money from foundations or from organizations abroad that open schools in Brazil because of an economic interest in teaching their native language.

- Most people cannot afford private education, so they have no choice but to send their children to the public schools. Many Brazilians are ashamed of the condition of these schools. The buildings often do not receive sufficient maintenance, and people from the area frequently make necessary repairs by themselves. The money that the government allocates to public schools sometimes does not reach its intended destination. Additionally, there are many rural areas—mainly in the northeastern, northern, and midwestern parts of Brazil—where schools are simply nonexistent; thus, children must travel by bus or buses to another town to attend school. Occasionally, a farmer may donate land for a school. If no qualified teacher is available, an individual who knows how to read and write and knows something about math or biology is invited to teach. In addition, most public schools cannot afford books, special colored pencils, or technical equipment, and the classrooms are seriously overcrowded.

- Overall, school enrollment in the fundamental grades (for children ages 7 to 14) has reached about 90 percent. However, less than half of those who enter first grade complete all eight grades of fundamental schooling and go on to high school. Part of the problem is that children in rural and low-income populations need to work to help support their families. In 1990, 18 percent of children between the ages of 10 and 14 were earning an income. One recent attempt to keep children in school involves giving students a grade or a number of credits after they finish a course rather than when they finish the normal school year.

TEACHING STYLE

- Public schools are typically teacher-fronted, whereas teachers in private schools often adopt a learner-centered approach to teaching.

- The teacher makes an explanation using visual aids or reading materials, then students are given exercises to do in pairs or groups or as homework.

- In private schools, there is one teacher for every three subjects through the end of fourth or fifth grade, after which there is one teacher for each subject.

- In public schools, many teachers in grades one through four teach subjects for which they have little or no familiarity.

- Foreign language classes use a large variety of materials. Extra books are read to improve vocabulary, videos are used for listening comprehension (students have to answer questions or write about a video), and oral presentations and role plays are used for developing speaking skills.

LEARNING STYLE

- Students ask questions by raising their hands whenever they have doubts about their work.

- Pair work and group work is common in classrooms at private schools and in some public schools.

- Children play games in and out of the classroom, with teacher supervision.

- Teenagers play games in the classroom to review materials taught.

- At first, it may appear that Brazilian students are confused about their long division. Instead of using the method familiar to teachers and students in the United States, as in $3\overline{)18}$, students in Brazil reverse the order of the integers and turn the long division symbol upside down, so that the preceding example appears as $18\underline{)3}$. In both methods, the answer is the same: 6.

INSTRUCTIONAL SETTING

- The number of female teachers has always been larger than the number of male teachers. In preschool and fundamental grades, almost all the teachers are women.

- Public schools do not always look appealing. Money for maintenance is scarce, and allocations may be mysteriously diverted away from the school. Many rural schools are maintained by local volunteers.

- All public schools have blackboards, some have audio and video equipment, and a few have computer labs. There is usually a snack bar and a gymnasium for physical education classes.

- Private schools have blackboards, audio and video equipment, computer labs, cafeterias, and fewer students per class than public schools. The buildings at private schools are well kept and repaired continually. There is usually a separate recreation area for play. Some private schools also have auditoriums and special places to practice sports.

- Girls and boys study separately in Catholic Schools, but elsewhere they are placed together in the same class.

- Catholic or Adventist groups run a small percentage of the schools.

- English classes are typically more crowded than the other language classes.

ACTIVITIES

- Physical education is part of the curriculum in all schools.

- Music lessons are offered in all private schools but not in all public schools. Generally, music is offered as a children's subject.

- Field trips to museums, zoos, parks, and hydroelectric dams are organized if the locations are within driving distance from the school. Because of Brazil's size, the types of trips can vary greatly.

- All schools have *futebol,* or soccer, teams. Private schools offer a variety of after-school activities, often at an extra cost. These activities include volley-ball, basketball, swimming, chess, art, dancing, gymnastics, judo, and foreign language study.

DISCIPLINE AND CLASS MANAGEMENT

- When a student's behavior is particularly bad, he or she is usually sent to the school director. The student may be suspended or expelled after two warnings or immediately if the violation is severe.

- Teachers can choose to discipline students in the classroom by assigning additional homework or research or by asking them to leave the classroom.

- A common discipline problem is noise. Students who are not paying attention may talk or shuffle in their seats and, at the university level, may even get up and leave the class.

- Public schools tend to have harsher disciplinary practices than do private schools, and boys reportedly tend to get away with worse behavior than do girls.

TEACHER-STUDENT RELATIONSHIP

- The relationship of the teacher to the student is most like a counselor and sometimes like a disciplinarian. A teacher can be a student's friend, but that relationship must not interfere with the student-teacher relationship. A friendship should not determine a student's grade or cause jealousy or concern on the part of other students. A relationship outside the school should be kept separate from the relationship that exists in the classroom.

- Students are taught to respect and obey their teachers.

STUDENT-STUDENT RELATIONSHIP

- Students are tolerant and cordial with one another and, therefore, work well with others.

- Because students are congenial and also afraid of appearing boorish, they often have difficulty saying no. To appear polite, they might say, "I'll see" or "Maybe" at times when they never intend to oblige a particular request or invitation.

- Students believe that it is wrong not to assist a peer who asks for help—even during exams.

- Students are competitive and want individual recognition, so some cooperative activities that will be graded may not be effective.

Protocol

NONVERBAL BEHAVIOR

- A kiss or two on the cheek is a common way to greet a friend or even a new acquaintance. Both females and males can kiss females, but males never kiss males except their father or grandfather. An old expression that is still used is "Three kisses for marrying." Therefore, platonic friends are careful about keeping the kiss on the cheek to one or two. The first time that a man and woman are introduced they may kiss three times, but only once or twice thereafter.

- Males shake hands and sometimes give a hug to a special friend.

- Brazilians stand closer when talking face-to-face than do North Americans or Europeans; physical touch is acceptable, and eye contact is more prolonged.

- Rubbing one's fingers sideways underneath the chin when listening means that the person speaking does not know what he or she is talking about.

- The North American gesture of placing the thumb and index finger together to mean "ok" is very obscene in Brazil. It is better to use the thumbs-up gesture.

IMAGES

- Students are very knowledgeable about American pop and rock music.

- Brazilians love to dance. The bossa nova of the 1960s has been replaced by the lively Brazilian rhythms and dance movement of samba, *forró, lambada,* and *pagode.* Samba is a popular dance among all ages, and samba schools compete during Carnaval. Girls do not wait for the boys to ask them to dance; they enjoy dancing samba in groups.

- Soccer is a favorite pastime. Five World Cup championships for Brazil are the source of great national pride. Some people joke that if a war erupted at the same time as a soccer tournament, the battle would have to wait until after the game ended.

- A sport that is unique to Brazil is *capoeira.* It is a type of artistic fight-dancing performed to music and involving skills of gymnastics, balance, and power.

FORMS OF ADDRESS

- Students usually address their teacher with *professor* or *professora,* but forms of address vary from school to school. In some schools, students address their teachers by first name. In other schools, students must use the more formal *Senhor or Senhora*.

- Brazilian culture and people are informal. Its people are often referred to or addressed by title plus first name (e.g., "Professor Paulo," "Doutora Julia."

DRESS

- The preprimary and fundamental schools usually require children to wear uniforms—T-shirts with the school's symbol, bermuda shorts or trousers, and a sweater with the school colors. Teenagers in secondary schools are sometimes required to wear uniforms. University students, too, have a school t-shirt that they may wear.

- Evening dress is not casual, and Brazilians take great care with their appearance when going out at night with friends. Brazilian girls often wear short dresses, tight-fitting tops, and high-heeled sandals for parties or dances.

- Nowadays, most young people wear American brands of tennis shoes, jeans, and T-shirts.

POLITE/IMPOLITE TOPICS AND BEHAVIORS

- Direct personal confrontation is avoided.

- Arriving late to an appointment or dinner party is expected behavior.

- It is customary to ask an individual about his or her family when you greet each other. It is considered impolite if you forget to do this.

- It is usual and not taboo to ask how much money an item cost or how much money someone makes.

- It is acceptable to discuss personal health care, such as plastic surgery or birth control.

GIFT GIVING

- Gifts are usually given for birthdays, Christmas, Mother's Day, Father's Day, Valentine's Day, or any other special occasion or party, such as a farewell party, wedding, or anniversary.

- When a Brazilian gives a gift, the wrapping paper is skillfully and beautifully folded into pleats so that tape and ribbon are not required.

- Young people often elaborately fold their personal correspondence.

? **Problem/Solution**

PROBLEM

Why are many of my Brazilian students having trouble making friends with students from other cultures, especially native English speakers?

SOLUTION

There may be a problem involving stress and rhythm. By stressing words that should be unstressed—pronouns, auxiliary verbs, prepositions—and speaking with a low pitch, Brazilians may give the erroneous impression that they are rude, irritated, or uninterested. Draw your students' attention to this phenomenon and give them practice with rhythm by clapping on stressed words. Having students recite limericks or rhythmic chants with a metronome, which might be available from the music classroom, is also helpful.

PROBLEM

I can tell from my Brazilian student's behavior that I have clearly offended him, but I don't know exactly how. Is there something I should know about hispanic culture to communicate better with him? How do you say *I'm sorry* in Spanish?

SOLUTION

First, Brazilians speak Portuguese, not Spanish. Second, many Brazilians do not consider themselves hispanic. Portugal, not Spain (from which the word *hispanic* emanates), colonized Brazil, leaving a linguistic and cultural heritage that differs from that of Spain.

PROBLEM

Many of my Brazilian students seem to swallow the endings of some words. Why does this happen, and how can I correct this?

SOLUTION

The Portuguese language does not have long vowels, so when Brazilian students say such English phrases as *I'm very happy* or *I feel bad,* they may sound like *I'm very hap* or *I feu bad.* To correct this, try providing your students with a hint (e.g., tapping your foot or some other object) whenever they make this mistake, then allow time for them to repair the error.

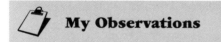 **My Observations**

Colombia

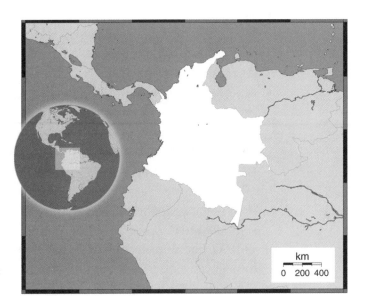

 Focus on Colombia

Capital: Bogotá

Population: 38,580,949

Size: 439,734 sq. mi. (1,138,910 sq. km.)

Location: northwestern portion of South America, bordering Brazil, Ecuador, Panama, Peru, Venezuela, the Caribbean Sea, and the Pacific Ocean

Climate: Stable year-round; determined by altitude. Colombia rests on the equator.

Monetary Unit: Colombian peso

Urban/Rural Life: 73% urban. 21% of Colombians live in extreme poverty. 3 out of 4 poor people live in rural areas. Per capita income is approximately the equivalent of U.S.$5,300.

Religion: 95% Roman Catholic

Languages: Spanish (national and official), English on the islands of San Andrés and Providencia, hundreds of indigenous Amerindian languages and dialects

Ethnicity: 58% mestizo (Amerindian-Spanish), 20% white, 14% mulatto, 4% black, 4% Amerindian

Government: democratic republic with legislative, judicial, and executive branches

 Personal Snapshot

Colombian students these days suffer from stereotyping perhaps more than do most of their peers. What outsiders know about Colombia is generally confined to a handful of negative topics—drugs, civil war, kidnappings. Classroom discussions of current events in the news compel Colombian students to serve as representatives of their country and to explain the violence that they themselves do not understand. These issues are highly personal. Few Colombians can claim that they know no one who has been victimized by the country's raging political, social, and economic battle. Talking about the violence can be more traumatic than any of us imagines. On a recent trip to the country, I went horseback riding through the lush, verdant hills outside Medellin. "Your country is so beautiful," I commented to one of my fellow riders, a university student. He answered: "There is a saying in Colombia. *God gives each country either peace or paradise.* It's obvious which one He's given us."

✦ Cultural Closeup

- Colombia is named after explorer Christopher Columbus and was settled by Spaniards in the early 16th century. Well before the arrival of the Spaniards, however, Colombia had been part of the great Aztec and Mayan empires. More than 10 million Amerindians lived in this rich, highly organized culture. Among them were mathematicians, astronomers, and skilled artisans.

- For 10,000 years before the Spanish conquest, Colombia's people represented a broad range of ethnic, cultural, and linguistic communities, having distinct traditions but living in harmony with each other. The Spaniards introduced slaves from Africa into the population as well as a vision of political, cultural, and religious cohesion. The result was a great intermixing of the races, or *mestizaje.* Today, most Colombians celebrate their rich heritage but are unable to conclusively identify their ethnic or cultural roots.

- One of the most identifiable traits of the Colombian people is an intense desire for self-improvement. They are extremely hard-working people who tend to fill each day with an abundance of activities aimed at enriching their lives. Thus, it is not uncommon for a Colombian to work a long day and then attend an English or fitness class in the evening. Colombians direct their penchant for hard work not only at bettering their individual lives but at contributing to the improvement of their organizations, institutions, and country.

- Nobel Prize–winning Colombian author Gabriel García Márquez argues that Colombians have a well-developed capacity to adapt to new environments due to their pre-Colombian and colonial histories, both of which involved the integration of very different ways of life.

- Until the middle of the 20th century, Colombia's educational system was considered by many to be repressive and conformist. Creativity and critical-thinking skills were discouraged, and the Catholic Church had a strong influence on the curriculum. Today, massive educational reform is underway. Not only is Colombia looking to eradicate its social and economic ills through education, but great emphasis is being placed on the education of the poor. The majority of Colombia's poor receive very little formal education; nonetheless, 91 percent of Colombians are literate, and the country enjoys a 90 percent primary school enrollment.

- Unlike many of their Latin American peers, Colombians tend to be more conservative in interpersonal dynamics, appearance, protocol, and philosophy. Some claim Colombian culture to be one of quiet elegance. Colombians are a warm but not particularly effusive people whose trust and friendship is won in little time. They are extremely hospitable and will go to great lengths to accommodate a visitor. Once friendship has blossomed, it becomes a very important part of a Colombian's life, and Colombians expect to spend a great deal of time with true friends. In fact, such friendships typically last a lifetime.

🎓 Educational Panorama

- Colombian schools recognize two calendars. Calendar A runs from the end of January to mid-June, with a break from mid-June until mid-July, and finishes in mid-November. Calendar B extends from September through the end of November, with a break until early January, ending at the end of June.

- Roughly three-quarters of Colombian children begin elementary school; one-third of them finish.

- Most Colombians refer to their elementary and secondary school as *colegio;* students may erroneously translate this word literally into English as "college."

- After seventh grade, students who do not wish to continue formal schooling have the option of either studying on their own or attending a special institute to prepare for a certificate that may be used in lieu of a high school diploma for application to the university.

- Throughout the educational system, the Colombian government is attempting to institute a new grading format whereby students' success and progress are measured by the achievement of established *logros* (competencies). This system will replace the older tradition of assigning numeric grades to a student's performance. To attain the established *logros,* a student may work at his or her own pace after school or during vacation. A student still owing certain *logros* may advance to the next grade.

👁 A Closer Look

POLICY

- Public schools are generally coeducational, while private schools will enroll only boys or only girls.

- Created in 1974 for primarily rural populations, the *Escuela Nueva,* or New School, features multigrade classrooms, flexible promotion from level to level, individual and group study, rural orientation, specially trained teachers, mastery learning, and active learning. One of Colombia's goals for the future is to become a "truly bilingual nation," with English serving as the second language of the population. The government sees an objective of this magnitude as a necessary step in bringing the country into the

COLOMBIA

Level/Age	Hours/Calendar	Curriculum	Required	Class Size	Exams	Grades	Classroom Setup	Homework
Preschool, or *guardaría*, ages 1–4	Variable hours depending on parents' needs	Colors, shapes, numbers, left/right, opposites, social skills, hygiene	No	10–20	At end of *guardaría*, *prekinder*, kindergarten, and *transición* children take tests and interviews that determine readiness for the next level.	N/A	Large round tables or small tables for 2 students	N/A
Prekinder, ages 4–5	Variable hours depending on parents' needs	Same as above plus connect the dots, using scissors, drawing	Yes, unless child passes skills tests	20	Same as above	Pass/Fail for individual competencies (or *logros*)	Same as above	Bring items to class
Kindergarten, ages 5–6	Mornings or afternoons	Introduction to regular academic courses such as math, science, social studies, music, etc.	Yes	20	Same as above	Same as above	Desks arranged in rows with students sitting two to a table or in horseshoe shape if group is small	Some simple homework
Transición, ages 6–7	7:00 A.M.–2:00 P.M. Mon.–Fri. Calendar A: Feb. to Nov. Calendar B: Sept. to Jun. Breaks for Christmas, *Semana Santa*, and national holidays	Reading, writing, math, Spanish (English in some schools), social studies, science, arts, history, physical education, (religion)	Yes	20	Same as above	E = *excelente* (excellent); B = *bueno* (good); A = *acceptable* (acceptable); I = *insuficiente* (unsatisfactory)	Same as above	Heavy, including worksheets and simple research projects in which parents participate
Primaria, grades 1–5; ages 7–11	Same as above or an afternoon shift with an equal number of seats	Same as above at higher level	Yes	25–30	Short answer essays. No multiple choice, fill-in-the-blank, or true/false. Two to three major tests plus a final exam.	Same as above	Same as above	Heavy reading, essays, projects
Secundaria (or *bachillerato*), grades 6–11; ages 12–17	Same as above	Math, geometry, calculus, trigonometry, physics, algebra, world history, Spanish literature, English, arts, physical education, philosophy, chemistry, health, computers, (religion), (2d foreign language)	Yes, (up to 14 years of age)	25–30	Longer essays plus occasional fill-in-the-blank, multiple-choice, true-false. Students must pass an entrance exam (ICFES) for access to universities.	Same as above	Same as above or individual desks in rows	Workbooks, exercises, library research projects
University, age 18–23	Same as above	Curriculum varies according to type of institution: university, technology institute, technical professional institute, or military academy. A variety of distance-learning degree and certificate programs are offered. Students take 6 classes at a time for a total of 5 years.	No	15–50 (larger classes in initial semesters)	Short quizzes, assignments, 3 major exams (each worth 20–25%), 1 final exam (worth 30–35% of final grade). Tests involve closed questions, problem solving, projects; multiple-choice questions are not used much.	1–5 with 3 as pass/fail level 4.6–5.0 extremely high, 4.0–4.59 excellent, 3.5–3.99 good, 3.0–3.49 sufficient, 0.00–2.99 failure (individual class assignments and tests may be graded on a 0–100% basis)	Same as above, with TV/VCRs available, computer labs, few classrooms with internet access	Heavy reading assignments, projects

21st century with a greater chance to eradicate poverty and increase the overall stature of Colombia and Colombians. For the present, the goal of bilingualism remains in the theoretical realm while educators and politicians debate both the means to achieve the goal and its viability.

TEACHING STYLE

- Classes are teacher-centered, with plenty of lecturing and the expectation in many schools that students will write verbatim notes from the teacher's lecture. This is particularly true of dictation exercises that are common at the primary level. Teachers tend to be very strict and demanding, as well as traditional. They tend not to consider themselves the students' friend. The teacher generally does not invite discussion of concepts taught in class.

- Typically, a teacher will deliver his or her lesson standing at the front of the room. It is less common for teachers to circulate around the classroom.

LEARNING STYLE

- Although most Colombian students are strongly kinesthetic, they do not often receive instruction that is designed to address this particular learning style. In addition to having strong kinesthetic tendencies, Colombian learners are also highly visual.

- Students are expected to stay quiet in class and to listen politely. On the whole, students do not participate actively in class.

INSTRUCTIONAL SETTING

- Classrooms are small and crowded. Desks may be old and in poor condition.

- There is little decoration on the walls of the classrooms. In the primary schools, one may find a map of Colombia or a portrait of national hero Simon Bolivar, author Gabriel García Márquez, or another prominent Colombian, with the exception of the president of the republic.

ACTIVITIES

- In more affluent school communities, students may elect to participate in choir, sports, band, orchestra, dance, and theater groups. Students in poorer schools may be limited to organized basketball and soccer activities.

DISCIPLINE AND CLASS MANAGEMENT

- Teachers invest a relatively large amount of time trying to keep students quiet. When a student misbehaves, he or she is sent to the coordinator, who requires that the student sign a black book. The coordinator may then call the student's parents or send the student home. Violations that merit disciplinary action often include talking back to the teacher, fighting, smoking, or failing to observe the school's dress code.

TEACHER-STUDENT RELATIONSHIP

- Good teachers are friendly and respectful of students' space, ideas, individuality, and feelings. Some teachers may use grades to manipulate students' behavior.

- Students often complain about grades and may even attempt to negotiate a better grade with the teacher.

STUDENT-STUDENT RELATIONSHIP

- Classmates often become excellent friends, as they stay together in the same class throughout their primary and secondary school years. It is not unusual for classmates to spend a night or an entire weekend together on a frequent basis. A child's friends can easily become a part of the family.

Protocol

NONVERBAL BEHAVIOR

- Colombians maintain closer proximity to their conversation partners than do their North American counterparts, but they are less likely than their Latin American peers to touch one another.

- The gesture used for "ok" in the United States (placing the thumb and index finger together) is not used in Colombia except when the circle made by the fingers is placed over the nose. This is the gesture to suggest homosexuality.

- It is not appropriate in Colombia to go barefoot in public or to put feet on chairs or tables.

- Public yawning is considered extremely rude.

- It is considered bad luck to lay one's purse or book bag on the floor.

- Indicating the height of a person requires a different gesture from the one used to indicate the height of an animal. Palm down refers to animals. When the palm is held vertically, as if one were about to shake hands, it refers to human beings. Confusing the two gestures risks offense.

- Colombian gestures are charming by almost any standard and are common among men and women alike. They consist primarily of flourishes of the hands, accompanying speech.

IMAGES

- Colombians are outwardly gregarious, fun-loving people. They laugh easily and make conversation with little effort.

- The Colombian flag generally does not hang in Colombian classrooms. However, it is common for schools to hold flag-raising events on a regular basis. During such an event, the national anthem is sung, and individual students are awarded before all their peers for meritorious academic performance or good citizenship.

FORMS OF ADDRESS

- Teachers are normally addressed simply with *profesor* or *profesora.*

- Children and adolescent students may be called by their given names.

- Teachers should address a student's parents with *señor* or *señora* plus the family name.

- Many Colombians have two family names. In the name *Luz María Vargas Arcila,* the second to last name in the series, *Vargas,* comes from the father's side of the family, and the last name in the series, *Arcila,* derives from the mother's side. If Luz María Vargas Arcila were a teacher, she would be called "Señora Vargas."

- It is common nowadays for an individual whose economic or professional position is relatively high to be addressed with *doctor* or *doctora.* For example, a secretary may call her boss "Doctor Armando," and a painter may call the lady of the house "doctora."

DRESS

- Students in private schools wear uniforms: boys wear dark or khaki-colored pants, a polo shirt, and a blazer; girls wear a jumper and blouse with white socks and low-heeled, rubber-soled shoes. Once a week, students will wear sweat suits to school all day long if they have a physical education class. In schools where no uniform is required, students nonetheless must dress conservatively. Shorts, for example, are not allowed for either boys or girls.

- Colombians are generally very careful about dress. They are at once fashionable and tasteful in their attire, and they are fastidious in terms of cleanliness. Polished nails and/or well-manicured nails for women are a must in many circles.

- It is unusual for Colombian women to leave their homes without wearing makeup, jewelry, and pantyhose. They do not wear shorts or sneakers in public. Affluent women will not wear their gold and gemstones in public for fear of being mugged.

POLITE/IMPOLITE TOPICS AND BEHAVIORS

- Such subjects as poverty and the escalation of violence in Colombia are appropriate for discussion. It is not unusual for Colombians to question others about the social problems in their countries as well. With regard to the United States, a typical question concerns the perceived lack of concern for manners and education among North Americans.

- Sexuality (including homosexuality) and a woman's age are two subjects that are largely off-limits in conversation except among one's closest friends.

- Colombians typically engage in vigorous debate about their country's political and economic situation. They may be quite critical of their government, and arguments may erupt between friends over political issues.

- It is not considered impolite to ask the cost of items purchased or the amount of one's salary.

- Young married couples may be quizzed endlessly about their plans to have children.

- Both men and women enjoy discussing the performance of the country's national soccer team.

- The term *gringo* to refer to a North American does not have a pejorative connotation in Colombia as it does in the U.S.

GIFT GIVING

- Colombia produces a great variety and abundance of beautiful flowers and plants, which make excellent gifts.

- Colombia has many holidays, including Secretary's Day, Doctor's Day, and Teacher's Day. A card or an inexpensive gift of a book or chocolates is appropriate in each case.

- September is the month of *amor y amistad,* "love and friendship." Throughout the month, secret friends leave each other small gifts, such as fruit, chocolates, an original poem, or something humorous and creative. At an end-of-the-month party, a larger gift is opened, and the receiver may also guess the identity of his or her secret friend.

- Parents and students sometimes send gifts to the teacher as a means of gaining a more favorable grade.

- A wrapped gift may be opened in the presence of the gift giver so that the recipient may show his or her appreciation and enjoyment.

- An enthusiastic expression of gratitude is expected when receiving a gift; a written thank-you note is not required but is appreciated.

? 💡 Problem/Solution

PROBLEM

I like to give my students problems to solve either individually as homework or in class as a group exercise. However, I find that my Colombian students seem lost when I ask them to generalize theoretical or abstract notions to practical situations. They want me to show them how, and once I give an example, it is not uncommon for them to produce something that is almost identical to the example. This strikes me as immature and lazy. Is it?

SOLUTION

By and large, Colombian students are not taught critical-thinking skills. They are expected to reproduce what has been presented, and they memorize content with great determination. They may have heard how important it is to think independently and may espouse as much themselves, but they lack sufficient critical perspective and inspiration to transform an idea of their own into a plan that can be presented to others. You can help your students by first talking about independent, critical thinking—not just the benefits, but also the process. Give plenty of examples, and assign tasks that incrementally move them from small to larger challenges.

PROBLEM

I assigned my students the homework task of answering the questions that test reading comprehension at the end of their unit. When I collected the papers, I found that the answers submitted by three of my students were exactly the same. Why did they feel they had to cheat?

SOLUTION

You may be misinterpreting the motives of the three students in question. They probably sat together to do their homework, and from their perspective, they were helping each other. They were operating from the idea that two heads are better than one, and their goal was to learn from one another and provide the correct answers to the questions posed. You need to talk with your students about the benefits of generating answers independently and show them how to develop critical-thinking skills. Also, discuss with them the code of ethics of your classroom, focusing on the reasons for their existence.

PROBLEM

One of my students, a beautiful Colombian girl, comes to class everyday wearing the tightest clothes I've ever seen. Should I tell her that she is dressing inappropriately?

SOLUTION

The meaning of images differs from culture to culture. In U.S. culture, people who wear tight-fitting or revealing clothes are sometimes thought of as exhibitionists, as being in need of elevating their physical appearance above their intellectual abilities, or as likely to be engaging in questionable sexual behavior. In Colombia, there are no such associations. In fact, despite their preference for tight-fitting clothing, women in Colombia are less likely to be sexually active before marriage than are their U.S. counterparts. Today, Colombian women comprise large portions of the university student and professional populations and are much less affected by the traditional *machista* culture than their mothers were. Physical beauty is celebrated and respected in Colombia, and women and men alike spend a great amount of time making themselves publicly presentable. You may want to raise your student's consciousness about the cultural associations made in the United States between behavior and dress and then allow her to determine her own response.

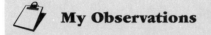 **My Observations**

Côte d'Ivoire

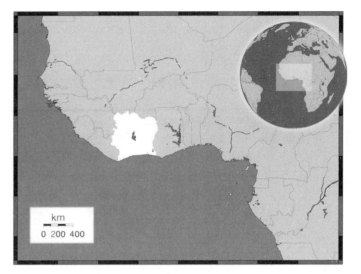

 Focus on Côte d'Ivoire

Capital: Yamoussoukro. Abidjan is the administrative center.

Population: 14,500,000

Size: 124,503 sq. mi. (322,469 sq. km.)

Location: western Africa, bordering Burkina Faso and Mali to the north, Guinea and Liberia to the west, Ghana to the east, and the North Atlantic Ocean to the south

Climate: tropical along the coast; semiarid in the far north. Seasons include warm and dry, hot and dry, hot and wet. Average temperature is between 77 and 86 degrees Fahrenheit, with ranges spanning from 50 to 104 degrees; temperatures are higher in the south.

Monetary Unit: CFA franc

Urban/Rural Life: 44% urban; 56% rural

Religion: 60% Muslim, 12% Christian, 25% indigenous

Languages: French (official), 60 native dialects

Ethnicity: 60 ethnic groups, including Akan, Kru, Voltaic, Mande, and Malinke

Government: multiparty presidential republic

 Personal Snapshot

My first teaching assignment was in Côte d'Ivoire (the Ivory Coast). When I first started teaching, I resolved that I would never give students orders, that I would explain to them what I considered to be best practices and advise them. About six weeks into the trimester, during the first test, students asked me where on the folded sheet of ruled paper they should write their names. Many teachers in the school had strict rules about that: for example, last name in capitals and first name in small letters or each name in a small box on the paper. I told them to write their names anywhere, that I didn't care where it was as long as it was easy to find. Most students wrote their names on their paper and proceeded to take the test. About midway through the one-hour test, I noticed that one student still had not started. I asked him why, and he said that he didn't know where to write his name. "Anywhere,"

I said to him. There was still no action on his part. I got angry and pointed to a spot on the paper. "Here," I said. "Why?" he asked me. "Because I'm the teacher, and you're the student," I replied. Not only that student but the whole class breathed a sigh of relief. I was finally acting like a teacher. I kept my goals of developing independent learners, but I saw that it would be a long, slow process. There could not be an immediate change from one system to another.

Cultural Closeup

- The concept of community is extremely important in the Ivorian culture, and emphasis is placed on the needs of the group rather than on the needs of the individual. Ivorians favor cooperation over competition.

- The extended family includes parents, children, grandparents, aunts and uncles, cousins, in-laws, and sometimes people not related by blood or marriage. Older members of the family are addressed as "auntie" or "uncle."

- A friend is someone who is considered a part of the family. As such, that person would be willing to make whatever sacrifices were necessary to help the family. The reward for taking on this responsibility is respect and acknowledgment from the family for helping.

- There is great respect for age and status in the culture, age taking precedence over status and over gender. Within age-groups or social groups, members are considered equals.

- For some Catholics and indigenous groups, there is great respect for and belief in the spirits of ancestors, who are honored with celebrations on the anniversaries of their deaths. Believers expect they will be reborn into the same family. Among those groups, it may also be commonly believed that things do not happen without a reason. If an event cannot be explained logically, its occurrence may be ascribed to evil spirits or witches.

- Time is viewed more often in terms of the present and past, and less importance is given to the future. Time is defined in broad terms, by events that happen, for example, instead of by the hour or by the day. A scheduled meeting will not start until the arrival of the senior person.

- Decisions are made in an unhurried manner. It is important that all members of the group share their opinions before consensus is reached. It is also important to avoid confrontation with or offending others. This may result in a person's saying "yes" when, in fact, "no" is meant.

- Hospitality is highly valued. It is important to take good care of one's guests by feeding them well and conversing with them to make their visit as pleasant as possible. When guests prepare to leave, they literally ask for the road. After this request, they are invited to stay longer, which they do. The request is repeated three or four times before the guests actually leave. They are then escorted to their car by their host.

Educational Panorama

CÔTE D'IVOIRE

Level/Age	Hours/Calendar	Curriculum	Required	Class Size	Exams	Grades	Classroom Setup	Homework
Preschool, ages 3–5	Varies	No set curriculum	No	Varies	None	None	Varies	None
Kindergarten, ages 5–6	Oct.–Dec. and Jan.–June, 8:00 A.M.–12:00 P.M. Mon., Tues., Thu., Fri.; breaks at Christmas and Easter	Art, social skills	No	Usually 10–15, with a maximum of 20	None	None	Varies	None
Elementary, grades 1–6, ages 7–12	Oct.–Dec. and Jan.–June, 8:00 A.M.–12:00 P.M. and 3:00 P.M.–5:00 P.M.; Mon., Tue., Thu., Fri.; breaks for Christmas and Easter	French for the first 6 months if child does not speak it, reading, writing, arithmetic, history, geography, natural sciences, music, art, physical education	Yes	21–25	Standard exams administered at end of school. Certificate of elementary education determines entrance to secondary institution.	0 (lowest)–20 (highest). Grades are weighted—e.g., French and arithmetic more than history. Averaging a 10 means "just passing."	Desks in rows. Classrooms are decorated with student work. Students often work in groups.	For the first 4 years, not a lot of homework is assigned. Years 5–6 see students doing more homework.
Middle, grades 7–10, ages 13–16	Oct.–Dec. and Jan.–June, 8:00 A.M.–12:00 P.M. and 3:00 P.M.–5:00 P.M. Mon.–Fri. (no class on some Wed. afternoons); breaks at Christmas and Easter	Reading, writing, arithmetic, history, geography, natural sciences, music, art, physical education	No	40–50	Standard exams administered at end of school. Certificate of lower cycle allows continued study at *lycée*.	Same as above	Desks in rows. Students often work independently.	Amount of homework varies. Much homework is memorization.
High, grades 11–13, ages 17–19	Oct.–Dec. and Jan.–June, 8:00 A.M.–12:00 P.M. and 3:00 P.M.–6:00 P.M. Mon.–Fri. (no class on some Wed. afternoons); breaks at Christmas and Easter	2 tracks: literary or science	No	40–50	Standard exams administered at end of school. Certificate qualifies for university entrance.	Same as above, with grades weighted within each field—e.g., in literary track, English more than math; in science track, physics more than history.	Desks in rows. Students often work independently. Group projects are occasional.	Amount of homework varies but is typically a lot because class time is not enough to cover all material. Much homework is memorization.
University, age 19+	Oct.–Dec. and Jan.–July; breaks at Christmas and Easter	Varied	No	20 in seminar groups; 500–700 in lectures	Exams are administered in July. If students fail an exam, another is offered in Sept.	0 (lowest)–20 (highest). Averaging a 10 means "just passing."	Classes are often held in auditoriums. Desks are arranged in a semicircle, with room for two students/desk.	Typical for university work

👁 A Closer Look

POLICY

- Educational policy is determined by the Ministry of National Education and Scientific Research. The ministry is responsible for educational development, including determining curricula, textbooks, and teaching methods; preparing the qualifying exams; and licensing teachers, administrators, and private educational institutions.

- Public schools are relatively tuition-free, costing the equivalent of approximately $20 per year, but families are increasingly being asked to contribute more toward the cost of their children's education. Tuition-free secondary schools run by the state are limited, and many families cannot afford to send their children away to those schools that charge tuition. Government-funded universities have begun asking students to pay tuition. Private schools include both Roman Catholic and Muslim schools. Roman Catholic schools are partially funded by the government.

- In rural areas, students may study inside a one-room schoolhouse or outside under a shade tree. Materials may be limited or even nonexistent. In the urban areas, schools are typically built of cement. Classes are often large, and split schedules may be instituted to accommodate the large numbers of students. The literacy rate of Côte d'Ivoire is approximately 64 percent.

- The school system is an adaptation of the French system, and debate continues on whether to continue in that tradition. French is the language of instruction. After primary school, students may begin Western language instruction. In the 1990s, primary school enrollment was approximately 1.5 million, secondary and vocational school enrollment was about 423,000, and students enrolled in the National University of Côte d'Ivoire numbered 21,000.

TEACHING STYLE

- Classrooms are generally quiet. In elementary school, students raise their hands for permission to speak and stand when responding to a teacher's question. In middle school, students are expected to raise their hands, but they need not stand when responding.

- Teachers use a variety of instructional materials, such as pictures, overhead transparencies, and realia from science labs. Generally, teachers do not prepare a lot of extra handouts or worksheets for the students.

- Students begin to learn note-taking in middle school by copying information from the board; in high school, students are exposed to the lecture format and begin note-taking in earnest.

- It is commonplace for teachers to move around the classroom during the lesson in order to have better eye contact with the students.

LEARNING STYLE

- In elementary school, middle school, and high school, students work alone or in pairs or groups, depending on the type of class. Working in pairs or small groups is typical of science classes; working alone is typical of, for example, reading or literature classes. Group work is more common in elementary school; the tendency in middle school and high school is for students to work alone. Group work is sometimes seen as an opportunity for certain members of the group to do nothing.

- Students in the first few years of elementary school are given little homework, typically reading or practicing one lesson. As students reach the middle and high school levels, the amount of homework assigned increases. However, even in high school, more work is done in class than is assigned as homework. The reverse is true for the university.

- Students are expected to do and turn in all required homework on time. Teachers will rarely accept homework late. Students who fail to turn in their homework receive a grade of zero.

INSTRUCTIONAL SETTING

- In elementary school, middle school, and high school, students occupy the same classroom throughout the school day.

- Classrooms in the elementary schools are often decorated with students' drawings and class work.

- In elementary school, middle school, and high school, one student per classroom is responsible for assigning chores to the other students in the room for keeping the room neat and clean. The student is either chosen by the teacher or elected by classmates.

- Students are not provided with lockers and thus carry their books and/or personal items with them throughout the day.

- In elementary school, students are often required to line up outside the classroom before entering. In middle school and high school, the teacher usually arrives after the students and leaves before them.

- In some private and public schools, students spend one hour a week doing community service, such as cleaning.

ACTIVITIES

- There are very few school-sponsored activities.

DISCIPLINE AND CLASS MANAGEMENT

- Depending on the teacher, a student might be selected or elected by classmates to serve as class spokesperson and take student concerns to the teacher. This student may also act as the teacher's assistant and be responsible for taking attendance.

- Teachers and parents meet regularly to discuss student progress.

TEACHER-STUDENT RELATIONSHIP

- Teachers are very respected in Côte d'Ivoire. Students show their respect by coming to class on time and by listening to and not interrupting the teacher.

- Students who arrive late to class must knock and wait outside the room until the teacher tells them to enter.

- It is common for teachers to address their students as "my son" or "my daughter."

- Teachers are considered the authority in the classroom. Students are, however, free to disagree with a teacher or dispute a grade if they do so in a respectful manner.

STUDENT-STUDENT RELATIONSHIP

- Although relationships among ethnic groups are cordial, students tend to form friendships with classmates from the same ethnic group.

Protocol

NONVERBAL BEHAVIOR

- Direct eye contact is common between friends. Direct eye contact with someone who is older or holds a higher-ranked position may be seen as disrespectful. Staring is also considered disrespectful.

- Friends may be greeted with hugs, kisses, or handshakes, depending on the closeness of the relationship. Touching a friend's head, arm, hand, back, or shoulder is not considered inappropriate behavior but would not be done in public.

- People generally stand close to one another when talking. They are also used to talking simultaneously rather than taking turns.

- Laughter may be a sign of nervousness or uncertainty of oneself. Laughter is also used as a way to cope with life's disappointments, from something as simple as having a cold to losing one's job.

IMAGES

- There is an Ivorian saying that *the man moves to the city but takes the village with him.* Family and village traditions are the foundation of the Ivorian culture.

- Ivorians frequently advise, "Be patient." Ivorian people are used to waiting. Whatever is not finished today can be finished tomorrow.

- Friendships between men and women are common.

- Regarding group decision making, the Ivorians say, *We join together to make wise decisions, not foolish ones.* It is important that all members of a group be able to share their opinions before consensus is reached and decisions are made.

FORMS OF ADDRESS

- In business situations, titles are very important and should be used. It is common to use the titles *Monsieur, Madame,* or *Mademoiselle* in the workplace. Titles may even be used among friends at work, depending on the closeness of the relationship or the presence of high-level personnel.

- Teachers may be addressed by the titles *Monsier, Madame,* or *Mademoiselle;* by the title *Professeur;* or even, in some instances, by first name. Students are commonly addressed by their first names.

DRESS

- Uniforms are required for students in the elementary, middle, and high schools. Boys wear khaki pants with khaki shirts. Girls wear blue skirts and white blouses.

- Students are not allowed to wear sandals, open-toed shoes, hats, or caps to class.

- Teachers are expected to dress professionally, but it is not uncommon for them to wear dressy jeans.

- Native costumes are worn on special occasions—weddings, holiday celebrations, and so on—and are considered formal dress. Both men and women dress colorfully and stylishly. In large cities, office dress is more formal: men wear suits, and women wear tailored African dresses.

POLITE/IMPOLITE TOPICS AND BEHAVIORS

- It would be considered impolite to discuss social class even among friends, especially if people present are from different classes. It is not considered impolite to ask what salary a person earns.

- Interrupting someone and speaking loudly to someone are considered rude. Speaking softly is a sign of respect.

- It is impolite to refuse an offer of food or drink. It is important to accept something the first time it is offered.

- When entering a room full of people, it is polite to greet everyone in the room, beginning with the person closest to you. Remaining seated when an elder enters the room is a sign of respect.

- When greeting people, it is important to shake hands and to use people's titles. With elders, shake hands if they offer theirs; if they do not, greet them verbally.

- When conducting business, it is impolite to begin discussing the business matter immediately. It is proper to first greet the person and inquire about the person's health and his or her family's health and general welfare.

GIFT GIVING

- Gift giving is very common in Côte d'Ivoire. Gifts are signs of friendship and respect and are given to celebrate birthdays, anniversaries, weddings, and funerals. Typical gifts include clothing and perfume. Wine and sometimes champagne are commonly given as gifts in all but the northern parts of the country. Men and women often give each other flowers on Valentine's Day.

- Teachers in the elementary schools often receive gifts from their students at Christmas and at the end of the school term. Gifts of chocolate or food, often homemade, are commonly given. During the school year, children will bring *attieke,* steamed ground cassava served with fish, as a gift to their teacher.

- Bringing a gift when invited to someone's home is appreciated but not required. Wine would be appropriate for such a gift.

- When receiving a gift, the recipient usually asks the giver whether the gift should be opened then or saved until later.

? 💡 Problem/Solution

PROBLEM

Why don't my Ivorian students assume more responsibility for their own learning and depend less on me?

SOLUTION

In Côte d'Ivoire, students highly respect their teachers and are more apt to depend totally on their teachers for guidance and instruction. Explaining the concept of taking responsibility for one's own learning as part of the culture of the English-speaking classroom may help. Have students compare this cultural concept to their home country experience. Asking students to generate ways they can take more responsibility for their own learning might also help.

PROBLEM

I am having difficulty getting my Ivorian students to cooperate while doing group work. They seem eager to share their ideas and opinions, and it is not a problem to get them to talk. But when it comes time to put together the product, it seems that they are content to let the others take the lead and do all the work. As a result, some of the other students do not want to work with them. How can I get the Ivorian students in my class to take responsibility for their share of the group work?

SOLUTION

If your students are new to the United States, they may not be familiar with the concept of group work, and the solution may be as simple as explaining it to them. As a rule, students in Côte d'Ivoire tend to work alone. They are not accustomed to working in groups except perhaps at the elementary school level. Assigning responsibilities to each student in the group may alleviate some of the problem.

PROBLEM

Why is my Ivorian student overly concerned about the final exam for my class? The exam is still weeks away.

SOLUTION

Typically, standard exams are administered at the end of the school year in Côte d'Ivoire. Passing the exam determines whether the student may enter the next school, that is, proceed from elementary to secondary school or from secondary school to the university. Familiarizing your student with the U.S. educational system and outlining what it takes to pass your class will more than likely ease the anxiety he or she is experiencing.

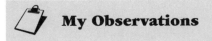 **My Observations**

Cuba

Focus on Cuba

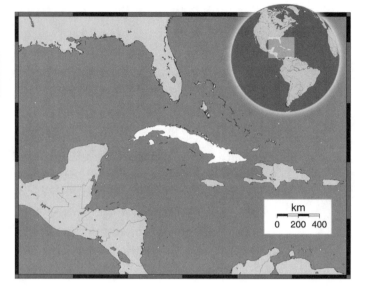

Capital: Havana *(La Habana)*

Population: just over 11,000,000

Size: 42,804 sq. mi. (110,861 sq. km.)

Location: Atlantic Ocean, just south of the Tropic of Cancer, between the Gulf of Mexico and the Caribbean Sea, about 90 miles (150 km.) south of the Florida Keys

Climate: tropical and humid, influenced year-round by the warming currents of the Gulf Stream; average temperature 80 degrees Fahrenheit; active and often violent hurricane season June to November.

Monetary Unit: Cuban peso, U.S. dollar in tourist areas and *dollar stores* (establishments where, formerly, diplomats and foreign visitors, and now Cuban citizens, can purchase scarce consumer goods)

Urban/Rural Life: 75% urban, 25% rural

Religion: mainly Christian (mostly Roman Catholic [25%], but some Protestantism); also *Santería* (a mixture of Catholicism and African traditions) and the remnants of a formerly significant Jewish community. Cuba has officially been an atheist state for most of the Castro era; however, it was declared secular in 1992.

Languages: Spanish (official)

Ethnicity: mainly Spanish and African origin, as well as Chinese, Haitian, and European

Government: socialist republic

Personal Snapshot

"I love Cuba," said the pretty, blonde-haired, blue-eyed former dental student. "I love my country. I love the food. I love the people. I don't care about the politics." She looked at me wistfully. "Then why did you move to the United States?" I inquired. "We have nothing," she replied, shaking her head. "No soap, no paper, no cars, no clothes, no meat, . . . nothing."

✦ Cultural Closeup

- Dramatic social and political changes swept through Cuba in the second half of the 20th century, beginning with Fidel Castro Ruz's takeover of power in 1959. With assistance from the former Soviet Union, Castro turned Cuba into a Communist country. The government controlled every aspect of the economy, and all private property was nationalized.

- The Communist government has seen to it that its Communist ideology permeates every facet of life, and political indoctrination starts at an early age. Cuban schoolchildren start their day by saluting the Cuban flag and singing a song honoring Cuban patriot Ernesto "Che" Guevara. Secondary and high school students sing anthems and recite speeches about important figures of the Cuban revolution. The ideological content of Cuban school textbooks is controlled by the government and designed to reflect the Communist perspective and emphasize the revolutionary message. Letters and sounds are taught using military concepts—*f* is for *fusil* (rifle), *gu* is for *guerrilla*—and word problems in math are about Cuba's symbolic lawsuit with the United States. Literature containing a negative view of Communism is banned. Teachers and other education workers are considered "soldiers" in the cause of protecting children from influences "contrary to their Communist formation."

- Due to the intolerance of political ideas opposing Communism, Cubans are often forced to be duplicitous. They have a public face shown by membership and participation in political organizations, for example, and a private face under which they teach a different set of values at home. Many Cubans must play this game if they wish to keep their jobs, have their children gain access to the university, and spare their families from harassment.

- Cubans today are faced with an extremely difficult economic situation. Since 1961, the United States has maintained a trade embargo against Cuba that prohibits the latter from importing products from and exporting products to the United States. When Soviet assistance to Cuba ceased after the collapse of the Soviet Union in 1991, poverty in Cuba increased, and there is now a lack of many goods, among them toiletries, medicines, paper, books, fuel for transportation and agriculture, and basic commodities, such as beef, milk, chicken, and eggs, which are in short supply due to Cuba's grain shortage. To ensure that all Cubans have equal access to food, many goods are rationed. According to recent data from the United Nations Financial Accounting Office, Cuba ranks last in per capita daily caloric consumption when compared to 11 other Latin American countries.

- Castro's Communist government has been intolerant of religious beliefs. In 1962, Catholic schools were seized and shut down, and Cuba was declared an atheist state. People who practiced their religion were denied education (access to the university) and employment. In 1991, Cubans regained the right to practice religion. In 1992, an amendment to the Cuban constitution declared the state secular. Nevertheless, churches may not establish institutions, such as schools, in Cuba, nor do they have complete access to the Cuban media.

- Food is very important to Cubans, and they enjoy eating together with their families and friends. Due to Cuba's strapped economy, there may be little hope of buying a nice car or a beautiful new home, but it is still possible to enjoy a good meal on occasion. Many families try to eat something special on Saturdays and Sundays.

- Cubans love to dance and will do so at almost any occasion. They especially participate in dance on July 26 (the national holiday), on New Year's Eve, and during Carnaval. The most popular dance is called the *casino* and is similar to *salsa*.

- National holidays in Cuba are January 1, New Year's Day and the anniversary of the revolution; May 1, International Worker's Day (Labor Day); July 26, National Rebellion Day and the anniversary of the Moncada attack; and October 10, the anniversary of the beginning of the War of Independence. Unofficial holidays that are important to Cubans include *Noche Buena* (Christmas Eve), the period of Epiphany in early January, *Semana Santa* (Holy Week, before Easter), and Carnaval. The last is traditionally celebrated in the days before Lent but has been moved to July in Santiago de Cuba to commemorate the revolution.

- Prior to the revolution, the Cuban family unit was very close. Today, however, many Cuban parents feel that their authority is being undermined by the Communist government's requirement that young people participate in social activities outside the home and by the practice of sending secondary school students to country boarding schools, or *las escuelas al campo,* for most of the year. Relationships within the family unit are also being strained by overcrowding in homes due to housing shortages. It is not uncommon to find three generations living together in one apartment.

- Despite a large amount of political contention, Cubans have a strong sense of nationalism and *Cubanidad,* or cultural identity. As an island country, Cuba's natural boundaries led to the development of a shared language and culture among its citizens.

- Cubans value collective wealth, interdependence, brotherhood, and loyalty to one's peer group—a combination of Hispanic and socialist elements. These values contrast greatly with American capitalism, independence, and individualism.

Educational Panorama

- Less than 5 percent of Cuba's higher secondary schools are urban. The Cuban government, drawing on the writings of José Martí and Ernesto "Che" Guevara, believes in the combination of mental and manual labor.

CUBA

Level/Age	Hours/Calendar	Curriculum	Required	Class Size	Exams	Grades	Classroom Setup	Homework
Day care, ages 6 mo.–4 yrs.	Sept.–June, 7:00 A.M.–4:00 or 6:00 P.M. Mon.–Fri.	Group play intended to develop basic knowledge, interests, and social skills, with a focus on cleanliness, achievement, and structured learning; seen as an opportunity to develop socialist values at an early age. Gender stereotypes are purposely discouraged.	No	25–40	None	None	Small tables and chairs, arranged in groups; special areas for painting, reading, and career role playing	None
Preschool, age 5	Sept.–June, 8:00 A.M.–12:30 P.M. Mon.–Fri.	Play intended to develop basic knowledge, interests, and social skills. Painting, drawing, ABC's, cutting and pasting, singing, etc. Children whose parents work stay for organized after-school activities.	No	25–40 or even 50	None	For behavior only	Tablelike desks for two students, arranged in rows	None
Primary, grades 1–6, ages 6–11	2 semesters Sept.–June, 8:00 A.M.–12:30 P.M. Mon.–Fri.	Basic arithmetic, science, basic literacy skills and composition in Spanish, English, geography, ideological orientation. Children whose parents work stay for organized after-school activities.	Yes	25–40	Written midterm and final examinations each semester	90–100 = excellent; 80–89 = above average; 70–79 = pass; below 70 = fail.	Tablelike desks for two students, arranged in rows	Daily written homework: exercises, paragraphs, essays, projects, reports, etc.
Basic secondary, grades 7–9, ages 12–14	2 semesters Sept.–June, 8:00 A.M.–12:30 P.M. Mon.–Fri.; activities in the afternoon	Spanish, English, the sciences, technical drawing, math, foundations of political knowledge, physical education, home economics for girls, shop for boys. Students in country schools do agricultural labor for half the day.	Yes	25–40	Written midterm and final examinations each semester	Same as above	Tablelike desks for two students, arranged in rows	Same as above
Technical and professional secondary, grades 10–12, ages 15–18	2 semesters Sept.–June, 8:00 A.M.–4:00 or 6:00 P.M. Mon.–Fri.	Completion of basic secondary school is required. Students may choose higher secondary school instead. Technical and professional studies lead to either a "skilled worker" or "middle-level technician" qualification. English and military preparation are required.	Yes	25–40	Written midterm and final examinations each semester	Same as above	Tablelike desks for two students, arranged in rows	Same as above
Higher secondary, grades 10–12, ages 15–18	2 semesters Sept.–June, 8 A.M.–12:30 P.M. or 1:00–4:30 P.M. Mon.–Fri.	Preuniversity studies leading to a *bachillerato* (secondary school leaving certificate); English and military preparation required. Students in country schools have classes in the morning or afternoon and do agricultural labor during the other shift.	Yes	25–40	Written midterm and final examinations each semester. Students may apply to university upon successful completion of higher secondary level.	Same as above	Tablelike desks for two students, arranged in rows	Same as above
University, age 18+	2 semesters Sept.–July, days and times vary.	A *licenciatura* or *título profesional* (professional diploma) requires 5 years of coursework (in medicine, 6); a master's degree (*maestría*), 1–2 years; a *candidato a doctor en ciencias*, 4–5 years. A *doctorado* is presented after thesis. All degrees require courses in English, scientific communism, and historical and dialectical materialism.	No	As many as 25–40; 10–20 generally, not more than 30	Oral examinations and *preguntas escritas* (written quizzes)	2–5: 5 = excellent; 4 = good; 3 = average; 2 = poor.	Long tables, arranged for seminars	Self-study and preparation; papers, reports, presentations

For this reason, basic secondary school students are required to spend 45 days a year at country boarding schools, where they spend half of each day working in the fields. Students in higher secondary school mostly attend country boarding schools, where they, too, spend half of each day picking oranges, planting crops, and so on. Students may only go home from country boarding schools on a weekend pass.

- Conditions in the country boarding schools are often dismal. Students complain about terrible food and having to use outhouses. Most of the schools are simple wooden structures with bare cement floors, in which rows of bunk beds have been set up, as many as 60 to 70 in one room. Sometimes, boys and girls must sleep in the same room. It is common for a Cuban family to try to get a doctor's excuse to prevent their child from having to attend a country boarding school.

- School officials in Cuba create a personal dossier for each student. This dossier records not only a student's grades but his or her political and religious activities as well. A negative entry in this dossier can prevent a student from being admitted to the university and/or obtaining a desirable job. After graduation, the dossiers follow students to their jobs, where supervisors continue to enter notes.

👁 A Closer Look

POLICY

- According to all sources, the Cuban educational system is excellent. Cuba's literacy rate is 96 percent, second only to Argentina among Latin American countries. A recent study by the United Nations Educational, Scientific, and Cultural Organization (UNESCO) of the quality of education in the Caribbean and Latin America ranked Cuba as number one. Pro-Castro sources claim this success is the result of the revolution's emphasis on education.

- The educational system of Cuba in no way resembles the prerevolution educational systems—neither the system in the Spanish colonial period, when education was only available to the wealthy urban Spanish population, nor the system during the period of occupation by the United States, when school enrollment rates never went beyond 60 percent and when the literacy rate stagnated around 72 percent. After the revolution in 1959, one of the first goals of the new government was to completely reform the educational system, not only to increase the accessibility of education and improve the educational level of the general populace, but also to serve as a medium in which to disseminate nationalist and socialist values and create a new culture. Castro considered education an important tool in creating a "new man"—one devoted to Communism and the "new society."

- Educational reform in Cuba can be characterized by four main phases: the expansion of formal schooling in the 1960s and the Literacy Campaign of

1961, the reforms of *Perfeccionamiento* (improvement) in the 1970s, the policies of *Perfeccionamiento Continuo* (ongoing improvement) in the 1980s, and the adjustments in the 1990s in what is known as the Special Period. In the expansion phase of the 1960s, the focus was on bringing basic education to the general populace, with an eye toward ending the disparities between races, genders, and urban versus rural populations. *Perfeccionamiento* sought to bring about qualitative improvements in the organization and unity of formal education. *Perfeccionamiento Continuo,* originally conceived as a recommitment to socialistic values and an *error correction* phase, shifted its focus to survival strategies as the economic crises of the 1990s caused the Special Period, which was marked by shortages of educational resources and an exodus of teachers into higher paying professions, such as tourism.

- The Cuban Ministry of Education controls the curriculum of Cuban schools, and ideological content is a top priority. Students use *ideologically correct* textbooks, and class exercises reflect Communist theory and anticapitalistic themes. Teachers are required by law to begin classes with 15 minutes of discussion about a current or historical event from the Communist perspective.

- The Ministry of Higher Education controls courses and programs, teaching methodology, and the allocation of student places. Only students who have completed the higher secondary school and received a *bachillerato,* a special diploma awarded at the end of a rigorous program, may apply for the university and sit for university entrance examinations. A student's political attitude and his and her participation in youth organizations are acceptance considerations. There are only a limited number of slots available in each major, and no student is guaranteed his or her first choice of major. The best students (both academically and politically) are assigned to the most desirable careers (international tourism, buisness, agriculture). The number of universities in Cuba has increased from 3 at the time of the revolution to 40 today.

- Education in Cuba is free to all. In return, students who complete a degree in higher education must work for a period of years in a position designated by the government.

TEACHING STYLE

- Starting in primary school, classes are taught mostly in lecture format in traditional, teacher-fronted classrooms, in which the teacher does most of the talking.

- Textbooks are loaned to students and returned.

- Aside from a blackboard and chalk, there are very few other instructional materials available, due to the shortage of goods, especially paper.

- At the university, teachers lecture or lead discussion-type seminars in which the students participate actively by commenting on assigned literature, giving presentations, and so on.

- Teachers in primary school through higher secondary school may ask questions of students during class, and students are expected to stand up when giving an answer. Students ask questions by raising their hands and waiting to be called on.

- Teachers in Cuba are generally very well trained and well prepared, and lessons are delivered with firm confidence.

- In primary school through higher secondary school, teachers write almost everything on the blackboard, and students must take notes. This changes drastically at the university, where students are expected to learn more independently.

LEARNING STYLE

- Most work is done individually within the Cuban classroom at the primary and secondary levels. At the university level, both individual and group work is common.

- Homework is taken very seriously, and Cuban students spend a lot of time completing their assignments. This activity is reinforced during planned after-school activities at the secondary schools and country boarding schools, where monitors ensure that homework is completed at required evening study sessions. Homework is also often completed with the assistance of parents or friends.

- Memorizing information is considered quite important, as are critical-thinking skills.

- It is very common for Cuban students to form after-school study groups. Generally, these groups will be arranged by subject. Sometimes, study groups are a necessity due to Cuba's difficult economic situation: two or three students may have only one textbook to share.

INSTRUCTIONAL SETTING

- School buildings in Cuba are often simple square buildings, many of which were formerly police buildings or military facilities appropriated during the expansion of education in the 1960s. Today, many of these buildings are well worn and in need of paint or repair. Though the climate tends to be hot and humid for much of the year, schools are not air-conditioned.

- The country boarding schools tend to be simple wooden constructions ("like a shed," reported one teacher) with bare cement floors. They tend to have outhouses for restrooms.

- Power cuts, or *apagones,* are a regular occurrence in Cuba. Since Cuban schools have no air-conditioning, few or no computers, and very little other technical equipment, the power outages do not affect instruction greatly. They do, however, interrupt evening study sessions in the country boarding schools.

- Classrooms in Cuba are often decorated with pictures of Cuban revolutionary heroes, such as Fidel Castro, José Martí, and Ernesto "Che" Guevara, as well as with the national emblem of Cuba. They may also have bulletin boards with information to help and/or motivate students, such as math tables. Pro-Communist and anti-American slogans, such as *Viva Fidel* [long live Fidel] and *Patria o muerte, venceremos* [country or death, we will win] are often displayed in the schools.

- Cuban students store their books and belongings in their desks. It is rare that they need to wear coats to school, but if they do, they simply hang them on the backs of the school chairs. There are no lockers for students.

- Given the Cuban emphasis on combining manual and mental labor, students are expected to help keep the school clean and to help care for the school grounds.

- Transportation to and from school remains a problem in Cuba due to a lack of vehicles and to shortages of fuel. For this reason, students at the country boarding schools, who once received weekend passes to return home, may be required to remain at school every other weekend.

ACTIVITIES

- Students are required to participate in political activities. Primary school children automatically become *pioneros,* akin to Boy and Girl Scouts, and participate in neighborhood watches, cleanups, recycling collections, campouts, and marches. Secondary school children join the Federation of Middle School Students. They attend rallies, do agricultural labor, and receive military training. Students who intend to go on to the university are expected to join and participate in the activities of the Union of Young Communists, the youth branch of the Communist Party, in which they receive more military training and attend conferences, rallies, and marches. University students may also join the Student University Federation.

- Cultural activities and sports round out the Cuban educational experience. Once a year, for example, the school sports games are held. At this competition, the best athletes aged 11 to 16 are invited to be tested for the Schools for Sports Initiation. At these special schools, students are coached and encouraged to participate in higher-level competitions, with the goal of attending one of the Schools of Higher Athletic Performance after graduation.

DISCIPLINE AND CLASS MANAGEMENT

- Students in Cuba have great respect for their teachers. When teachers enter the classroom in the primary and secondary schools, their students rise to greet them.

- Classrooms in Cuba maintain, in general, a disciplined atmosphere. Teachers run their classrooms with a friendly but firm hand. Disciplinary actions depend on the nature of the offending incident and the teacher. A teacher may embarrass a student who has not done his or her homework or may purposely ask an offending student more difficult questions on an oral exam. Teachers can, moreover, hit a student, and some do, either with a hand or with a ruler. This type of punishment seems more common during after-school activities, when an adult monitor, rather than a teacher, is attending the students.

- Starting in secondary school, each class elects class monitors, whose job is to assist the teacher and help keep order. There is generally one monitor for every subject of study, and the best students in each subject are chosen. General duties of the class monitor might include reviewing with the class until the teacher arrives, going over homework assignments, or tutoring students in need of assistance. While the position is considered an honor in secondary school, few students seem to want the job at the university level.

- Students are expected to be on time for class, and a student who is more than 10 to 15 minutes late will not ask to be admitted to the classroom.

- Political dissention of any kind is not tolerated in a Cuban classroom, and students who dare to express an anti-Castro or anti-Communist view can expect to be punished and to have a note of the incident put in their permanent personal dossiers. Such a note could prevent a student from entering the university. Very serious offenders can be put in prison for *re-educación,* Marxist indoctrination classes.

- Although it is uncommon, a student has the right to dispute a grade. This generally does not happen, however, because retesting until the student passes the exam or class is a common practice.

- Parents in Cuba are very involved in their children's education. It is customary for teachers to meet formally with parents three to four times a year. Moreover, parents are welcome to drop by to inquire about their child's progress, and they do so frequently.

TEACHER-STUDENT RELATIONSHIP

- Teachers develop warm relationships with their students and become almost like family members. This is particularly true in primary school, due to the fact that the students have the same teacher for grades one through four and for grades five and six.

- Cuban teachers are seen by their students as being well trained, well prepared, and very caring. Teachers assume the responsibility of guiding and motivating their students, and they push them to succeed. They also make themselves accessible to their students; a teacher who stays after class to assist students is valued.

- Though intimate relationships between teachers and students are not legal, they seem to be fairly common, especially between male teachers and female students and especially at the country boarding schools.

STUDENT-STUDENT RELATIONSHIP

- Due to all the time that Cuban students spend together, they tend to develop strong bonds, and they are warm, friendly, and helpful toward each other. These relationships are reinforced by the socialist philosophy that the common good and goals of the group are more important than individual success or achievement.

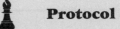 **Protocol**

NONVERBAL BEHAVIOR

- Cubans, in general, are very warm and friendly people, and they express this warmth in their mannerisms. They smile a lot, and they greet each other warmly, often with hugs and kisses or at least by shaking hands. Men may exchange a hug (*un abrazo*) as a sign of affection. One Cuban woman stated that when she immigrated to the United States, one of the first things she had to learn in greeting and conversing with Americans was "Don't touch!"

- Like many Latin Americans, Cubans tend to stand close to each other when conversing, and they may tap conversation partners frequently on the arm, shoulder, or back.

- In the classroom, it is common for a teacher to touch a student, and an encouraging pat on the back would not be considered offensive. When greeting a teacher outside of school, the hug and the kiss given to close friends is completely acceptable.

- When held behind someone else's head, the hand gesture of vertical horns (raised index and pinky fingers, with the thumb clasping the other two fingers) means that the person's spouse is cheating on him or her. However, this gesture is often used in jest—for example, when photographs are being taken.

- The hand gesture used to mean "ok" in the United States (placing the thumb and index finger together) means the same thing in Cuba.

IMAGES

- Cubans, both children and adults alike, participate in an activity involving the phrase *el que no salte es yanqui,* meaning "he who doesn't jump is a Yankee." In this activity, the phrase is shouted out by numerous participants, which causes everyone to hop up and down to avoid the insult of being called a Yankee—in other words, an American.

- Paintings and photos of José Martí and Ernesto "Che" Guevara may be seen all over Cuba. Martí, the central figure in Cuba's struggle for independence from Spain, wrote voluminously about economic, racial, and gender equality. Guevara helped organize Castro's coup in 1959 and is considered a role model by socialists. He died leading the guerrilla movement in Bolivia.

- A typical sight in Cuba is a late 1950s or early 1960s automobile. Few vehicles were brought into the country after the 1960s, and Cuban mechanics are known for their ingenuity in repairing and maintaining these cars. It is not uncommon for a "new" vehicle to be built entirely of parts from other vehicles. In general, the Cubans are a resourceful people, making the best out of what they have.

FORMS OF ADDRESS

- In Spanish, men are addressed with *señor* and women with *señora.* In Cuba, an additional form of address is often used to get a person's attention: *compañero* for a man and *compañera* for a woman mean "comrade."
- A form of address common between men is *compadre,* which literally means "godfather" but actually means "my friend."
- Teachers are addressed with *maestro* (masculine) or *maestra* (feminine). University professors are addressed with *profesor* or *profesora.*
- At all levels of instruction, teachers generally address students by given name.
- Students address each other by given name, nickname, or, occasionally, last name.

DRESS

- All Cuban students are required to wear the same uniform: a white shirt, red shorts or a red skirt, and a blue scarf in preschool; the same in primary school but with a red scarf; a white shirt and yellow shorts or a yellow skirt in middle school; a blue shirt and dark blue trousers or a dark blue skirt in secondary school. In the university, only medical students have a uniform—dark blue trousers or a dark blue skirt and a white coat.
- Teachers and professors in Cuba dress casually but conservatively in simple dresses and/or slacks and shirts—even in T-shirts and jeans. Teachers cannot afford expensive clothes, and there is a clothing shortage in Cuba as well. Teachers are expected to be well groomed: men do not have long hair, and women wear little makeup.
- The *guayabera,* a popular Latin shirt, is considered acceptable business attire and is, in fact, worn by the heads of businesses and companies and by academic deans. Conservative suits and ties are seldom worn except when doing business with a foreign company.

POLITE/IMPOLITE TOPICS AND BEHAVIORS

- Given the consequences to Cubans of criticizing Fidel Castro or Cuba's Communist government, political topics are best avoided in Cuba. When meeting Cubans who have immigrated from their country, political topics still may not be a good choice, due to political contention within the Cuban community itself. Cuban points of view on politics can vary considerably, and a particular Cuban immigrant's view depends on when he or she left Cuba.

GIFT GIVING

- Small gifts are given among family members for typical occasions, such as birthdays, weddings, Mother's Day, Father's Day, and perhaps Valentine's Day.

- When a gift is given, it is customary to open it in front of the giver.

- It is not common for guests to bring a gift when invited to a home in Cuba for dinner, and it is certainly not expected, since little is available in Cuba to bring. However, a small gift would be graciously accepted.

- When visiting in Cuba, it is a nice gesture to bring things of which Cuban citizens are in short supply: for example, small bottles of toiletries, medicines, paper products, and writing supplies.

? ☼ Problem/Solution

PROBLEM

One of my Cuban students asks me a lot of questions about issues involving procedures and paperwork, such as registration procedures, graduation requirements, financial aid eligibility, and so on. He even asks me about issues unrelated to school, such as health and car insurance. I sometimes do not feel qualified to assist him. What should I do?

SOLUTION

Cubans accustomed to socialist systems in which their needs were met and their decisions were made for them are often overwhelmed by U.S. bureaucracy, which places the main responsibility for seeking information and services on the individual. Try to assist this student as best you can by reading through the materials (the college catalog, the insurance forms, etc.), and/or direct the student to appropriate advisors. Also try to be patient. Cubans deeply value their education, and they will go through much to achieve academic success. Remember, most Cuban newcomers to the U.S. educational system have spent the majority of their lives in a socialist educational system that gave them very little choice with regard to selecting a career path and no choice of courses once the major field of study had been selected. These students are likely to be baffled by the variety of programs offered at even the high school level, let alone by the variety of degree programs offered at a university, by the complications of selecting electives versus nonelectives, and so on.

PROBLEM

My Cuban students do not seem to pronounce consonants at the end of words and some syllables. How can I help them with their pronunciation?

SOLUTION

The sounds *b, v, w, s, ch, d, th* as in *either, f, g, k, p,* and *t* are often not pronounced at the ends of words in Cuban Spanish; they occur, but remain *unaspirated.* In other words, the vocal apparatus is in place, but the articulation is withheld. This makes Cubans' English (and for some native Spanish speakers, even their Spanish) difficult to understand. Moreover, some Cuban speakers pronounce *n* as *ng* and *r* as *l* before another consonant or at the end of a word. Your students will need a lot of practice learning to hear the differences between these consonant sounds.

PROBLEM

I have heard Cuban immigrant students complain about how unfriendly people are in their new homeland. They say that most of their teachers do their job without seeming to care and that their fellow students are not as helpful as those back home were. How should I respond to this complaint?

SOLUTION

These students are probably influenced by a combination of cultural influences. First, there is the idea of the *ideal* Cuban teacher. In Cuba, a good teacher is one who is accessible and available to help students, one who takes interest in and shows concern for the students. In return, a teacher is treated almost like a family member. This type of relationship may be difficult to duplicate under the demands of a modern, time-conscious culture. Second, interdependence and loyalty to one's peer group are greatly valued in Cuba, and these values carry over to the school system. Peers are expected to help one another, and they gladly do so—by forming study groups, for example. Your Cuban students are probably shocked by the individualism and competitiveness demonstrated by students in many Western cultures. A casual discussion about the differences between these two value systems may help to make your Cuban students feel less intimidated and more welcome.

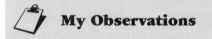 **My Observations**

Egypt

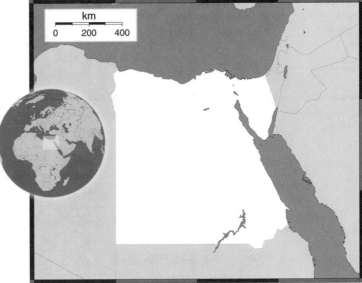

 Focus on Egypt

Capital: Cairo

Population: 68,359,979

Size: 386,662 sq. mi. (1,001,449 sq. km.)

Location: northeastern Africa; bordered by Libya to the west, Sudan to the south, the Gaza Strip and Israel to the east. The Mediterranean Sea lies to the north, the Red Sea to the east.

Climate: mild winters (Nov.–Apr.), with temperatures from 68 to 88 degrees Fahrenheit; hot summers (May–Oct.), with temperatures from 88 to 104 degrees Fahrenheit; rainfall minimal except along Mediterranean coast

Monetary Unit: Egyptian pound

Urban/Rural Life: 45% urban, 55% rural

Religion: 90% Sunni Muslim, 8.5% Coptic Christian, 1.5% other Christian

Languages: Arabic (official)

Ethnicity: Hamitic and Semitic Arabs

Government: republic

 Personal Snapshot

My intensive academic ESL class was like many others in that it included many student-centered activities, and I often made use of cooperative learning, with students assigned to small groups. I viewed my role as that of a facilitator, one who guided students in their language learning. As the semester progressed, so did the students, and I thought everyone was comfortable with the way I had structured the class. One day, a colleague walked into my office and said he wanted to share what he had overheard a student saying about my class. To my surprise, he told me that he had heard one of my Egyptian students wondering out loud when I would begin teaching the class. The student indicated his frustration in not knowing what would be asked on the final exam, asking how he could pass my class if I didn't teach him what he needed to know. I then realized that not all students automatically adjust to the North

American educational system or understand the many ways there are of learning. In class the next day, I made it a point to address the difference between teacher-centered and student-centered classrooms and did my best to help this student realize that I was teaching and that he was learning.

⟶✦⟵ Cultural Closeup

- In Egypt, the family is considered the cornerstone of society. The Egyptian family is an extended one, comprising grandparents, aunts, uncles, cousins, nephews and nieces, and in-laws.

- Marriage has great importance in Egyptian society, and although it is becoming more common for young people to choose their marriage partners, arranged marriages still exist, especially in the countryside.

- In many villages outside of the city, a married woman's status rises when she has children, especially if she gives birth to sons.

- Education is the mark of the modern man or woman. Although getting an education does not guarantee one a good job with a good salary, it is the goal parents set for their children. Parents are willing to sacrifice to give their children a good education. Most people believe that to succeed in school, students need private lessons, and parents are willing to pay the cost of tutors for their children.

👁 A Closer Look

POLICY

- Educational policy is determined by the Ministry of Education. Education is compulsory through middle school, that is, to approximately age 14. Education is free at all its different levels, although private schools charge tuition. The Book Sector of the Ministry of Education provides students with textbooks from kindergarten through the end of secondary school.

- The curriculum focuses on basic skills, self-education, and the use of technology. Religious education is included in the curriculum, as are foreign languages and Arabic. Science and math play an important role in education as well, and the Ministry of Education promotes the educational use of computers, televisions, and language labs and the use of the Internet in the classroom. The curriculum in the secondary school is two-track: general, or college preparatory, and technical.

- There are both private and public schools in Egypt. The private schools are supervised by the state and include primary, preparatory (middle), secondary, and technical schools. These types of private schools tend to offer a higher standard of education and, thus, are becoming increasingly popular.

Educational Panorama

EGYPT

Level/Age	Hours/Calendar	Curriculum	Required	Class Size	Exams	Grades	Classroom Setup	Homework
Preschool, ages 3–4	Varies	Basic social skills	No	Varies	None	None	Varies	None
Kindergarten, ages 5–6	Oct.–May	Varies from school to school	No	35	None	None	Varies	None
Elementary, grades 1–5, ages 6–11	34 weeks, 45-minute periods, 24–30 hours/week Sat.–Thu.; 2 terms, with 2-week vacation mid-year at the end of Jan. or beginning of Feb.	Grades 1–3: reading, writing, math, and religion; grades 4–5: use of basic skills	Yes	45	Achievement tests and oral performance tests to get certificate at end of cycle. Students must pass a special exam to go to intermediate school.	A single written exam at end of term; evaluations sent to parents throughout the school year	Desks in rows. Students stay in the same classroom with the main teacher most of the day and spend 1–2 hours with another teacher.	A lot of homework is assigned.
Middle, grades 6–8, ages 12–14	Same as above	Reading, writing, math, social studies, and religion	No	40	Students must pass a special exam to go to secondary school.	A single written exam at end of term; no grades throughout year; 3 written exams at end of year for basic education completion certificate	Desks in rows. Students stay in the same classroom, and teachers change classrooms throughout the day.	A lot of homework is assigned. Either the parents help, or a tutor is hired.
High, grades 9–11, ages 14–17	Same as above	General: humanities, social studies, math, and science; technical: agriculture, communication or industry (3 years or 5 years)	No	40 40	Students must pass a standardized exam to pass to the next level. There is a nationwide exam for each subject. Grades decide the future of a person.	Two written exams at end of term; no final grades. General secondary stage certificate exam leads to general secondary stage certificate. Exams at end of 3/5-year cycle lead to diploma. Final exams include sections on translation, composition, novels, linguistics, and poetry. Students who fail 1–2 subjects during their senior year can retake the relevant exam(s) during the summer.	Desks in rows. Students stay in the same classroom except for lab classes. Teachers change classrooms throughout the day.	Homework is assigned but is not so important. More emphasis is placed on the standardized exam.
University, ages 17–22	Oct.–June; vacation July–Sept.	Varied: law, engineering, etc. All students in the same group take the same courses during the year.	No	600–3,000 in lectures, divided into sections of 40 students taught by teaching assistants	Midterm exams (30% of final grade) and final exams (70% of final grade)	90+ = Excellent (varies according to field); 80–89 = very good; 70–79 = good; 60–69 = acceptable; 0–59 = fail.	Students attend classes in large lecture halls.	Few quizzes are given, and little homework is assigned, because emphasis is on exams.

- Higher education in Egypt includes both university and nonuniversity education. There are public universities in Egypt, and a limited number of private universities have appeared in the last decade. Egyptian universities are independent institutions: they are academic and cultural in nature. The best universities are usually located in the cities.

- The university presidents and deans of colleges are appointed by the Minister of Higher Education, who also sets educational policy.

- Students are chosen to attend public universities based on their grades. Students who attain good grades in high school can attend better universities and have more choices of field of study. The top fields of study, open only to those with the highest grades, are medicine and engineering. Although the number of women enrolled in universities is beginning to increase, it still remains relatively low.

- In the last decade, the private universities have improved, but they are still not considered to be as good as the public universities. Students lacking the grades to enter the public universities often attend the private universities.

- Government-operated training institutes are open to those who have completed the basic cycle (nine years), and vocational education offers certificates for programs of varying lengths. Institutes offer four- or five-year programs, including specialty training in acting, dance, and film production. Teacher training is a five-year program for which a certificate can be issued. Vocational schools offer two-year programs and issue certificates in such subjects as accounting or computer science.

- The Ministry of Education encourages continuing education for its population. Students who graduate from technical schools may go on to the university level and may even choose from a number of alternatives for completing the university level, including finishing via correspondence courses for students enrolled at open universities.

- Education and culture became a priority in the country in the 1990s. Overall goals included developing education at all levels in the school system and improving the quality of education. Previously, teaching positions held little status in the country, and many teachers left to teach in other Arab countries. Teaching salaries have since improved, and training programs for teachers, including sending teachers abroad for teacher training as well as technology training, are being instituted. However, many teachers continue to add to their income by giving private lessons. In 1990, tutoring was made legal, and the pay for tutoring was regulated by the government.

- Additional goals of the Ministry of Education include increased attention to religious and artistic activities, to nutrition and health care, and to increasing literacy among the country's population. Literacy classes and vocational training are offered at schools in rural areas or small villages, in an effort to reach the approximately 45 percent of the population who cannot read or write.

TEACHING STYLE

- An ideal teacher is defined as one who is friendly but reserved and strict. By being too friendly toward a student, a teacher may send the message that he or she will not fail the student regardless of poor academic performance.

- Memorization is important to passing the exams at the end of the school cycle. To pass tests, students write down and memorize everything said by the teacher. Personal opinion is not encouraged; written text is viewed as authority. Teachers do not use games as learning tools in the classroom.

- There are no choices in the yearlong programs; the curriculum is set. Research and library skills are not taught. Private schools offer classes in foreign languages.

LEARNING STYLE

- Students work individually most of the time, occasionally in pairs, and seldom in groups. Students feel safe when they are silent and become self-conscious when required to speak in a group. Depending on their degree of religiousness, some women, mainly Muslim women, may feel nervous when working with men.

- Students raise their hands to answer or are called on to answer by the teacher. Students receive praise for work well done.

- Students are not exposed to collaborative or cooperative learning and thus are unfamiliar with the dynamics of group or pair work.

- Learning is teacher-centered.

INSTRUCTIONAL SETTING

- Chairs or desks are usually arranged in rows. If the class is small, chairs may be arranged in circles.

- In most classes, a class leader is elected at the beginning of each school year.

ACTIVITIES

- School sports include soccer, basketball, handball, and volleyball.

- After-school activities include agriculture, computers, cooking (for girls), theater, and drawing. In private schools, these activities may come during long breaks between class terms.

DISCIPLINE AND CLASS MANAGEMENT

- Students are expected to be on time for class. If late, they knock on the door and ask to be admitted. They apologize for their lateness. Students must request permission to use the restroom.

- In high school, when the teacher steps into the classroom, students stand until they are told to sit.

- Turning in homework late may result in a lower grade; not all teachers accept late homework.

- Attendance is mandatory. A student is not allowed to take exams if his or her attendance falls below 70 percent. Letters threatening dismissal may be sent to the student's family.

TEACHER-STUDENT RELATIONSHIP

- Many Egyptian teachers consider themselves friend and father or mother to their students. If a student is doing poorly in school, the teacher may ask the parents to come in to discuss the problem, but the teacher will not go to the student's home. Every month, the parents receive a report on—or attend a parent-teacher meeting to discuss—the student's status.

- The demeanor expected of teachers is reflected by the common Egyptian belief that a teacher must be loved by his or her students. At the same time, teachers do not often joke with their students.

- Students tend to worship their teachers. Students see themselves as the recipients of information fed to them by their teachers.

- Teachers show respect for their students by listening to their problems and treating them in a friendly manner.

- Students show respect for their teachers by obeying them and by the way they talk to them—for example, by not asking personal questions of them.

- If students are doing poorly in class, families may hire a tutor to give their children extra lessons. Often, the classroom teacher is hired as the tutor.

- Teachers are seen as authorities, and students will not disagree with them. Students tend to feel that disagreeing with the teacher may result in failing the course. Turn taking is not well defined, and interruptions by students are very common.

STUDENT-STUDENT RELATIONSHIP

- Students tend to group themselves by common interests and view their classmates as a big group of friends.

- Saving face is an important part of the Egyptian culture. Supplying answers to a classmate during an exam, behavior viewed as cheating in a North American classroom, is seen as helping a classmate in an Egyptian classroom. Supplying answers helps the student supplied save face by not failing the exam.

Protocol

NONVERBAL BEHAVIOR

- It is common for men to embrace or kiss when greeting each other. However, casual touching on the arm or back or head is appropriate only between boys or between girls. For some people, depending on their religious beliefs, any touching of another person of the opposite sex is forbidden.

IMAGES

- Egyptians hold the elderly in high regard and show their respect for old age in sayings and proverbs, such as *He who is one day older than you knows a whole year better than you.*

- The saying *He who lives with a group of people for forty days becomes one of them* reflects the value Egyptians place on companionship.

- The proverb *Whoever taught me a letter, a slave should I be to him* reflects the Egyptians' great attitude of respect toward teachers.

FORMS OF ADDRESS

- In elementary school, preparatory school, and secondary school, such titles as *abla* and *ustez* are used when addressing female and male teachers, respectively. The English word *mister* is also becoming very popular in many schools.

- The title *doctor* is used for any teacher in the university, whether or not he or she holds a doctorate degree.

- Teachers address students by first name.

DRESS

- Uniforms are worn in private and public schools. In public schools, students are asked to wear specific colors—blue pants and white shirts, for example. Students are thus uniformly dressed at an affordable cost. Girls' uniforms consist of skirts or pants, a blouse, and a tie.

- Outside of school, girls generally wear skirts that are below the knee and do not wear sleeveless blouses. Neither girls nor women wear shorts or blouses with revealing necklines.

- Egyptian girls and women pay much attention to their appearance. They iron their clothes, fix their hair nicely, and wear makeup. Egyptian women are often described as elegant in their dress, a reference to their not dressing casually.

POLITE/IMPOLITE TOPICS AND BEHAVIORS

- It is generally considered impolite to discuss outside one's family the special affairs of the family or any problems occurring within the family. Because of the teacher's role as father or mother figure to the student, a student may approach a teacher to discuss a personal or family problem.

- Sex issues are discussed in some high school religion classes as part of the government curriculum; the religion teacher is the same gender as the students.

- Students are not accustomed to discussing controversial issues, such as abortion, euthanasia, or gun control.

- It is considered impolite to openly admire another person's belongings or possessions. Envy is to be avoided, and it would be inappropriate to say, "I wish I had a car like yours." People do, however, often offer compliments. Such comments as "You look nice today. Your necklace is very pretty. Where did you buy it?" are acceptable and appropriate.

- When greeting someone, it is considered polite to ask about the person's health and family.

GIFT GIVING

- Students usually give gifts to their teachers on Mother's Day or Father's Day and at the end of the school year.

- It is not acceptable for students to give teachers presents for no apparent reason. By doing so, a student would be suggesting that he or she expects some favor from the teacher in return. Likewise, accepting such a gift suggests on the part of the teacher that he or she is willing to do something for the student in return; that is, the teacher is accepting a bribe.

- Outside of school, gifts may be given on birthdays, Mother's Day, and Valentine's Day and for weddings and the birth of a child. Typical gifts include flowers, chocolate, and jewelry. Money is given as a gift at weddings and at a celebration on the seventh day of a child's birth.

- A gift should not be opened in front of the giver.

? 💡 Problem/Solution

PROBLEM

My Egyptian student seems more concerned about passing the tests in my class than about any other aspect of the class, including learning. Doing homework, participating in discussions, and giving presentations seem unimportant to him. What can I do to make him realize he is going to fail my class if he doesn't do every task that is required?

SOLUTION

Your student may not understand the basics of the Western educational system. In Egyptian schools, the goal of learning is test-driven, and to pass tests, students focus on memorizing everything the teacher says. Explain to your student that in his host educational system, learning is seen as a process and thus is both knowledge- and test-driven. It is important for you to explain clearly to your Egyptian students your expectations regarding their performance.

PROBLEM

Recently, before I administered a test to my class, I told the students that they were to keep their eyes on their own papers and that cheating would not be tolerated. Halfway through the test, I was totally surprised to see two of my students sharing answers. I warned them and finally had to separate them. Why did they so blatantly disregard my instructions?

SOLUTION

The issue here seems to be more cultural than academic. Saving face is an important part of Egyptian culture. Rather than let a friend lose face by doing poorly on a test, an Egyptian student will offer that friend help—to the point of supplying answers during a test. Explain to the students the North American concept of *academic dishonesty* to help them understand the possible consequences resulting from helping a friend by providing test answers.

PROBLEM

In the conversation class I teach, I often bring in news articles or show short film clips. I try to find topics that will stimulate conversation among my students, and I find that I have the most success with controversial topics, such as same-sex marriages, euthanasia, and gun control. Although usually very talkative, some of my Egyptian students tend to hang back and not speak up much during discussions on such topics. What can I do to bring them into the group?

SOLUTION

There are two possible explanations for your students' behavior. First, the dynamics of pair and/or group work may be new to your Egyptian students and may require some explanation on your part. Egyptian students tend to feel safe when they are silent and to become self-conscious when they have to speak in a group. Second, your Egyptian students may be uncomfortable talking about issues considered taboo in their country. Dividing your class into several groups, offering each group a choice of topics, some controversial and some not, and allowing your students to choose which group to join will bring them into a group without making them uncomfortable.

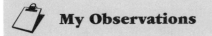 **My Observations**

Haiti

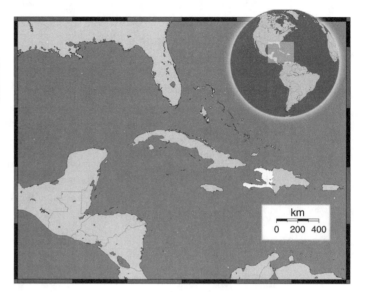

 Focus on Haiti

Capital: Port-au-Prince

Population: 6,867,995

Size: 10,714 sq. mi. (27,750 sq. km.)

Location: western third of the island of Hispaniola in the northern Caribbean Sea

Climate: tropical along the coast (average temperature 70 to 95 degrees Fahrenheit); subject to hurricanes; semiarid in the eastern half where the mountains cut off trade winds (average temperature 50 to 75 degrees Fahrenheit)

Monetary Unit: gourde, divided into 100 centimes

Urban/Rural Life: 80% live in abject poverty; 70% depend on agriculture.

Religion: 80% Roman Catholic, 16% Protestant. Half the population practices voodoo.

Languages: French and Haitian Kreyòl (both official)

Ethnicity: 95% African descent, 5% mulatto (African-European)

Government: democratic republic with legislative, judicial, and executive branches (with both a president and a prime minister)

 Personal Snapshot

The very popular Haitian proverb *Piti, piti, wazo fe nich li* [Little by little, the bird builds its nest] reflects how I see Haitian students learning English—*piti, piti.* Because of a very poor education system and a high rate of illiteracy, Haitian students are arriving in the United States and Canada with huge gaps in their learning. Transcripts might indicate that they are in high school, but once they are in the classroom, deficiencies in their learning appear. Some of these students show up in the 11th grade and do not even know how to hold a pencil. The theory behind BICS (Basic Interpersonal Communication Skills) and CALP (Cognitive Academic Language Proficiency) allows for five to seven years for students to develop cognitive-academic language. How can they do it in two years (i.e., 11th and 12th grades) if they cannot even read or write? To teach these students, I often have to start with the alphabet, which is basically the same in English and the Haitian languages, and go from there—*piti, piti.*

⟶⟨⟶ Cultural Closeup

- Elements of Haiti's culture come from African traditions. The majority of Haitians are pure descendants of African slaves brought to the islands by French owners of Haitian sugar plantations during the 17th and 18th centuries.

- Voodoo combines African religious beliefs and rituals with beliefs and symbols of Roman Catholicism. Although most Haitian people claim to be Roman Catholic, almost all of them practice voodoo in some form. This uniquely Haitian religion believes in *louas,* or spirits, that are believed to help families by either bringing good fortune or harming enemies. In return, families must offer gifts of food, drink, or flowers during the rituals. Drums are almost always involved with voodoo rituals, as are dancing and drinking near a family altar.

- Haitians have a vibrant oral culture full of jokes, riddles, proverbs, and folktales. Families often gather in the evening to listen to a story. The storyteller will ask, "*Krik?*" and if the family wants to hear the story, they will answer, "*Krak.*" The most common folktales involve the quick-witted and mischievous Ti Malice and his dim-witted friend Bouki. Here is a short example: One day, Ti Malice went over to Bouki's house. When he arrived at the *lakou* (farmyard), he was shocked at what he saw, and he watched for some time. Bouki was playing dominoes with his dog! Ti Malice said, "Bouki, what a brilliant dog you have! He can play dominoes." "I don't know," said Bouki. "He's not so smart. I beat him three out of five games already!" Hundreds of proverbs exist in Haitian culture. One popular proverb reflects the difficulty of life in Haiti: "*Dye mon, gen mon*" [Beyond the mountain is another mountain]. Another proverb points to Haiti's social division and to the suspicious nature of Haitians: "*Li pale franse*" literally means "He speaks French," but the phrase's implied meaning is "He is deceiving you."

- Since the 1987 constitution, Haitian Creole, or Kreyòl, and French have been the two official languages in Haiti. Everyone speaks Kreyòl, but only a few people speak French. Prior to 1987, French was the language used in government, business, and education. This language difference further increased the gap between the upper and lower classes.

- Some Haitians, especially those educated in French before 1987, are very critical of books written in Kreyòl. Furthermore, since French was the language of the upper class, many Haitians continue to see it as a prestige language and, therefore, claim they speak French even if they do not.

- About 2 percent of the population is considered to be wealthy, controlling about 44 percent of the national income. Approximately 80 percent of the population lives in abject poverty. Some families are so poor that they send their children to work as *restaveks,* or domestic servants, in the homes of the middle class. It is estimated that there are 300,000 children, ages 4 to 17, living as *restaveks.*

- Immigration to the United States and Canada has been high. One in six Haitians now lives outside of Haiti, mainly in south Florida, New York, Boston, Chicago, and Montreal.

- Common-law marriages, called *plasaj,* are considered normal, and having more than one in a lifetime is acceptable.

- Extended, supportive families are part of the traditional Haitian culture. In fact, the extended family often includes half brothers and half sisters that are born to either the mother or the father. However, the siblings do not regard each other as anything other than full siblings, and they live harmoniously in one household.

🎓 Educational Panorama

- A large gap exists between public and private educational facilities, and since over 75% of schools are private schools run by charitable or religious organizations, variations occur in the curricula.

- Less than 50 percent of Haitians can read and write.

- The dropout rate is very high, but there is no age limit for going back to school. Thus, it is possible to have a 40-year-old student in a class full of children.

👁 A Closer Look

POLICY

- Major educational reforms took place in 1978. In 1987, Kreyòl gained approval for use in Haiti's primary schools. One setback has been the slow development of affordable teaching materials in Kreyòl. Another impediment has been the lack of adequate teaching facilities and an insufficient number of teachers due to limited government funds.

- Private or religious organizations operate nearly 75 percent of Haiti's schools, but not many students can afford to attend them. Additionally, there are inconsistencies in curricula. Even though there is an established Department of Education, coordination between the public and private schools is ineffective. Additionally, most private schools in Haiti do not permit students to take final exams if their account is not paid up.

- For every teacher in the countryside, there are 550 school-aged children. Moreover, dropout rates for primary students in rural areas may be as high as 80 percent.

HAITI

Level/Age	Hours/Calendar	Curriculum	Required	Class Size	Exams	Grades	Classroom Setup	Homework
Preschool, ages 4–5	Mornings Sept.–June, 5 hours/day	Krèyol, hygiene plus social, spiritual, and cultural development.	No	25–30 or low as 12 in private schools.	None	None	4–8 students per table, 1 table for discipline. No teacher's desk. Shelves for supplies.	None
Kindergarten, ages 5–6	Oct.–July, 5 hours/day	From national Dept. of Education	No	45–50 in public schools, 25–30 in private schools	None	None	Same as above. TVs, VCRs, library, and desks rather than tables in some private schools.	None
Elementary, grades 1–6, ages 6–12	4–6 hours/day mornings or afternoons Sept.–June	Study skills, reading, writing, math, environmental sciences, Krèyol and English or French	Yes, to age 12	45–50 same as above	At end of the 3d, 6th, and 9th years, students take a national exam, which are multiple choice and matching.	1–10, 1–20, or 0–100%	Students sit in rows of benches facing the teacher, who is in front of a chalkboard.	Little, if any, but mainly in math and English or French
High, grades 7–12, ages 12–18	Same as above	Students choose between classical, technical, or professional programs.	No	50–60	At the end of the 11th and 12th years, a standard government exam is given. The first, called *reto*, must be passed before starting the last year, called *philo*. Few pass philo.	1 – 10, need 6 or higher to pass, or 0–100%	Same as above	Little in comparison to American schools
University, age 18+	Sept.–June, up to 8 hours/day	Licenses in nursing, theology, civil engineering, agriculture, pharmacy, dentistry (3–5 years); master of anthropology, education, business (4–6 years); doctor of medicine (7 years)	No	80 in public schools; up to 50 in private schools	Essay questions are given whenever appropriate to challenge students to synthesize information and go beyond the rote memorization they are used to.	0 – 100%. Passing is 65% and above.	Same as above. No computer labs.	Research papers

- Education in Haiti remains at the lowest level in the Western world. Approximately 50 percent of the adult population cannot read or write. Despite these problems, many Haitian students have succeeded and gone on to universities and colleges in Europe and North America.

- In very poor areas, preschool through early elementary teachers become very creative at adapting anything and everything for their classes. For example, plastic containers found in the garbage are transformed into playthings, room decorations, illustrations for counting, or containers for demonstrating plant growth.

TEACHING STYLE

- Most lessons are characterized by teacher-fronted lectures.

- Tests and quizzes are very strict and formal.

- Students are called on by their last names to answer questions concerning specific details of the lesson.

- Teachers do not help their students learn to analyze and synthesize information.

- In rural schools, where books cannot be afforded, teachers write entire lessons on the chalkboard, and the students copy every word onto their papers.

LEARNING STYLE

- Rote learning and memorization of details is the norm.

- Students speak only when asked a question.

- Students attach great importance to their grades, even to the detriment of learning.

INSTRUCTIONAL SETTING

- Rural schools usually do not have running water or electricity, and most do not even have sets of class books. Some schools in the capital, Port-au-Prince, and some private schools have better facilities, including running water and electricity.

- Since there are not enough books printed in Kreyòl, some schools continue to use French textbooks and maintain elements of a classical curriculum, emphasizing literature.

ACTIVITIES

- Soccer or volleyball is played after school or on Saturday.

- Young children have many outdoor activities: *lago* (a type of tag), *marelle* (a game similar to hopscotch), and *osseletes* (a game using goat bones as dice).

- Wealthy Haitians enjoy water sports, such as snorkeling, diving, or sailing.

DISCIPLINE AND CLASS MANAGEMENT

- Corporal punishment is permissible both at home and at school.

- Parents are sometimes asked to come to the school and discipline their child in front of the entire class.

- Besides disciplining by hitting or spanking, a teacher may ask a student to stand on one leg with his or her arms outstretched for a set amount of time.

TEACHER-STUDENT RELATIONSHIP

- A formal relationship exists between the teacher and the student, and the teacher has total authority.

- At the higher education levels, students are very likely to challenge the teacher's opinion, as well as to challenge their grade on a particular assignment or exam.

- There is no concept of PTA (Parent-Teacher Association) in Haiti, and parents believe that the teacher knows what is best for the students. Parents never visit the schools unless there is a discipline problem with their child.

STUDENT-STUDENT RELATIONSHIP

- A strong sense of hierarchy exists in Haitian schools. For example, third-year students hassle or bully second-year students, second-year students hassle first-year students, and first-year students hassle new applicants. However, within each class, there is a strong sense of support. A student with a problem is almost always accompanied by one or two fellow students when he or she approaches the teacher for consideration.

- Students are very cooperative with one another in finding creative ways to cheat during a test. Giving the correct answer and receiving a high grade is more important than knowing why an answer is correct.

♟ Protocol

NONVERBAL BEHAVIOR

- When students have to leave class, they hold up an index finger until they are out the door. This is not necessarily meant to call attention but is seen as polite, almost as if it makes the student invisible while slipping out of the class.

- Eye contact with elders is avoided.

IMAGES

- Haiti is mountainous but does not have the lush, tropical forests that one would imagine. Due to the exploitation of hardwoods and the increase of agriculture, only 2 percent of the land remains forested.

- Because of poor nutrition or other gastrointestinal problems, students occasionally eat chalk from the classroom. They are told it is a source of calcium.
- Because of poor health conditions, life expectancy is only 49 years.
- Corn, rice, and tropical fruits are the main foods.

FORMS OF ADDRESS

- A teacher may be addressed as "my dear teacher." *Pwofesè* is used for both male and female teachers. The words *msye* (mister), *madanm* (missus), and *madwazèl* (miss) are also used, without a last name, to address the teacher.
- Teachers address their students by last name.

DRESS

- Students and teachers are expected to dress well for class, which means a shirt, tie, and slacks for young men. Shorts, T-shirts, and sandals are not worn in class.
- Uniforms are required, but few students can afford them.

POLITE/IMPOLITE TOPICS AND BEHAVIORS

- It is polite for every student to pay the director a personal visit at the beginning of the semester to present himself or herself.
- It is considered disrespectful for children to stare at adults.

GIFT GIVING

- A new student might bring the principal or teacher a live guinea hen, presenting it by the feet, with the bird's head hanging down and the feet tied together.
- A principal or teacher in rural Haiti would be delighted to receive a practical rare item, such as a pencil sharpener, from a foreign visitor.

? 💡 Problem/Solution

PROBLEM

Whenever I ask my Haitian student to express her opinion, she looks at the floor in silence. How can I encourage her to respond?

SOLUTION

Two things are happening here. First, Haitian education is mostly rote memorization, so she is confused by an opinion question. Secondly, Haitian students refrain from direct eye contact because it is considered disrespect-ful. Therefore, you need to explain to the student that there are no right or wrong answers to opinion questions, and the ability to think for oneself is highly valued in North American schools. Also, you need to explain that teachers in her new homeland value eye contact.

PROBLEM

One of my biggest problems involves teaching new words or concepts. For example, my class may discuss animals in a zoo, but my Haitian students have no idea what a zoo even looks like. How can I best introduce my Haitian students to new concepts?

SOLUTION

Living on an island with little diversity and few books and where only 1 in 25 homes has a television does not give students much background schemata or life experience. Try to coordinate with other teachers for field trips, and increase your use of realia and video.

PROBLEM

I just don't think that my Haitian students are making any progress in learning English. What's wrong?

SOLUTION

They are probably isolating themselves within their own community of Haitian speakers and not taking advantage of opportunities to immerse themselves in the English language. Stress the importance of finding oppor-tunities to speak and listen to English. Also, make frequent announcements about school and community activities, such as sports, movies, volunteer work, and various clubs. Something else that you can do is to prepare a class lesson on prejudice and tolerance. Haitian students may feel embarrassed by the "refugee" label, and may therefore be keeping to themselves to avoid rejection.

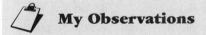 **My Observations**

Japan

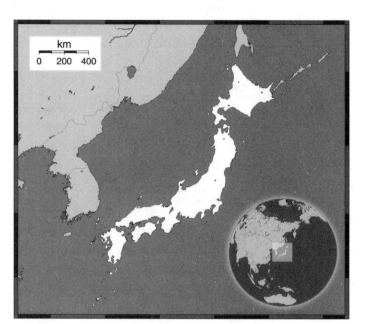

 Focus on Japan

Capital: Tokyo

Population: 126,000,000

Size: 145,882 sq. mi. (377,835 sq. km.)

Location: archipelago off the eastern coast of Asia and separated from the Asian continent by the Sea of Japan

Climate: varies widely; mean temperature 41 to 61 degrees Fahrenheit; typhoon season from August to October

Monetary Unit: yen

Urban/Rural Life: 78% urban, 22% rural

Religion: 84% Shinto or Buddhist

Languages: Japanese (national and official)

Ethnicity: mainly ethnic Japanese; 2 to 3% *hisabetsu buraku,* descendants of premodern occupational groups, and Ainu, originally thought to have migrated from Siberia; small groups of Koreans, Chinese, Vietnamese, and Filipinos

Government: parliamentary democracy under a constitutional monarchy

 Personal Snapshot

Some years ago, I taught a linguistically and culturally heterogeneous group of intermediate-level conversational English students. Among them was a group of approximately five young Japanese girls, whose whole body language told me volumes about the excruciating shyness that overcame them when they were asked to contribute to class discussion. To improve their class participation, I tried everything from humor to the threat of a low participation grade to no avail. Thinking they would feel more comfortable in a small group of their peers, I gave the class a simple problem-solving exercise, but I noticed that there wasn't a peep coming from the Japanese group during the exercise. In frustration, I basically cried, "What are you doing?" Silence. "Are you talking to each other at all?" Silence. "Are you thinking? Are you thinking about what to say?" Silence. I hoped all we were experiencing was a cultural phenomenon, so as a last resort, I asked the students to come to class the next day prepared to present a role play reflecting a typical classroom, typical student behavior, and typical teacher activity in their home culture. The following day, the girls, portraying typical students in Japan, sat quietly side by side as the student chosen to portray the typical Japanese teacher lectured and erroneously wrote on the board "2 + 1 = 4." The students consulted with each other in whispers each time the teacher asked one of them a question. They bowed as the teacher arrived and departed, but the periods before and after the teacher was in the room were filled with an unexpected mayhem. Eyes opened figuratively as well as literally that day, and my class was fortunately never the same.

➤✦← Cultural Closeup

- Japan has been called a *vertical society* because of the many layers that exist in that country to distinguish one person's status from another. Age is a particularly important feature of the vertical society, so regardless of ability or merit, the person who is oldest is given the most respect and accommodation. He or she is also addressed by others using a special kind of language reserved only for those of high social rank.

- The concept of group or community is highly valued in Japanese culture, to the extent that most Japanese feel uncomfortable when singled out for either praise or criticism. Their culture emphasizes strength through unity, and they recognize that it is easier to achieve something together rather than individually. This is perhaps why conformity is seen as a virtue rather than a vice.

- Shame is an important element of Japanese culture. When a person violates a rule, he or she will very likely be ridiculed in front of others, which is naturally a highly undesirable punishment.

- The expression *onko-chishin* refers to one of the greatest sources of pride among most Japanese—tradition. Ideas, ceremonies, and art forms are deeply valued, and vigorous efforts are made to preserve them. In addition to their long history and traditional practices, the Japanese are also proud of the physical beauty of their country and of their people's attitude toward hard work and tenacity.

- One reason so many Japanese people are described as quiet or reserved is that they have a particular perspective on communication. They believe in the notion of *ishin-denshin,* or shared communication that needs no words. They ascribe a much greater role in communication to circumstance and environment than to mere words. People are expected to "tune in" to each other and to interpret one another's implied meanings.

- There is a Japanese saying that "*Ishi no ue nimo sannen*" [a cold stone becomes warm if one sits on it for three years]. In Japanese culture, individuals are urged to follow through with plans and to make great sacrifices to reach their goals. Perseverance is one of the most cherished assets and is seen as the key to resolving difficult problems.

Educational Panorama

JAPAN

Level/Age	Hours/Calendar	Curriculum	Required	Class Size	Exams	Grades	Classroom Setup	Homework
Preschool, ages 0–6	8 hours/day + evening care	Play, nap, basic courtesy	No	15–20	None	None	Small tables and chairs	None
Kindergarten, ages 3–6	4 hours/day	Arts, social skills	No	15–20	None	None	Same as above	None
Elementary, grades 1–6, ages 6–12	Apr.–Mar., 8:30 A.M.–3:30 P.M. Mon.–Sat.; 40-day summer break	Art, music lessons, English, calligraphy (or *shuji*), recess, cleaning duty; ethics and home economics in grades 5–6	Yes	25–40	Five regular tests each year	Good, average, or poor	Desks in rows, pairs, or "islands" of 4–6 desks pushed together. Classrooms are often decorated with student artwork.	Students receive a fair amount of homework.
Middle, grades 7–9, ages 13–15	Same as above	Japanese, math, calligraphy, science, social studies, Chinese literature, world history, foreign language (usually English)	Yes	30–40	Five regular tests each year	1 (lowest)–5 (highest)	Teachers move from room to room to teach their subject to different classes of students. Desks are most commonly arranged in single rows but may be put in pairs or "islands" for special projects. Classrooms contain few personal touches, and there are few decorations on the walls.	Students expect to be assigned a considerable amount of homework for their classes. The teacher is expected to correct these homework assignments thoroughly.
High, grades 10–12, ages 16–18	Same as above. But students may attend full- or part-time.	Focus in high school varies according to type of school: academic, agricultural, technical, etc.	No, but 97% of middle school graduates continue.	30–50	To get into high school, students must pass a rigorous high school entrance examination.	Same as above	Students sit in rows of neatly arranged individual desks facing the front of the classroom. The teacher stands behind the teacher's desk at the front. Desks may be rearranged for occasional group work.	Handouts, exercises, worksheets, workbooks for college-bound students
University, age 19+	Apr.–July and Oct.–Mar.	Undergraduate and graduate degree programs in all fields	No, but 45% of high school graduates continue.	50–300 in lectures; much smaller seminar groups	To enter the university, students take the national standard exam and a university specific exam. Competition to the best schools is fierce.	*Kanji* grades: superior, good, possible (to pass the course), and impossible (will not pass)	Same as above	Students are not required to do much homework at this level except in seminar classes (*zemi*), where they work closely with their professor.
Juku, or cram schools, ages 11–19	After school	Music, sports, foreign languages, preparatory courses	No, but 50% of 5th and 6th graders attend; 80% take music or sports.	5–20	Students who fail the entrance examination will frequently study for a year or 2 years to achieve the score necessary to eventually enter that school.	No grades, but test scores and rankings are reported	Same as above	*Juku* homework essentially doubles homework from regular school but is considered more important and more challenging.

👁 A Closer Look

POLICY

- In 1871, Japan established Monbusho, the ministry of education, science, sports, and culture. One year later, Monbusho developed a full national educational system, based on Western educational practices. Japanese laws provide for a basic public education for all citizens. This provision allows citizens from all walks of life to compete for admission to institutions of higher education, eliminating the differences that formerly existed between the social classes in the area of education.

- Educational policies, curricula, textbooks, and qualifying exams are centralized under Monbusho, with a course of study set for each school level. In response to the internationalization of Japanese society and the influence of technology, Monbusho has begun to revise the national curriculum on all levels. It is striving to implement curricular changes in the area of emotional education and personal well-being. The goal of this reform is to help students develop into well-rounded, creative individuals with critical-thinking skills and the ability to more readily express their individuality.

- Many middle and high school students attend *juku,* or special tutoring schools, after regular school hours and often late into the night, to supplement their school lessons and prepare for the high school and university entrance exams. It is believed extremely important to get into the "right" high school or college, because this virtually guarantees that the individual will gain lifetime employment with the "right" company. Many students who do get accepted to the better high schools face the prospect of a commute of over an hour in each direction—by train, by bike, or on foot—to attend a school that will provide them with future advantages. Since competition to enter the best schools is strenuous, pressure to do well on entrance exams is equally severe.

- *Juku* are extremely advanced and rigorous. In fact, sometimes, students who attend academic *juku* advance several levels ahead of their public school lessons and subsequently become bored with their regular classes.

- Parents of elementary students also send their children to *juku,* with the hope of giving these young students an advantage over their peers. Popular subjects include music, sports, and foreign languages, although elementary school students often attend a *juku* to prepare themselves for the entrance examinations for private junior high schools.

TEACHING STYLE

- Lessons at the elementary school level are very child-centered, and nurturing the students is considered important. Teachers use a variety of instructional materials, such as videos and picture books, and games are often incorporated into the instruction at this level.

- Starting in middle school, students receive direct instruction from the teacher in a lecture format. They take notes, and they answer questions by raising their hands or waiting for the teacher to call on them. Some teachers require students to stand when giving answers.

- At the university level, the lecture format dominates, although teaching style may show more variety in the smaller seminars.

- Until recently, foreign language instruction in Japanese schools relied heavily on the Grammar-Translation Method, an approach that emphasizes grammatical accuracy and translation of literary texts. Today, more and more foreign language classrooms in Japan have begun to gravitate toward a more communicative approach to foreign language teaching, which stresses comprehensibility, fluency, and spontaneity.

LEARNING STYLE

- Students rarely volunteer to make contributions to the lesson. In fact, some teachers report cases of their high school students sleeping through lectures. Sometimes, asking questions is construed as challenging the teacher's authority or implying that the teacher is not competent. Another reason students are hesitant to ask questions in class is that they do not want to stand out or show off. Instead of asking the teacher questions to clarify a point in the lesson, students commonly ask each other, even while the class is in session. This behavior is not considered disrespectful so long as it does not disturb the whole class.

- Students are hesitant to share their opinions openly in large classrooms or in public but will share their opinions in small groups or outside the classroom.

- At the elementary level, students are assigned and enjoy group projects. By the time they reach middle school, students are generally assigned more individual work than group work. If they work in groups, students tend to prefer being with members of their own gender.

- At the university level, students do not always attend the larger lecture classes on a regular basis. Being admitted to a university or college does not always mean that students will take their studies very seriously. For many students in a liberal arts program, this time period is often viewed as the vacation they have worked so hard in junior high and high school to achieve and as a break before entering the workforce, where they will receive the training necessary for their specific job.

INSTRUCTIONAL SETTING

- In elementary school, middle school, and high school, students are responsible for the cleanliness and appearance of their classroom space, the hallways, offices, bathrooms, and general campus grounds. During the daily cleaning period, each student is assigned a specific cleaning task. University students are not expected to clean their classrooms and lecture halls.

- Regardless of Japan's reputation for technological sophistication and innovation, instructional technology has not in the recent past been widely introduced to many schools. However, education reform plans now call for all schools to be equipped with computers and multimedia technology.

- The elementary school, middle school, and high school classroom is occupied throughout the day by the same class of students, who perform almost all school tasks and activities together, forming a close group bond among classmates. Thus, the homeroom is a special place for the students, and the teachers who arrive in the room to teach are more or less visitors.

- Many older Japanese school buildings are plain concrete-type structures with many windows. Classrooms are of a uniform size, generally located along a common hallway. In older schools, the buildings often have no insulation, heating, or air conditioning.

- The educational environment is strictly supervised. Such things as bicycle parking spaces and shoe style are predetermined for the student.

ACTIVITIES

- Athletic, cultural, and academic extracurricular activities are offered at all levels, although participation is most prevalent in junior high school. Students frequently arrive at school an hour or two early or remain at school until sunset to participate in clubs and practice for school events.

- Every school has organized annual events set by Monbusho (the Ministry of Education), including sports day, student-organized show-and-tell presentations, athletic competitions, musical performances, and theatrical performances. Organized events are not considered optional. Students are encouraged to work together in competitions, performances, and other school-sponsored events.

- Annual field trips are common at all grade levels. Elementary school students frequently take day trips to local attractions or historic locations. Secondary school students engage in longer excursions lasting up to a week. Usually, an entire grade level will participate in an educational field trip together.

- University students will frequently attend educational and social functions out of a sense of obligation to the group of which they are currently a part, even if they do not have motivation from a personal interest in the event. This may explain why Japanese students may have high attendance at events but may show little interest or participate minimally in the proceedings.

DISCIPLINE AND CLASS MANAGEMENT

- Teachers receive a great deal of respect in Japan. The authority of the teacher is generally unquestioned.

- From kindergarten through high school, a student representative nominated by classmates assists the teacher in some of his or her duties.

- Students rise and bow as the teacher enters and leaves the room in elementary school, junior high school, and high school.

- Individual teachers are responsible for meting out class discipline within their own classroom.

- Disciplinary measures used by the teacher depend on the nature of the misconduct and might include shaking the head, ignoring the offending student, making the class or student stand or kneel on the floor for a period of time, sending the student to the principal's office, taking the student to the staff room and scolding him or her until the student is suitably penitent, and administering corporal punishment.

- Male teachers are considered to be less lenient than are female teachers.

- With some teachers, students may be punished for giving a wrong answer in class.

- Shame and humiliation are often used to get students to conform to group rules.

- Disruptive students are rarely thrown out of the classroom, because no student may be denied the right to an education.

- The teacher is expected to visit the home of each student once a year.

TEACHER-STUDENT RELATIONSHIP

- A teacher plays a variety of roles with his or her students: friend, counselor, and disciplinarian. The job of teachers is not only to supervise the academic growth of their charges but also to oversee the development of the students' social consciousness. Homeroom teachers, in particular, have almost a parental role to play in Japanese schools. They serve in this capacity with the same group of students for one to three years and are essentially jointly responsible with the parents for the students' well-being and behavior in and outside of class. For example, if a student is absent from school, the homeroom teacher will call the parents. Students often feel a deep sense of gratitude to their homeroom teachers long after they have finished school, and it is considered natural to invite a homeroom teacher to a student's wedding and to inform homeroom teachers about major events in students' lives.

- Academic failure is unthinkable to the average Japanese teacher. In fact, it is rare for a student to be allowed to fail. Teachers assume responsibility for making sure that their students will succeed. The maxim "If the student hasn't learned, the teacher hasn't taught" is widely accepted by teachers, students, and their parents.

- Outside of school, teachers take on the responsibility of organizing and leading students' clubs and sports teams, if they are not already given the responsibility of acting as homeroom teacher.

STUDENT-STUDENT RELATIONSHIP

- Students in the same classroom form close bonds by learning and working together. Group bonds are also formed through formal competitions and sports events in which classes participate as a team.

- Students often arrive at school before the teacher does, and they use the time interval to clean and prepare the classroom for the teacher.

- After-school activities, including sports, are used to help students develop strong *sempai-kohai* (junior-senior) relationships. The fine art of addressing and relating to one's superiors begins in elementary school. Any students above the learner's current grade are considered *seniors*. Through *sempai-kohai* relationships, students learn the formal or polite forms of speech, as well as deference to superiors, which is vital to functioning effectively in Japanese society.

Protocol

NONVERBAL BEHAVIOR

- Bowing is still used among Japanese in formal social situations, but it is primarily seen among the older generations. Japanese bow when being introduced to another person, when meeting an acquaintance, and when thanking, apologizing, and making requests.

- Spatial experience is important in conversation. The preferred distance between Japanese speakers is greater than that between English speakers.

- Long pauses may occur before responses. These pauses may express as much meaning as the spoken word. The Japanese use the term *ishin-denshin* to describe a special intuitive understanding that may take the place of words.

- Laughter may be a response to an embarrassing or confusing situation.

- Direct eye contact is sometimes seen as rude behavior.

- The hand gesture used by many English speakers to mean "ok" (placing the thumb and index finger together) means "money" when used in Japan.

- The Japanese point the forefinger at the nose to indicate "I," much like people in the United States point the forefinger to the chest with the same meaning.

- The thumbs-up sign in North America is a gesture of approval or support, but in Japan, the same gesture means "boyfriend." Holding the hand in a fist and raising the pinky finger means "girlfriend."

- Some Japanese may rub their heads when embarrassed by either praise or criticism.

- The *three banzai cheer* is used to wish others good fortune and is called out by a group of people during a celebration. Three times, the people raise both hands in the air and shout, "banzai!"

IMAGES

- There is a Japanese saying that *the nail that stands up will be pounded down.* What Westerners might call individuality or eccentricity in behavior and outward physical appearance is often considered inappropriate in Japanese culture.

- The display of a common identifying symbol or article of clothing, such as a baseball cap, reinforces one's relationship to and concern for the group.

FORMS OF ADDRESS

- The Japanese usually address each other by last name with *san* attached at the end. This address is appropriate in all social situations, particularly if the addressee's profession is not known. Most Japanese students do not expect this custom to be used outside of Japan; therefore, many are eager to adopt nicknames or alter their given name. Some older or more traditional students might object to the informality and familiarity of certain classrooms. The use of *san* or of *mister* plus last name might facilitate adjustment.

- The title *sensei* is used with teachers and other professionals.

- The forms *chan* and *kun* indicate familiarity and would be inappropriate in business settings or with acquaintances.

DRESS

- Uniforms are required in almost all Japanese schools, although students may dislike them. Teachers have the authority to enforce the dress code, which varies in severity of restrictions from one area to another. For example, some schools have haircut requirements as well as uniform standards. An identification badge is worn on the uniform.

- Young Japanese people tend to dress very fashionably; however, older adults dress, as a rule, conservatively. Colors tend to be traditionally dark: navy, black, and dark gray. Men with professional careers wear white shirts (not colored shirts) with suits. Women wear dresses more often than pants.

- Women wear simple jewelry; men may wear a watch and wedding ring.

- Cologne is not typically worn by either men or women. Wearing heavy cologne may imply that one has not bathed.

- Older women seldom wear high heels, although younger women will wear whatever shoes are in style in Paris. Students wear plastic slippers in school and keep their shoes in their lockers.

- Kimonos, which may cost thousands of dollars, are worn only on special occasions—weddings, coming-of-age days, and other celebrations. A kimono may be passed on from generation to generation or given to a woman as a wedding gift.

POLITE/IMPOLITE TOPICS AND BEHAVIORS

- Most Japanese would consider a question regarding their religious beliefs to be impolite.

- It is considered impolite to give advice to a Japanese person unless he or she is a close acquaintance or family member.

- Japanese do not discuss their desires or wants, especially while they are guests in someone's home.

- Japanese may become offended if comments are made on the way they discipline their children. It may be seen as interference.

- It is poor policy to call attention to anyone in a group by giving that person praise or blame.

- It is considered immature to criticize or correct the mistakes of others.

- Japanese are taught to refrain from talking back to a superior.

- Complaints are made as tactfully as possible to avoid their being construed as accusations.

- Personal questions about one's job, title, work responsibilities, and marriage are acceptable and are not considered impolite.

- Apologies are often used to show a wish to cooperate. Even in situations in which they are not at fault, Japanese often apologize for causing inconvenience.

- In Japan, giving praise is often an expression of kindness and is not necessarily an indication of approval.

- Both the denial of a compliment and abnegation of self and family are signs of modesty.

- Japanese do not strive to fill in pauses in conversation. Silence is a sign of empathy and communion with the other person.

GIFT GIVING

- It is very common to give gifts in Japan, especially at the new year.

- Gifts to teachers are usually given from the group, not from the individual student. They are not usually personal in nature.

- In Japan, the actual exchanging or giving of gifts is usually more important than the price or extravagance of a gift.

- The Japanese tend to be modest about the gifts they give, even if they are expensive. It is not unusual to hear the gift giver say, for example, "It's really nothing," regardless of the value or elaborateness of the gift.

- Invited guests to a Japanese home will often bring a cake, some flowers, or fruits.

- An obligatory or thank-you gift is usually not opened in front of the gift giver.

? 💡 Problem/Solution

PROBLEM

Some of my Japanese students don't always look me in the eye when I talk to them, which really bothers me. Why do they avoid eye contact, and how can I develop this nonverbal skill in them?

SOLUTION

The Japanese, in general, find direct eye contact with those whom they consider senior to them to be aggressive, rude, and unacceptable. It is natural for some of your Japanese students to find direct eye contact of any kind uncomfortable. This will be especially true for those who find themselves in situations in which they feel shame or embarrassment of any kind. As time goes on, you may find that this level of discomfort lessens as new generations of Japanese students become more comfortable with Western ideals and cultural practices. Meanwhile, you may want to have casual class conversations about the importance of eye contact in your culture. Discussion may help your students become more comfortable with this particular type of nonverbal communication.

PROBLEM

My Japanese students sometimes whisper with their friends in class when I ask a question. I don't particularly like this, because I feel they are telling each other the answer. How can I stop this?

SOLUTION

Japanese students are taught that mistakes are serious and that the consequences of mistakes are too embarrassing to risk. Therefore, they consult each other when questioned by the teacher. Japanese students are also taught not to question the teacher or any authority figure, which is why they may ask each other, rather than the teacher, for clarification. The best way to deal with this concern is to discuss the cultural differences in classroom behaviors. It will also help if your students understand that in most English-based instructional environments, questioning the teacher is encouraged, expected, and beneficial to the students' educational development. If it seems that students are turning to their friends when they should be turning to you, gently ask these students if they need help.

PROBLEM

My Japanese students don't always answer my questions right away, even when I believe they know the answers. How can I shorten their response times?

SOLUTION

Your students are most likely taking the time they need to become confident that they have formulated the correct answer for the question, to avoid making an embarrassing mistake. Try to initially count to 10 after asking your students a question, to allow them time to answer. As the course progresses, slowly decrease the amount of response time you give the students. Reassure your students that mistakes are a normal, important part of the learning process.

My Observations

Korea

Although the general term is used, the text applies primarily to South Korea.

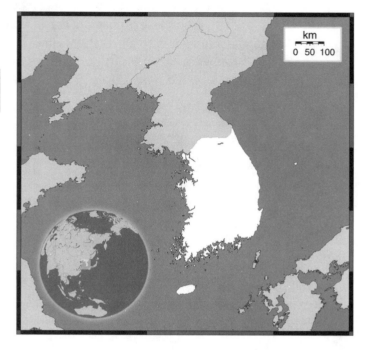

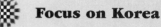 Focus on Korea

Capital: Seoul

Population: 46,884,800

Size: 38,023 sq. mi. (98,480 sq. km.)

Location: eastern Asia; southern half of the Korean Peninsula, bordering the Sea of Japan and the Yellow Sea

Climate: temperate, with rainfall heavier in summer than winter

Monetary Unit: won

Urban/Rural Life: 22% rural, 78% urban

Religion: 49% Christian, 47% Buddhist, 3% Confucian, 1% other

Languages: Korean (official)

Ethnicity: homogeneous (except for about 20,000 Chinese)

Government: republic

Personal Snapshot

When teaching in the public schools, I once received a new student in my class who was Korean. I sent home with the child a note saying that I would like to meet her parents. When her parents arrived as scheduled, I introduced myself. Although the meeting went smoothly, I sensed that something was wrong. I spoke to a colleague who had had Korean students in her class before, and she asked me how I had addressed them. I had called them "Mr. and Mrs. Kim." My colleague explained that it was likely that the couple felt awkward with my use of their last name without the appropriate title. In other words, I should have addressed them according to the type of employment they had. It would have been more appropriate for me to address them as "Doctor and Mrs. Kim." When I saw my student's mother again the next day, I explained the American custom of calling people by *mister* and *missus.* She thanked me for my concern, and as she left, she turned around and said, "Goodbye, Teacher Scheidler!"

⌖ Cultural Closeup

- The Korean culture consists of a vertical society. There are six levels of status, three up and three down. These levels are established by age (ten, twenty, or thirty years older and ten, twenty, or thirty years younger), and different levels of speaking are incorporated into the Korean language to accommodate the status levels. As a result, elders are greatly respected. Even if a person is one year older than another, he or she is treated with a higher level of respect by the younger person.

- A great many Korean beliefs can be traced back to the Tangun myth. This story of the son of the god of Heaven delineates the importance of harmony, human welfare, and national identity.

- The family has a strong bond which goes beyond the immediate family. The family members are responsible for one another, and they see themselves as a cohesive unit. Elders are greatly respected and ancestors are honored on such holidays as Chu-sok (around Sept. 21), the Korean equivalent of Thanksgiving.

- Educators are viewed as part of the extended family and, as such, are greatly respected. With a very high literacy rate, the importance of education can easily be seen. Great sacrifices by both the parents and the students are expected to ensure the students' success.

- Buddhism and Confucianism were the most prominent religions in Korea until the introduction of Christianity in the mid-1890s. Buddhism has had a great influence on the architecture in Korea as can be seen by the Buddhist temples. Associated with Confucianism is the ancient art of traditional calligraphy and painting. Artists, in general, are well respected in Korea, and traditional artists are frequently honored with the designation of national icon.

- Korean society is strongly influenced by Confucianism's Five Moral Codes and Three Moral Bonds of Human Relations. The Five Codes are: (1) Between parents and children, there shall be love; (2) Between the rulers and the governed, there shall be justice; (3) Between man and wife, there shall be distinction; (4) Between the old and the young, there shall be an order; (5) Between friends, there shall be trust. The Three Bonds are: (1) Parents love children; children respect parents and be filially pious; (2) Rulers be just; the ruled be loyal; (3) Man calls; wife follows.

◉ A Closer Look

POLICY

- The education system of Korea is governed by three levels of administration: the Ministry of Education nationally, offices of education municipally and provincially, and district offices of education locally. Each county has a school board and a superintendent, who serves for four years.

Educational Panorama

KOREA

Level/Age	Hours/Calendar	Curriculum	Required	Class Size	Exams	Grades	Classroom Setup	Homework
Preschool, ages 3–5	Hours vary. Students may attend 2–3 times/ week for a few hours.	Nonacademic, with a focus on physical and emotional development	No	22	None	None	Varies	None
Kindergarten, ages 5–6	180 days/year, 3 hours/day Mon.–Fri.	Physical, social, expressive (singing and dancing) language, inquiry activities, and basic literacy	No	22	Assessment tests are administered at midterm and end of year in all subjects.	None	Self-contained class-room with desks in rows	Rare
Elementary, grades 1–6, ages 6–11	Mar. 1–Aug. 31 and Sept. 1–Feb. 28, 4 hours/day in 1st and 2d grades, 5 hours/day in 3d and 4th grades, and 6 hours/day in 5th and 6th grades, Mon.–Fri.	Moral education, Korean language, basic English, mathematics, social studies, science, physical education, extracurricular activities (computer, language, chess, drama, etc.). Optional courses and practical arts are offered in grades 3–6.	Yes	35	In grades 3–6, students are given 1-hour exams in each subject area. These exams are generally essay. Verbal exams are given in the 5th and 6th grades.	Letter grades	Same as above	A small amount of daily homework is given.
Middle, grades 7–9, ages 12–14	Mar. 1–Aug.1 and Sept. 1–Feb. 28, 6 to 7 hours/day, Mon.–Fri.	Moral education, Korean language, mathematics, social studies, science, physical education, music, visual art, home economics, technology and industry, English, electives (Chinese characters and classics, computer science, environmental studies), extracurricular activities	Yes	40–45	Midterm and final exams are given in all subjects, assuming the format of essay and multiple-choice questions.	Students are ranked against peers in their classroom and their grade level. They are also given number and letter grades.	Students stay in their homerooms most of the day. Desks are arranged in rows.	Approximately 2–3 hours of homework assigned each day.
High, grades 10–12, ages 15–18	Mar. 1–Aug. 31 and Sept. 1–Feb. 28, 7 to 8 hours/day Mon.–Fri.	3 tracks: academic (college preparatory), vocational (commercial, technical, fishery, agricultural), and special (fine arts, science, sports, foreign language). The academic high schools are the most popular.	Yes	40–45	Midterm and final exams are given in all subjects. About 60% of students take exams for college admission.	Same as above	Students stay in their homerooms most of the day. Desks are arranged in rows.	Much homework is given.
University, ages 18–25	Mar.–June and Sept.–Dec. Hours vary.	2-year junior or vocational college or 4-year university followed by masters or doctorate programs	No	Varies	Midterm and final exams are given.	Letter grades	Varies	Varies

- Education is generally financed by central and local governments, families, and private foundations. In 1995, 84 percent of the Ministry of Education's budget was allocated to local governments, which distributed the money to local schools.

- A curriculum for each grade level is prescribed by the government to ensure quality across the board. The curricula are frequently revised to reflect changing needs and trends.

- Students in middle and high schools pay tuition and buy their textbooks. Students' entrance into high school is determined in two ways: in some areas, students must pass an assessment and then may apply to particular high schools; in other areas, students may simply apply to the high school they wish to attend.

TEACHING STYLE

- The Korean teacher, considered the giver of knowledge, generally stands in front of the class and lectures.

- Class discussion is rare in a Korean classroom, and students generally do not ask questions. Instead, they are more likely to be required to answer questions or to perform tasks at the blackboard.

- The teacher rarely groups students according to ability, nor do students typically participate in group activities, such as role playing, problem solving, and completing exercises together. However, the occasional group assignments are normally accompanied by explicit instructions, carefully articulated objectives, and clear criteria for success.

- Teachers give an abundance of homework. Students expect this, and parents demand it.

LEARNING STYLE

- The role of being a student is tantamount to a career. It is essentially a full-time job, and both students and parents make great sacrifices to ensure that a child receives the greatest benefit possible from schooling.

- Rote memorization is the primary learning style.

- Teachers in most classes welcome questions but few students ask questions because doing so makes them feel ashamed for not understanding in the first place.

- Although the schools are coeducational, after-school study groups are generally separated by gender, age, and grade level.

INSTRUCTIONAL SETTING

- Elementary students are taught in self-contained classrooms. Students may move to other rooms for music or art.

- Middle school and high school students remain in their homeroom class for most of the day. Teachers move from class to class, teaching their specific subject.

ACTIVITIES

- Music and sports (*tae kwon do,* soccer, baseball, swimming, basketball, and bowling) are common activities available to students after school.

- One hour of the school day is dedicated to special classes, such as computers, foreign languages, chess, or drama.

DISCIPLINE AND CLASS MANAGEMENT

- There are very few discipline problems in the typical Korean classroom. For serious offenses, either students are sent to the homeroom teacher or the parents are called.

- Because poor academic performance is perceived as a bad reflection on a child's family, teachers may use the prospect of disgrace and shame to motivate students to behave appropriately.

TEACHER-STUDENT RELATIONSHIP

- Teachers try not to embarrass students by pointing out their shortcomings in front of the whole class as such an act is the source of deep shame for students.

- The teacher is usually very serious and strict with students.

- Students show respect to the teacher. Direct eye contact with a teacher is considered inappropriate and even defiant. Students may nod their heads even if they do not understand. This is the student's way of showing respect for the teacher's efforts.

STUDENT-STUDENT RELATIONSHIP

- Students have close relationships with each other and interact according to the age, status, and gender distinctions of the vertical society in which they live.

Protocol

NONVERBAL BEHAVIOR

- A smile does not always mean happiness in Korea. It can be used as a greeting or to mean "I'm sorry." It is not typical to smile at strangers.

- Korean girls are commonly seen holding hands. Likewise, boys are often seen with their arms linked together or their arms around each others' shoulders.

- Students will submit paperwork by holding it out to the teacher with both hands.

- Korean men typically bow and shake hands when greeting each other. Women bow but do not shake hands with men.

- Women often cover their mouths when laughing.
- Koreans do not usually apologize for burping, sneezing, coughing, or even accidently passing gas. However, none of these occurrences is considered appropriate.
- Students will not look the teacher in the eye, because doing so is considered rude.

IMAGES

- Students strive not to offend their teachers. Therefore, it is common for them to remain silent in class even if they do not understand. The phrase *silence is golden* also applies to situations in which conflict may exist. In such cases, Koreans believe it is better to remain silent than to encourage conflict.
- It is risky to write a person's name in red ink. This is taken as a sign that the other person's mother will die.
- *Kimchi* is the national food of Korea. It is a very spicy pickled cabbage.

FORMS OF ADDRESS

- Students address teachers with the title *seon-saeng-nim* (teacher). It is not typical to address teachers with the titles *mister, missus,* or *miss*.
- In general, Koreans are addressed by last name plus appropriate title, such as *boojang-nim* (division chair) or *sajang-nim* (president). After a person retires from work, the highest title achieved (not necessarily the most recent title) is used.
- First names are very important in the Korean culture. It is not typical to call someone by first name until given permission to do so. The person's title is used instead. Calling someone by first name is usually reserved for friends that are of the same age. This rule applies to family members as well. For example, an older brother would be called by his title, "older brother," not by his first name.

DRESS

- In the past, uniforms were mandatory in schools everywhere in Korea. Now, each individual school may choose whether or not to require them.
- In public, Koreans generally wear Western-style clothing. The traditional dress, *hanbok,* is brightly colored and worn during national holidays.

POLITE/IMPOLITE TOPICS AND BEHAVIORS

- It is common to hear parents discussing their students' grades and college plans with other parents.
- To reduce conflict politics and religion are topics to be avoided.

- Children and young people show respect to their parents and the elderly by demonstrating obedience to them.

- It is typical to take off your shoes in a Korean home.

- Older people are greatly respected in Korea. Offering your seat to an elderly person or rising when they come into a room is appropriate.

GIFT GIVING

- Gift giving is common in Korea, especially on traditional family holidays, such as New Year's Day, the lunar New Year's Day, *Chu-sok* (literally, "bountiful abundance"), and Christmas. At weddings, funerals, or 60th birthdays, money is given in an envelope.

- Teachers are given gifts on two occasions: Teacher's Day and Thanksgiving Day. Appropriate gifts include cards, flowers, and makeup for female teachers or wallets for male teachers.

- It is common to bring a small gift when invited to someone's home. Fruit, cake, or other foods are acceptable.

- When receiving a gift, it is impolite to open it immediately.

- When giving a gift, it is traditional to downplay its importance.

- White chrysanthemums should never be given, as they are only used at funerals. Yellow chrysanthemums, however, are acceptable.

- Giving a handkerchief, knives, or scissors to a person signifies the end of the relationship. These items should only be exchanged if a minute amount of money is requested from the receiver (in other words, if the item is sold).

? 💡 **Problem/Solution**

PROBLEM

I have a Korean student who does not work well in groups. He usually hangs back while the other students in his group work. What should I do?

SOLUTION

Students in Korea are not accustomed to working in groups. If your groups are mixed by gender and age, this may make the student even more uncomfortable. Try to place Korean students with others of the same gender and age for a time until they become more comfortable.

PROBLEM

Having just corrected a stack of homework, I wrote a brief note to one of my Korean students, asking her to come see me. When this student saw the note, she looked positively shocked and very offended. What did I do wrong?

SOLUTION

Were you correcting homework with a red pen? If you wrote the note with that pen, especially if you wrote the student's name in red ink, you did something considered a bad omen in Korea. Writing a person's name in red ink is taken as a sign that the person's mother will die. Explain to the student that you were unfamiliar with the significance of your action in Korea. In the future, you may want to consider using a pen of another color as red has similar connotations in other countries.

PROBLEM

One of my Korean students unknowingly said an inappropriate English word during class. I took the opportunity to explain that the word was inappropriate and to give the class some alternative words to use. The student was profusely apologetic afterward and is keeping her distance from me. It wasn't *that* bad a word. Why did the student take my correction so hard? How can I repair our relationship?

SOLUTION

Koreans have great respect for their teachers. Regardless of how minor the infraction, it is likely that your student is extremely embarrassed because she feels that she offended you. Although it may be difficult to put your student completely at ease, you can offer your gentle assurances that you are not upset. Inviting your student to your office for a cup of tea might also show her your sincerity. Try steering the conversation toward cultural gaffes made by foreigners in Korea.

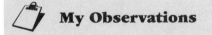 **My Observations**

Mexico

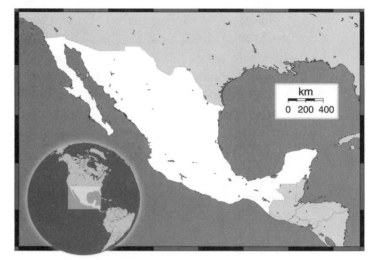

Capital: Mexico City

Population: 101,879,171

Size: 761,603 sq. mi. (1,972,550 sq. km.)

Location: between the United States to the north and Belize to the south; bordered by the Caribbean Sea and the Gulf of Mexico to the east and the Pacific Ocean to the west

Climate: varies from tropical to desert; average temperature 90 degrees Fahrenheit in summer, 85 in fall, 75 in winter, and 84 in spring

Monetary Unit: peso

Urban/Rural Life: 25% of the population lives in areas of less than 2,500 inhabitants, 26% in urban areas of 500,000 or more inhabitants, 14% in semirural cities, 14% in small cities, and 21% in medium-sized cities.

Religion: 89% Roman Catholic, 6% Protestant, 5% other

Languages: Spanish (official), Mayan, Nahuatl, other regional indigenous languages

Ethnicity: 60% mestizo (Amerindian-Spanish), 30% Amerindian, 9% European, 1% other

Government: federal republic with 31 states and 1 federal district

 Personal Snapshot

Like many Mexican people, I have fair skin and dark curly hair. But when I came to the United States to study English as a second language at a university, I was surprised to discover that some people doubted my nationality. They conceded that I was probably from some country in South America, but certainly not from Mexico. After all, Mexicans have dark skin and straight black hair. Or do they?

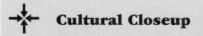 **Cultural Closeup**

- In Mexico, family always comes first, and the concept of family embraces extended systems of aunts, uncles, cousins, and sometimes close friends.

The family may be characterized as paternalistic; the father is considered the head of the family, but the mother's role is critical as well, since she is the one who offers the entire family moral and spiritual guidance.

- A person's socioeconomic status is obvious in Mexico. People behave differently according to their place in society. Behavior that is acceptable for a member of a certain class may be unacceptable for a person from another social class. For example, affluent and less affluent Mexicans each have their own speech styles. Using the speech style of the other class may create offense; more often, however, it is simply considered taboo, and people normally do not violate the unwritten rules.

- Even though Mexicans are very warm people, new arrivals are not automatically accepted into groups. However, newcomers are welcomed in time, and ties of friendship with them may become very strong.

- Machismo is an unwritten code of behavior among men. One of its tenets is that men are not to show fear or weakness. The popular saying *No te rajes* literally means "Do not break yourself," and it suggests that men must not show any sign of weakness under any circumstance.

- Mexicans pay less attention to time than do their North American neighbors. Neither the future nor the past are dwelt on, since we have no control over either. Thus, the present is all that really matters. One should live life fully and pleasantly.

Educational Panorama

- Basic education includes primary and secondary education.

- Since 1993, the federal government has provided free textbooks to all preschool and elementary school students.

- Secondary school was made compulsory in Mexico in 1993. Students can choose among several different types of school at this level, including: schools with a general, more conventional instructional curriculum; those that broadcast courses via television; those with a technical orientation; those for young people who have already joined the workforce; and schools for adults. Entry into secondary school requires the student to have completed primary school. After approximately three years of instruction at the secondary level, students have the option of studying for the baccalaureate, an advanced-level high school degree.

- Students over 16 years of age who have not finished their basic education can enroll in vocational schools for adults. Students who attend secondary school for workers prepare to enter the labor market. This type of program takes from three to four years to complete.

- The State provides special education at all levels, and it also offers remedial or compensatory education geared toward students from marginalized or rural areas of the country. Participating schools may receive financial assistance, materials and supplies, and teacher training from the government.

MEXICO

Level/Age	Hours/Calendar	Curriculum	Required	Class Size	Exams	Grades	Classroom Setup	Homework
Preschool, ages 3–5	3 hours/day, Mon.–Fri.	3 different grades by age; emphasis on play, creativity, affective factors, self-confidence, curiosity	No, but highly recommended	30 in public schools; 20 in private schools	Didactic games	Based on students' behavior and completion of tasks and activities	Students sit in circles and small groups, with the teacher at a desk in front of the class. Rooms are decorated with posters and students' work and have at least one blackboard. Many rooms have nap areas.	Basic writing assignments, drawing, painting, crafts
Primary, grades 1–6, ages 6–12	200 days/year Aug.–June, 4 hours/day Mon.–Fri.; morning, afternoon, or evening schedules; breaks for Christmas, *Semana Santa*, national holidays, Teacher's Day	Reading, writing, math skills, independence, initiative, development of intellectual skills, Spanish, math, science, geography, physical education, civics, art	Yes	50–60 in public schools; 30–40 in private schools	Written exams; mainly multiple-choice, open-ended and true-false questions; no essays. Students take subject mid-terms and final exams.	0–10. A grade of 6 is needed to pass. Public and private schools inform parents on a monthly basis as to students' progress.	Chairs are arranged in rows, with the teacher at the front of the classroom. Students do not change classrooms (except in some private schools). Rooms are decorated with students' work and books and bookshelves.	Teachers assign daily homework and occasional research papers.
Secondary, grades 7–9, ages 12–16	Same as above	Mastery of reading, writing, and oral skills in Spanish; problem solving in arithmetic, algebra, and geometry; also physics, chemistry, biology, history, geography, civics, foreign languages (English or French), art, and physical education; emphasis on preservation of natural resources	Yes	50–60 in public schools; 30–40 in private schools	Types of exams vary. Pop quizzes are common. Students take subject mid-terms and final exams.	Same as above. Some private schools may use other grading systems.	Chairs are arranged in rows facing the front of the classroom. The teacher usually sits at a desk in front of the class.	Homework is common, as are group assignments, oral presentations, research projects, and written reports.
Baccalaureate, ages 16–18	Same as above except 6 hours/day	3 types: general, technical, and professional; prepares students for more advanced study and gives a well-rounded scientific, humanistic, and technical education; includes study of research methodology	No	60 in public schools; 45 in private schools	Types of exams vary. Pop quizzes are common. Most schools have admission tests. Students take subject mid-terms and final exams.	Same as above	Same as above	Same as above. Community work may also be assigned.
Higher education, age 17+	Varies	3 subsystems: universities, technological institutes, and teacher colleges; degrees in humanities, arts, sciences, engineering, medicine, and teaching	No	Varies	Types of exams vary by institution. Some schools have admission tests. All schools require students to have the baccalaureate degree.	Same as above	Same as above	Varies

- Mexico's constitution states that public education should be pluralistic and multilingual. More than 62 indigenous ethnic groups receive instruction in their native languages.

- Higher education is comprised of autonomous state universities and private universities. Each institution establishes its own program of study, determines its own budget, and awards its own degrees and certificates. The federal and state governments fund public universities, of which there are more than 39 in the country.

- Students attending institutions of higher learning can choose among three degree options: a bachelor's degree (four to five years), a technical degree (three years), or a technological degree (two years). Graduate study is also available at many universities.

- Students who wish to teach can obtain a bachelor's degree from a teacher preparation program. Schools of education offer specialized training for prospective preschool, primary school, and secondary school teachers, as well as for students interested in special education or physical education.

A Closer Look

POLICY

- The federal government, through its ministry of education, the *Secretaría de Educaciòn Pública,* or SEP, is the main authority in educational matters. The SEP was created in 1921 and is responsible for establishing the curriculum for both public and private schools in Mexico. The SEP has made a concerted effort to encourage education and to reduce illiteracy.

- Both Article 3 of the Mexican constitution and the General Education Law govern the national education system in its entirety. Article 3 stipulates that every person must receive an education and that it is the responsibility of the government to provide basic education free of charge. Public education must be secular, that is, independent of any religious doctrine.

- In 1992, the National Agreement for the Modernization of Basic Education was ratified, and the federal government handed over the operation of preschool, elementary school, and secondary school services to local state governments. The entire curriculum was revised shortly thereafter, and new books were written.

TEACHING STYLE

- Mexican classes are normally teacher-fronted. In general, students are expected to listen and learn from the teacher, and students participate only when asked to do so. However, given the climate of educational reform in Mexico nowadays, teachers are slowly beginning to expect their students to participate more actively in class. They lecture less and facilitate more.

- Teachers generally do not create in-class activities aimed at developing critical-thinking skills in their students, but there are exceptions. Secondary school students often conduct experiments or build models in science class.

LEARNING STYLE

- Learning style varies among students. In general, they prefer to memorize information, since most of their tests tend to be multiple choice and so require memory skills.

- Mexican students prefer a high degree of structure in their classes.

- A global versus analytic approach to solving problems and digesting information is preferred by many Mexican students. They welcome the teacher's view of the big picture or significance of the details as they relate to a more holistic perspective.

- Students are accustomed to working both individually and in groups. There is more group work in the higher grades.

- Activities involving the use of one's hands, the manipulation of objects, or movement from one place to another are well received by Mexican students, who tend to be highly kinesthetic.

- At the baccalaureate level, one of the most dominant practices among students is taking dictation from the teacher's lecture, because most tests are taken more from the content of class sessions and less from books.

INSTRUCTIONAL SETTING

- Public schools rarely own a sufficient amount of media equipment, such as overhead projectors or computers. Private schools tend to be more fortunate in this regard.

ACTIVITIES

- Mexican students may participate in after-school activities such as sports or music, but they generally have few such options. Mexican high school students do not hold part-time jobs after school or engage in activities that divert their attention away from their studies.

DISCIPLINE AND CLASS MANAGEMENT

- Teachers are normally very strict with discipline. Talking while the teacher is lecturing is considered a violation of the student code of conduct.

- Students who misbehave in the classroom are reprimanded. Minor infractions, such as talking during the teacher's lecture or failing to complete a homework assignment, may be punished by requiring the student to leave the classroom. More serious violations, such as fighting, receive more severe penalties. For instance, students may receive several days' suspension from attending classes. Physical punishment of students is not common in the city schools but may occur in rural schools.

- The student code of conduct includes more than behavior. It also applies to physical appearance. For example, most schools require students to wear uniforms. Those who do not arrive at school wearing a uniform are asked to return home.

- Copying answers from a fellow student is not tolerated in Mexican schools. Students who are caught copying during a test are usually awarded a grade of zero.

- Students are expected to be in their seats before the teacher enters the classroom.

TEACHER-STUDENT RELATIONSHIP

- The relationship between teacher and student is cordial but distant. Teachers in primary school and secondary school rarely become friends with their students.

- Students view their teachers as a source of knowledge, not as potential friends.

- It is rare to find a teacher who acts as a counselor for students.

STUDENT-STUDENT RELATIONSHIP

- Relationships between and among students are often very close. Students who do not switch schools before graduation usually stay with the same group of classmates throughout their school years.

- Cooperation among students is one of the most dominant traits of young Mexican learners. It is fairly common for students to collaborate on assignments, and even while taking tests, classmates expect each other to offer help. This behavior is generally not tolerated by teachers, however. University students tend to be more competitive.

- Students begin their university studies as a cohort and remain with that cohort—taking the same classes together, often living together, and so forth—until graduation.

Protocol

NONVERBAL BEHAVIOR

- A handshake is appropriate when meeting someone for the first time. Kisses on the cheek may be exchanged between women friends or between a man and a woman, but Mexican men do not kiss each other on the cheek. The *abrazo,* a quick hug, is common among men.

- Mexicans may stand closer together while engaged in conversation than would people from the United States.

IMAGES

- In Mexico, people may appear to move slowly, to complete tasks unhurriedly, or to arrive far after the appointed time of a meeting. This cultural practice has often been called the *mañana syndrome,* suggesting that what is being expected today will probably occur tomorrow.

- Corn is ubiquitous throughout Mexico. As the culture's most important staple, it forms the basis of the Mexican diet. At least one meal a day contains corn and may consist of *tamales, tortillas, pozole* (pork and hominy stew), and *tacos.*

- A familiar sight on November 2 in Mexico is that of families making their way to the cemetery. This is the *Día de los Muertos,* or Day of the Dead. Mexicans refer to the celebration as *Hannal Pichan,* an ancient festivity that dates back to the time of the Aztecs. It was not a Christian holiday, but with the passage of time, it has acquired some Christian connotations. On this day, Mexican families remember their dead and celebrate the cycle of life. They often enjoy a picnic with their loved ones and feast on all kinds of special dishes, bread, and sugary confections shaped like animals or skulls. Families also decorate grave sites or altars with colorful flowers. In some cities, prizes are given for the best altars.

- The patron saint of Mexico is the Virgin of Guadalupe, and her image is ubiquitous. Many families maintain a small altar to the Virgin inside their homes.

- September 16th is Mexican Independence Day, a day when all Mexicans openly display their nationalism. At 11:00 P.M., everyone gathers in the *zocalo,* or city center, where the mayor rings the *campana de Dolores,* a special bell, thus reliving the moment when the fight for independence began.

- It is very common to see indigenous people in the big cities selling their crafts or dancing for the public. Members of the public often join in the dancing.

FORMS OF ADDRESS

- Mexicans have dual last names. The father's family name comes first, followed by the mother's family name. For example, if Miguel Rodriguez Torres and Maria Rivera Romero marry and have a daughter, they might name her Consuelo Rodriguez Romero.

- Students never address their teachers by first name. Instead, they are expected to use *señor, señora,* or *señorita* plus last name. They may also address the teacher as *profesor* or *profesora* (teacher).

- Teachers show respect for and distance from their students by using the students' last names. For example, a student whose name is *Mario Dominguez* may simply be called "Dominguez" by the teacher. Teachers may also address their students by title (*señor* or *señorita*). First names may also be used.

- Students must show respect for their teachers by addressing them with the formal pronoun *usted*. Outside of class, differences in socioeconomic status come into play when deciding whether to be formal or informal with someone in terms of pronoun choice. Someone may address another person with *usted* (formal "you") to show distance and respect, and the other person may use *tú* (informal "you") in response, to demonstrate that he or she does not belong to the same socioeconomic status as his or her interlocutor.

DRESS

- Dignity is an important part of Mexican culture, and this is reflected in the way Mexicans dress. People tend to dress up rather than down, and cleanliness is very important as well.
- Most schools require students to wear uniforms.
- Teachers tend to dress formally. Many male teachers wear a suit or jacket and a long-sleeved shirt. Female teachers may wear dress pants, skirts, or dresses. It is rare for teachers to come to school in jeans.

POLITE/IMPOLITE TOPICS AND BEHAVIORS

- It is not polite to address the topic of sex or sexuality in conversation. Although people recognize the existence of homosexuality, they will not discuss it openly. Abortion and out-of-wedlock births are also considered inappropriate topics for discussion.
- Mexicans are eager to please others and hesitate to hurt each other's feelings. To avoid open disagreement or offense, they may answer some questions indirectly and respond to requests in the same way.
- Money, politics, and religion are viewed as innocuous topics of conversation.
- In class, students are not supposed to be too relaxed. They should always be alert and ready to learn. Eating in class or putting one's feet on the desk is considered to be extremely rude.

GIFT GIVING

- It is common in Mexico for parents to send gifts of food or crafts to the teachers of their children, especially in rural areas. In cities, students buy presents (such as wine or cake) for their teachers for Teacher's Day, Christmas, birthdays, and at the end of the school year. In private schools, parents may get together to collect money to buy a present for the teacher. Students in the baccalaureate program pool their resources and together select gifts for their teachers.

? 💡 Problem/Solution

PROBLEM

I teach English to a group of Mexican university students in Mexico City. I have noticed that many of my students light up cigarettes and start smoking in the middle of my lesson. I have even noticed that other teachers smoke during their own lectures. It bothers me tremendously. What can I do about it?

SOLUTION

In Mexico, *la fumada,* or smoking, is quite common in schools of higher education. Even though it is considered acceptable by many students and teachers, not all professors allow their students to smoke in class. You could appeal to your students by explaining to them that you do not like them to smoke during your class. Out of respect for you, the teacher, they will probably refrain from doing whatever you tell them is offensive to you.

PROBLEM

I teach a group of Mexican high school students. Even though I try to spark their interest in the interactive exercises that I plan for the class, I have noticed that they prefer lectures, during which they take a lot of notes and seem to come alive. While I admire their diligence during lecture, I really want my students to participate in class much more. What can I do?

SOLUTION

Many students in Mexico are used to lecture-style classes. The teacher is considered their superior in knowledge, and the student's role is usually to take notes and to ask a few pertinent questions. Nevertheless, this situation is changing little by little. Explain to your students the benefits of group work and how they will learn much more through interaction. Make sure they know what they need to do to prepare themselves for class participation.

PROBLEM

My teenaged students really respond well to the journal assignments I give them. They're particularly willing to discuss their feelings and experiences regarding family life. Recently I asked the class to write about some of their frustrations regarding parental decisions. Everyone, except my Mexican student, poured his heart out, giving full vent to complaints and anger. Guillermo, however, wrote one sentence: "I'm sorry, but I'm not mad at my parents." Why wouldn't he share his real feelings with me? How can I get him to trust me?

SOLUTION

The commitment to family among Mexicans often means that adolescents relate to their parents in a more conformist, less rebellious way than do their stateside peers, and this can also prevent adolescents from bonding with their Anglo classmates. Guillermo was probably genuine in reporting his happy relationship with his parents. Next time, ask the class to write about peer relationships.

My Observations

Morocco

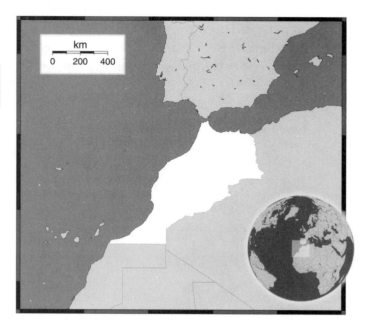

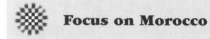 **Focus on Morocco**

Capital: Rabat

Population: 29,661,636

Size: 172,413 sq. mi. (446,550 sq. km.)

Location: North Africa; bordered by Algeria, Western Sahara, the North Atlantic Ocean, and the Mediterranean Sea

Climate: subtropical along the Mediterranean coastline; interior temperatures more pronounced

Monetary Unit: dirham

Urban/Rural Life: 50% of the population depends on agriculture, 26% on jobs in the service sector, 15% on industrial jobs, 13% of the population lives below the poverty line. There is 19% unemployment. Modern health services and good health conditions are common in the city but are less so in rural areas.

Religion: slightly under 99% Muslim, 1% Christian, less than 1% Jewish

Languages: Arabic (official), Amazigh (Berber) dialects, French, Spanish

Ethnicity: 99% Arab-Berber, 1% Jewish

Government: constitutional monarchy

 Personal Snapshot

I was always the best student in all my classes. My classmates would expect me to help them out during tests. Somehow, I would find a way to share information. I might let someone sitting next to me look at my paper. Soon, all the students in class would have my answer on their test sheets. We were definitely not ashamed of what we were doing. In fact, we were proud of the fact that we were outsmarting our teachers. They were very demanding and sometimes unfair with us, so we got back at them.

Cultural Closeup

- The word *Morocco* comes from the name of the former Moroccan capital, Marrakesh, and means "the Pass," a reference to the area's geographical function in the Atlas Mountains. Because Morocco is located west of the other Arab countries, some also refer to it using the name *Maghreb,* which comes from the Arabic word for "sunset."

- Numerous foreign invasions over time have contributed to the character of Morocco in the 21st century. It was first populated by the Berbers, a nomadic people of unknown ancestry. The area was invaded in the 12th century B.C. by the Phoenicians and later by the Carthaginians. In the second century A.D., Carthage was overtaken by Rome. In the fifth century, Germanic tribes conquered the region, and Byzantine rule was established. Following this period came the creation of several dynasties, which successfully incorporated under their rule areas now known as Algeria, Tunisia, and Libya, as well as major portions of Spain and Portugal. In the early 16th century, the migration of Moors and Jews from Spain helped reinvigorate a disintegrating country with marvels of art and architecture, but Spain invaded Morocco in 1859, taking control of much of the region. The French, too, sought and obtained portions of Morocco, which remained French territory until Morocco won its independence on March 2, 1956. Spain held the area known as the Spanish Sahara until 1976.

- Morocco is home to rich phosphate mines, control of which was the object of dispute for years. The primary players were Morocco and the Polisario Front, a Saharan nationalist group.

- Morocco supported the United States during the 1990 Persian Gulf War by sending troops to Saudi Arabia.

- Due to their long struggle with foreign invasion, many Moroccans are sensitive to the global expansion of the English language and of U.S. culture and its representations. Not only were the Spanish and French languages and cultures imposed on Moroccan society, but even before that, the native Berbers were dominated by the Arabs. Nonetheless, as Arabic and Berber decline in international importance vis-à-vis more powerful linguistic influences, such as French and English, pride in the native languages of Morocco has begun to fade, and Berber, especially, is seen as backward—the language of the underclass. English, is viewed functionally as the key to a better life, and French is viewed as a prestige language. More affluent Moroccans are likely to be able to speak French, but poorer individuals typically speak only Arabic or Berber. The ability to speak English is regarded as a very special asset.

- Morocco is an Islamic society, meaning that its people by and large follow the doctrine of a religion that is more than 1,400 years old. Its founder, Mohammad, was born in Mecca in A.D. 570 and became a prophet at the age of 40, when, it is said, the angel Gabriel visited him and gave him the words of the Koran to preach. One of the precepts of Islam is that God has complete authority over all we do in life. The Islamic phrase *in sha'Allah,* meaning "if Allah wills it," reveals a seemingly fatalistic view of life. One study of Moroccan schoolchildren reported that those who believed their success as students to be out of their hands were often the children who failed in school.

- Many people say that Islam is not only a religion but a way of life. In Morocco, training in the Koran is considered basic to a child's moral education and begins early in life to teach the value of discipline, respect for authority, love for parents and religion, and social responsibility.

- Moroccan society, while more liberal in many ways than other Muslim countries, is nonetheless male-dominated. Women are beginning to rise to higher levels of professional stature, but at the same time, girls tend to have less advantage and less privilege in school and in the home than do boys. For example, if the cost of the children's education places a strain on a family's budget, chances are that the male children rather than the female children will be given the opportunity to go to school. The government spends 25 percent of its resources on education, and since the 1990s, part of those funds has been designated for schooling for girls, who now constitute some 40 percent of school children in Morocco. This figure is continuing to rise.

- As a legacy of France's colonization of North Africa, there are now many Moroccan men working in France to support their families back home. Their employment significantly contributes to the upward mobility of their relatives back in Morocco and to the ability of their children to attend school. It is not uncommon, moreover, for families to eventually unite in France and for their children to attend French schools.

A Closer Look

POLICY

- At the end of secondary school, most students sit for the *baccalaureate,* an exam that consists of difficult reading passages, multiple-choice questions, prescriptive advanced grammar exercises, and a composition. Passing the exam frequently becomes the single educational focus of many students, and they may study night and day in preparation for this big exam. In class, too, teachers whose students are in their final year of high school will spend great amounts of class time preparing them for the "*bac.*"

- Morocco's school system is a reflection of two traditions: Islamic and French. The tradition of the *madrassa* (or religious school for boys and young men) represents the former and, though part of an ancient system of schooling for boys, still exists widely in Morocco, especially in rural areas. At a *madrassa,* a boy attempts to learn the text of the Koran by heart and studies the Islamic code of conduct; there are no grade levels. Modern education offers a broader curriculum and a more conventional system of advancement from one level to the next. However, students must take rigorous exams at the end of each level and at the end of elementary school, middle school, and high school. Many students fail these exams on the first try. The average child spends more than eight years in elementary school.

Educational Panorama

MOROCCO

Level/Age	Hours/Calendar	Curriculum	Required	Class Size	Exams	Grades	Classroom Setup	Homework
Preschool/ kindergarten, ages 4–6	Varies. Depends on parents' needs.	Social skills, games, songs, drawing, physical exercise	No	15–20	None	None	Small tables and chairs	None
Elementary, grades 1–6, ages 7–12	Sept.–June, 8:00 A.M.–6:00 P.M., with a 2-hour lunch break at home 12:00 P.M.–2:00 P.M.	History, geography, Arabic, religion, French (beginning in grade 3), science, physical education	Yes	15–20	Comprehensive end-of-cycle exam given in grade 6 (end of elementary school)	0–10, with 5 as pass/fail level	Two chairs or a small bench at a small table, which is bolted to the floor	Given every day
Middle, grades 7–9, ages 12–15	Same as above	History, geography, Arabic, religion, French, 2d foreign language (English, Spanish, or German), science, physical education	Yes, up to age 14	30–40	Comprehensive end-of-cycle exam given in grade 11 (end of middle school)	16–20 = very good; 14–15 = good; 12–13 = rather good; 10–11 = passing; 0–9 = unsatisfactory.	Same as above	Given every day. Depending on the teacher, the load may be light to extremely heavy.
High, grades 10–12, ages 15–18	Same as above	History, geography, Arabic, religion, French, 2d foreign language (English, Spanish, or German), physics, chemistry, philosophy, physical education. High school students may attend a *lycée*, or technical school. The *lycée* concentrates on preparing students for university; technical school is a place for students to learn a trade.		30–40	Baccalaureate exam given at end of high school	Same as above	Same as above	Same as above
University, age 18+	Same as above	Varies according to the type of institution: university, teacher training college, executive training institution, or engineering college	No	25–150	Comprehensive exams given at the end of each year	Same as above	Single desks	Heavy reading, with few writing assignments or tests to study for

- There is a severe teacher shortage in Morocco, complicated by the fact that nearly 50 percent of the population is below the age of 25. Teachers are very badly paid, schools tend to have very few resources, and many children in rural areas have no possibility of attending school.

- Education has been compulsory for students up to the age of 13 since 1962.

- The language of instruction in most Moroccan classrooms up until the university level is Arabic. French is studied beginning in third grade, and English is studied in high school. Arabic is the language of instruction in the first two grades. After that, either Arabic or French may be used as the language of instruction.

- The process of *Arabization,* or promoting the spread and use of Arabic rather than French or Berber outside the home, involves three objectives: fixing Arabic as the language of instruction, developing new Arabic terminology for phenomena that have only French or Berber expressions, and introducing Arabic into the broader community.

TEACHING STYLE

- Teachers are looked on as masters. Their job is to transmit knowledge to the students. Although this role is more prominent in the *madrassas,* it extends to the modern schools as well.

- During lessons, teachers sit at their desks or stand on a small platform in front of the class.

- Tests, never given in multiple-choice format, generally take the form of essays. Students are given a broad topic, such as "The most important characteristic of French culture," and are required to write essays drawing from content presented in lectures and books. A teacher may at times choose to give an oral test in class. In such tests, the teacher quickly quizzes the students on material that was previously presented in class. Students are graded on their oral responses.

- Approximately 70 percent of class time is teacher-centered. Foreign language classes tend to be the exception.

- Teachers often read directly out of the book or from lecture notes. In essence, they dictate the lesson while students strive to write down every word.

- Emphasis in pedagogy is usually placed on repetition, teacher control, and, in language learning, mechanical drill, with little student-to-student interaction.

- Many teachers, including many who say that they support such approaches, do not believe that pair and group work can be effective in Moroccan classrooms.

LEARNING STYLE

- Students assume that during exams they will be held accountable for what has been written on the board and presented in lectures during class time.

- Students prefer to work in small groups and to study together.

- Rote memorization and recitation is a common learning strategy in Moroccan schools. Even learning to read is done through this technique, and the subject is often a religious text.

INSTRUCTIONAL SETTING

- Classrooms tend to be serious places. A moderate amount of laughter is tolerated. Students may describe the atmosphere of the classroom as "stressful."

- Desks in Moroccan classrooms are often bolted to the floor or are too heavy to easily move into different configurations.

- Classrooms can be large and cold, often with poor acoustics and no electricity.

- Teachers and students generally have very limited access to library resources, photocopy equipment, and other instructional technology.

- Books are expensive and valuable, so students do not write in them.

- Boys and girls normally study in separate schools.

ACTIVITIES

- Aside from sports (soccer, basketball, volleyball), there are generally no extracurricular activities or clubs in Moroccan schools.

DISCIPLINE AND CLASS MANAGEMENT

- Students are penalized for arriving late to class, skipping class, and not submitting assignments. Late assignments receive a grade of zero, and students who arrive late to school are expected to apologize. Students who frequently miss class are not allowed to return to school.

- Students stand in a line outside the classroom while they wait for the teacher to arrive.

- Students may be required to stand when they are called on to speak in class. Students greet the teacher by rising from their seats.

- Many classrooms have an assigned student monitor, who is selected by the teacher.

- Students do not have the right to dispute a grade.

- Many teachers believe that the only way to keep a class under control is to exercise strict authority. Good behavior is often attributed to punishment or the threat of punishment. For this reason, teachers may cultivate fear in their students.

- Because of social problems, such as unemployment and a weak economy, Moroccan youth are increasingly characterized as frustrated and demoralized. This situation often results in behavior problems in class (insulting the teacher, talking out loud while the teacher is lecturing, arguing with the teacher about minor issues). In addition, the situation has prompted many students to stop taking their studies seriously or to stop attending school altogether.

- To resolve a discipline problem, a teacher may first discuss the problem with the student to try to get to the bottom of the student's unacceptable behavior. If the student's comportment does not improve, the teacher may call the parents. When this effort fails, a student may be dismissed from school.

TEACHER-STUDENT RELATIONSHIP

- A teacher who is unable to answer students' questions may be forgiven for being human, but students may feel embarrassed at the teacher's lack of knowledge or believe him or her to be a poor teacher.

- Although students are allowed to challenge the teacher and express opinions, most students refrain from doing so, because they believe that the teacher might punish them indirectly for speaking openly.

- Teachers generally do not meet with parents to discuss students' progress.

- By not abusing their authority, teachers show respect for their students. However, students and teachers often have an adversarial relationship, with one trying to get the better of the other.

- Overall, the student-teacher relationship is rarely close and friendly.

- Until the middle of the 20th century, literacy in Morocco was limited to a small population. In 1956, almost 90 percent of the population was illiterate. Teachers were part of a privileged group and were widely respected for their literacy skills. As literacy has spread throughout the country, the status of the teacher as the holder of special knowledge has fallen.

STUDENT-STUDENT RELATIONSHIP

- Students are discouraged from mingling with peers from different socio-economic groups.

Protocol

NONVERBAL BEHAVIOR

- Female students greet each other by kissing on the cheek. Male students shake hands.

- No touching should take place between a boy and girl. However, boys often hang on each other, walk arm in arm, or hold hands, as do girls.

- Children often kiss their father's hand in greeting or leave-taking.

- It is considered inappropriate to make eye contact with the teacher.

- The up-and-down waving hand gesture used in English-speaking cultures to mean "hello" is similar to the gesture used in Morocco to mean "come here." Therefore, its use may confuse Moroccan students.

IMAGES

- In Moroccan cities, traffic is notoriously heavy. Cars and mopeds compete with pedestrians for road access, and noise and air pollution are rampant.

- Classroom walls tend to be bare; however, it is not uncommon for a picture of the king of Morocco to hang on the wall.

- Moroccan women of all ages may be seen wearing henna on their hands, feet, and sometimes forehead and chin. Henna is a temporary reddish brown dye that is painted on the body in elaborate and beautiful designs. For special occasions, such as weddings, a group of women will gather for a henna party.

FORMS OF ADDRESS

- Students normally address the teacher by using the Arabic or French equivalent of *teacher, sir,* or *madam.*

- Teachers address students by last name.

DRESS

- While some Moroccan women wear the traditional *jelaba* (long-sleeved, loose-fitting robe) and *foulard* (head scarf), younger women are partial to more fashionable attire—e.g., short skirts, tight blouses, and high heels. Professional women wear business suits.

- Some public middle schools and high schools require female students to wear a uniform, often a white or pink dress. Girls are not allowed to wear makeup to school.

- No short skirts, shorts, or sleeveless blouses are allowed in school. However, jeans and Western clothing in general are considered permissible attire.

POLITE/IMPOLITE TOPICS AND BEHAVIORS

- The topics of sex and private life are taboo in the classroom.

- Many Moroccans are reluctant to discuss politics or religion except in the privacy of their homes.

- One of the most grievous insults to be made in Morocco is to call someone a donkey.

GIFT GIVING

- Students normally do not give gifts to their teachers.

- It is customary to give gifts on birthdays, when a baby is born, when someone gets married, and on the religious holiday *Ashoora* (around March 29), which commemorates the martyrdom of the Prophet Mohammed's grandson. While many Muslims regard *Ashoora* as a day of mourning, others feast lavishly on this day, wear new clothes, and give generous gifts to family members.

- It is not necessary to open a gift in the presence of the gift giver.

- Typical gifts include dates, flowers, perfume, clothing, compact discs, or something decorative.

- One is expected to bring a gift when invited to another person's home for the first time.

? 💡 Problem/Solution

PROBLEM

I wanted to invite some of my students to have coffee with me after class on a Friday afternoon, but I changed the day because I assumed that one of my students, who is from Morocco, would want to go pray at the mosque on Friday afternoon. When I happened to run into the student at a shopping mall at around 1:30 P.M. one Friday, I asked her if she was finished praying. She just laughed. Was she playing hooky from her religious obligations?

SOLUTION

Many Moroccan Muslims do not observe the traditions of the religion as orthodoxly as do people from other Muslim countries, particularly those in the Middle East. While they may not pray on Friday or go to the mosque, they will observe *Ramadan* by fasting, study Islam in school, and take to heart its teachings as they regard day-to-day living and ethics. It is appropriate to ask Moroccan students about the principles of Islam and to expect them to be strong believers in their religion, but it is inappropriate to expect that all Muslim cultures practice Islam in the same way.

PROBLEM

I had a student from Morocco who failed my course and was very disappointed. He came to me to discuss the matter and told me that he needed to pass because his parents would be angry if they found out he had failed. He argued that his only weakness was tests; his homework, class participation, and attendance were fine. I had no choice but to hold firm to the policy of my school. However, on the next day, I received several email messages and phone calls from other teachers of his whom he had approached asking for their intervention. How might I have avoided this situation?

SOLUTION

Academic failure is often a much more serious and less common issue among Moroccan students than it may be among their counterparts in some other countries, such as the United States. There is typically much at stake on both the emotional and the financial levels. It may also be the case that the student in question may have performed poorly on tests because he is not familiar or comfortable with the testing format in his new school. In addition,

Moroccan students may see policies as fairly flexible phenomena that are subject to change as the result of influence from the "right" person. Thus, it is important to make grading policies very clear to students and to stress that the criteria are firm. Teachers should also conference with students who appear to be failing to put them back on the right track if possible.

PROBLEM

My class was working on a unit writing assignment on current events, and I decided to ask the students to write a short composition briefly summarizing the main social issues and problems of their respective countries. My Moroccan student never turned in the assignment. When I asked the students to form small groups and share what they had written, the student joined the group but did not participate, and he asked to be excused early from class that day, claiming illness. What might have been wrong?

SOLUTION

Discussing Morocco's political or economic situation is considered not only taboo but dangerous. There are genuine risks to an individual's well-being if he or she engages in such conversation. Teachers are urged not to question their Moroccan students about the political or economic conditions in their country, even if the questions may seem innocent and are being asked outside of Morocco.

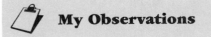 **My Observations**

People's Republic of China

 Focus on People's Republic of China

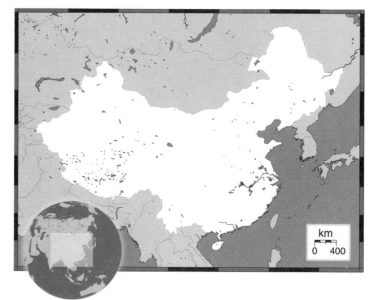

Capital: Beijing

Population: 1,261,832,482

Size: 3,715,392 sq. mi. (9,596,960 sq. km.)

Location: East Asia, south of Russia and Mongolia; bounded on the east by the China Sea

Climate: temperate with some desert; semiarid and tropical

Monetary Unit: yuan

Urban/Rural Life: 75% rural/agricultural

Religion: officially none; Taoism, Islam, Buddhism, and Christianity practiced and tolerated within limits

Languages: Mandarin Chinese (official), Mongolian, Tibetan, Miao, Tai, Uygur, Kazak, other dialects

Ethnicity: 92% ethnic Han, 8% representing 55 minorities

Government: socialist republic

 Personal Snapshot

Once while teaching a culturally mixed group of graduate students, I invited one young female student from the United States to come to the front of the room, as her classmates had before her, to give a brief oral report that she had prepared for the course. She bounced up to the head of the classroom, perched herself cross-legged on the desk, and began to speak with confidence and ease, as if she were surrounded by friends sitting with her on the floor of her apartment. I must admit that at first I wanted to roll my eyes when I realized that she apparently made little distinction between the casual setting of home and the more formal environment of the classroom, but I soon became engrossed in her report and joined her classmates in giving her a round of applause when she finished. At the conclusion of class, though, one of my Chinese students stayed behind. First, he insisted on erasing the blackboard for me, which surprised and delighted me, but then he made an even more surprising gesture: he apologized for his classmate. Although I assured him that I was not entirely offended by her behavior, it turns out that I was missing the point. He was not apologizing for her; he was apologizing for the entire class. In his mind, she had shamed the whole group.

✦ Cultural Closeup

- The Confucian values of hard work, sacrifice, personal accountability, and self-discipline did not die with the introduction of Communism to China. Learning for the sake of learning is still held to be the most laudable motive for study. Students are taught to seek the underlying moral message in educational texts and to themselves become models of exemplary character.

- China has been blessed with a long literary tradition, and students are accustomed to memorizing and reciting long passages of poetry even from the age of three years old. The literary influence can be seen in the compositions of Chinese students, which tend to be relatively flowery, making extensive use of metaphor and imagery. In addition, the written word functions among the Chinese as a symbol of power, authority, and truth. Thus, it is sometimes difficult for Chinese students to critique a text or to offer their personal opinion of its value.

- The Chinese talk of a cultural concept they call the *iron triangle*. Work, home, and the Communist Party or the State comprise the three mainstays of life, and they all come together in such a way as to surround the individual in the center. Some outsiders say that the iron triangle represents a lack of freedom and choice in a Chinese person's life. Others claim that the three sides of the triangle do not allow for the development of alternative passions or commitments.

- Because most Chinese come from an ethnically homogeneous society, it is not surprising that one of the more distinct features of Chinese culture is the value placed on collective, rather than individual, identity. The needs and interests of the self are often de-emphasized out of respect and consideration for those of the group, be it family, commune, school, professional group, military unit, or sports team. Most Chinese feel that individualism is consonant with selfishness. They hold that the communal worldview offers superior benefits, and they may be willing to follow a path prescribed by others even if doing so means personal sacrifice and disappointment. For example, due to the unmanageable size of its billion-strong population, China has adopted a One-Child Family Policy. Naturally, many couples long for bigger families, but under the prevailing circumstances, their personal desire for more children conflicts with the needs of the greater community. Adherence to the One-Child Family Policy is a matter more of patriotism than of fear of punishment. Simply put, elevating the needs of others above one's own is a way of life in China. Cooperation, not individualism, is regarded as the key to the strength and endurance of Chinese culture.

- Respect for the elderly is paramount, as is respect for authority, be it manifested in an individual or a text. Older teachers are more likely to enjoy the unfettered reverence of their students than are younger teachers.

- The Chinese are a gregarious, hospitable, and curious people. They enjoy light interpersonal interaction, mildly competitive games, jokes, plays, songs, cartoons, puns, and so forth. Most Chinese are fascinated by cross-cultural differences and are eager to discuss their own cultural traditions as well as those of others. Nonetheless, they are also a people who value personal modesty. It is unusual to hear a Chinese person boast about his or her accomplishments and abilities.

👁 A Closer Look

POLICY

- In China, education functions as both a right and an obligation. With such a large population, much of it rural, the challenge of educating the country's young is formidable, but it is absolutely necessary if China is to maintain its powerful presence on the world stage. Education also serves the state by promoting a socialist worldview and ensuring adherence to concepts particularly relevant to labor and production.

- While schooling is compulsory in China until the age of 15, it is difficult to guarantee, especially in rural areas. The government is particularly concerned about the country's low literacy rates in comparison with those of developed nations and has launched efforts to develop and expand the delivery of adult literacy education. Its goal is to completely eliminate illiteracy, regardless of age.

- To support the educational interests and aspirations of adults who have already entered the workforce, China makes it easier for them to pursue degrees in higher education. The government's expectation is that by doing so, work-related performance will improve. The country's goal is to enroll in higher education programs 700 out of every 100,000 adults.

TEACHING STYLE

- Classes of children stay together in cohorts for the first six years of school. Each class is assigned a *master teacher,* who is usually also the Chinese language arts teacher.

- Classes in almost all schools in China are large, with perhaps 60 or more students to a class. Given the size of the typical class, teaching tends to be formal and teacher-fronted.

- Teachers are figures whose authority is highly respected, and many students try to emulate their teachers. Teachers direct every classroom activity, generally giving very structured lectures that lead the students to produce a set of complete, detailed, and accurate notes. The model teacher is one

Educational Panorama

PEOPLE'S REPUBLIC OF CHINA

Level/Age	Hours/Calendar	Curriculum	Required	Class Size	Exams	Grades	Classroom Setup	Homework
Preschool, ages 3–4	Year-round except holidays; 30-min. class periods all day during the workweek	Games and simple learning activities	No, but working parents often need a place for their children.	50–60	None	None	Small tables with 4–5 students at each; mats on the floor	None
Kindergarten, age 5	Same as above	Practice for elementary school	No, but working parents often need a place for their children.	50–60	None	None	Desks in rows, with teacher's desk in front, facing the class. Children sit up straight with their hands behind their backs. They still have mats for naps.	None
Elementary, grades 1–6, ages 6–12	8:00 A.M.–3:00 P.M. 2 semesters, Sept. 1–New Year's and New Year's–July 20 or 30; 50-min. class periods and 10-min. recess Mon.–Fri.	Chinese, arithmetic, social studies, nature, sports, music, arts, labor; Pinyin orthographic system (Western-style letters for sounds) through grade 3, then Chinese orthography	Yes	50–60	Test at end of every unit; no final exams	Percentage system and letter grades (A, B, C, D). Passing = 60%.	Desks in rows. Children sit with their hands behind their backs only in the first 2 grades. Children go home for lunch and naps. Children stay in the same room all day, and different teachers come to them. There is no play space in the classrooms. There are large rooms for special activities, clubs, etc.	Hours of repetitive homework, such as writing, Chinese, and math, beginning as early as grade 1
Middle, grades 7–9, ages 12–15	Same as above	Sciences (chemistry, physics, geology, biology, etc.), morality, politics, geography.	Yes, through age 15	50–60 students in a class cohort	Test at end of every unit and major exam at end of each semester; high school entrance exam as well	Percentage system. Passing = 60%.	Desks in rows. Students change rooms for different classes. There are large common areas for clubs, sports, and other activities.	Hours of homework of a more varied nature including problem solving, writing, and languages
High, grades 10–12, ages 15–18	Same as above	Beginning foreign language studies, 2 hours a week, mostly grammar and reading	No	50–60 students in a class cohort	Test at end of every unit and major exam at end of each semester	Same as above	Desks in rows	Many hours of homework are given because getting into college is very competitive.
University, ages 18–22	36 weeks divided into 2 18-week semesters, with 2–3 weeks for review and resting and 11 weeks for winter and summer vacations	Mostly courses required for the major	No	20–30 students in a class	Quizzes, midterms, and final exams	Percentage system. Passing = 60%. Letter grades (A, B, C, D, P/F) are given for electives or less important courses.	Semicircular rows or rising seats, as in an amphitheater	Hours and hours of projects, studying, and assignments

who effectively critiques student performance, corrects students, and drills them. A teacher who does not measure up to these expectations may be considered delinquent. Games with a pedagogical focus, therefore, may be viewed as a waste of time.

- Teachers are expected to be strict, well prepared for class, knowledgeable, creative, stimulating, and accountable for students' success.

- In general, most teachers do not expect a great deal of participation and discussion, if any, from their students. In fact, teachers who demand the expression of opinions may be regarded as insensitive by their students.

- It is common for a teacher to teach from a seated position at his or her desk, which is often set on a small platform at the front of the classroom.

LEARNING STYLE

- Students sit up straight. They are expected to sit and listen, and they read or write only when instructed to do so by the teacher. They raise their hands and wait until the teacher calls on them.

- Chinese students pass through their various educational levels as an intact group and spend a significant amount of time helping one another with whatever work is to be done.

- Students expect to work hard and will accept as much work as the teacher is ready to assign.

- Grueling exams are an integral part of the Chinese student's school experience. Cramming is a necessary and normal by-product of such a situation, and students generally have finely honed study skills.

- In China, most students are loath to proffer an opinion or reaction to issues that are addressed in class. This is partly due to the widely shared belief that young people are far too inexperienced to generate responses that would be sound, interesting, or worthy of attention.

- Given the group-oriented nature of the Chinese people, group problem solving or planning comes naturally to most students. They are skilled at participatory activities such as these and understand the roles and tasks that must be played to arrive at a mutually satisfactory conclusion.

- Contrary to what many people believe, Chinese students often greatly enjoy competition in the classroom, perhaps because it is largely absent in the other parts of their lives. They may particularly appreciate being allowed to elect classmates for certain roles or to declare a particular student a winner.

- Most students will turn away from and possibly resent being singled out for praise, but they tend to enjoy being on stage. Performing is a routine and enjoyable part of school life, and students are usually not embarrassed to sing or recite poetry in front of their peers.

INSTRUCTIONAL SETTING

- Few schools are equipped with instructional technology, such as televisions, computers, and video cameras, and not every school has a library on campus. In some regions, electricity shutdowns occur on a fixed schedule.

- While textbooks are provided by the school, parents must buy whatever additional materials children may need for school.

- College students often live in very simple dormitories with as many as four students to a small room, a single desk, and a fluorescent light. They sometimes congregate in the evening in a classroom and study silently until the early hours of the morning.

ACTIVITIES

- Field trips at lower levels may be not instructional in nature but, rather, opportunities for play and amusement. Class outings typically take place in the spring and fall.

- Students may join a variety of clubs—educational, recreational, and political. Special periods are set aside for club activities during the school day, and there are also after-school events.

- Many schools in China have excellent sports teams for basketball, soccer, and table tennis, for example, but the teams do not receive extensive media coverage as they do in such countries as the United States.

- Movies may be shown on large, outdoor screens when weather permits.

DISCIPLINE AND CLASS MANAGEMENT

- Awards are given to students who sit up straight and are quiet in class.

- Teachers send notes home with children who misbehave. Receiving such a note is a source of shame to the whole family. It is typical for people to be concerned about what their neighbors think or how their behavior may reflect on their family, business, or school.

- Students who fail the regular school year go to summer school. Some consider summer school a form of punishment.

- An elected class monitor will frequently approach teachers with advice on how to handle and manage their particular class collective. This arrangement is thought to contribute to the general good order and stability of the entire academic community, as well as being an effective means of communication between the class and its teacher.

TEACHER-STUDENT RELATIONSHIP

- Written comments on papers and tests are not considered private in China. Thus, students may share the teacher's remarks with other students. Comments and communications meant to be private are delivered verbally.

- Some teachers develop close—almost parental—relationships with students and become very involved in the more personal and private aspects of the students' lives. Nevertheless, the formality of the teacher-student relationship is unlikely to diminish as a result of this closeness.

- Chinese students show respect and affection for their teachers by erasing the blackboard after class; helping the teacher move, sort, or distribute materials; and staying after school to assist with a variety of tasks.

- Given the Chinese culture's emphasis on community rather than individualism, Chinese students tend to expect a great deal of involvement and supervision from their teachers. Self-reliance and independence are not assets that are actively promoted. Teachers often find that presenting students with models helps them complete tasks more efficiently and with more confidence.

STUDENT-STUDENT RELATIONSHIP

- Over the first six years of schooling, all spent with the same classmates, Chinese students form strong bonds with each other, which may last a lifetime.

- Students pass through middle school, high school, and college in tight-knit groups that are not only academic but social. Student leaders are elected, and their role is often to provide personal advice and guidance.

- In college, social groups are usually made up of roommates or classmates pursuing the same major. A strong sense of identity, pride, and loyalty quickly grows out of these associations.

Protocol

NONVERBAL BEHAVIOR

- Students do not maintain eye contact with the teacher while he or she is lecturing. They tend to keep their eyes down and to concentrate on the lecture. In general, eye contact is considered another form of communication. The eyes are averted to convey respect for certain people.

- Contrary to what many Westerners believe, the Chinese do not bow when greeted or introduced. A handshake is always appropriate.

- Nonverbal insults are decidedly few in Chinese culture, and they tend to be relatively mild in intent. For example, one gesture that aims to convey contempt is raising the little finger in the air. An adult may suggest that a child feel shame by rubbing the index finger up an down several times under the eye.

IMAGES

- The dramatic image of the Chinese saying *The lead bird* [flying in a V formation] *gets shot* represents the average Chinese person's reluctance to publicly voice controversial opinion.

- The expression *The empty cart squeaks loudest* reflects the belief that individuals who are excessively verbal and opinionated do not have much of value to share.

- Large public outdoor posters promoting various policies of the state are seen everywhere in China. Large photos and paintings of Chairman Mao and the current leadership are also much in evidence. Outdoor advertising is also ubiquitous in Chinese cities.

- Chinese students are taught to make beautiful drawings and calligraphy writings on the blackboard with colored chalk. Board work, in general, must be very neat.

- Although billboards, brochures advertising services, and newspapers and magazines are most often written in Chinese characters, a romanized spelling system called *Pinyin* was developed to aid Westerners who may understand spoken Chinese but who are unable to read the language. It is common to see Pinyin in tourist areas.

- Despite the apparent absence of religion in China, Buddhism is practiced there, as are a handful of Western religions. It is considered inappropriate to photograph any Buddhist image without permission.

- One sight most unique to China is that of masses of bicycles moving silently through the streets or parked in front of buildings. While public transportation in China's big cities consists of subways, trolleys, and buses, many people prefer the convenience of the bicycle, as well as the opportunity it affords riders to avoid overcrowded vehicles.

- An image that exists only in the mind's eye in China is that of the *iron rice bowl.* It is a representation of the commitment to every person in the country that he or she will be guaranteed a job for life. Those who do not have jobs are not considered unemployed. The Chinese say they are "waiting for employment." The iron rice bowl has many obvious benefits, but one of the policy's shortcomings is the complacence it sometimes creates, resulting in poor work performance or absenteeism.

- Foot binding is a tradition of the past. The practice involved curling and wrapping a woman's feet to make them appear smaller, and allegedly, more beautiful, but it is still possible to see some very old women in public whose feet were bound when they were children. In general, Chinese regard such traditions with scorn and embarrassment.

FORMS OF ADDRESS

- In Chinese names, a person's family name comes first and is followed by a given name that is often very descriptive, with such meanings as "Golden Morning" or "Little Flower." Common family names include *Wu, Han, Chen, Zhao,* and *Wang.*

- All Chinese teachers may be addressed as *laoshi,* which is not a rank but a form of address of considerable respect, even more so than is *professor* in English. Chinese students of English will frequently address a teacher as "Teacher Jones" or "Teacher Mike," for example, or just "Teacher." Students refer to a teacher by last name (e.g., "Jones,") as they often do each other.

- The Chinese prefer formality in their forms of address, even on the job. Titles, such as those for plumber, engineer, postal worker, and so on, are simply appended to the person's family name.

DRESS

- In some schools, students wear uniforms all the time. In others, uniforms are only required once a week, due to expense. Both boys and girls wear a white shirt with some kind of kerchief around the neck. Girls wear dark skirts; boys wear dark pants. Both may wear canvas shoes with rubber soles.

- From the revolution until recently, Chinese of all ages and positions and of either gender have worn what some Westerners call the *Mao suit,* a simple cotton ensemble consisting of loose-fitting pants and a matching, long-sleeved, collarless jacket, often complemented by a cap of matching color. Today, many young people are moving more toward Western dress. In some colleges, students wear casual Western-style dress to class, as do their teachers. Nevertheless, the Mao suit is the preferred mode of dress for older people; older women are never seen wearing skirts or dresses.

- For funerals, it is important for the principal mourners to wear new clothes, although there is no special costume. The deceased is dressed in new clothing that is quilted, because it is assumed the afterlife is cold.

- Red, not white, is the color for weddings. For example, a bride may wear a new, bright red silk jacket on her wedding day.

POLITE/IMPOLITE TOPICS AND BEHAVIORS

- Death, sex, homosexuality, religious beliefs, and prodemocracy ideas are among the most obvious examples of topics to be avoided in public. Governmental policies are not openly discussed unless one intends to praise them. It is acceptable to address the differences between China and other countries, but not for the purpose of advocating adoption of other countries' policies, activities, or values.

- The topic of Taiwan, or the Republic of China, is very sensitive. The mainland Chinese believe that Taiwan rightfully belongs to China, and they are expecting the two to be reunited in the future.

- Among personal issues, the Chinese do not consider the amount of one's salary and the cost of purchases to be off-limits in conversation; and age is likely to be a welcome topic, because many people are proud of the years they have accumulated.

- It is polite to concentrate on what a speaker is saying but impolite to stare at him or her. The same rule applies to students speaking with teachers and to younger people speaking with elders.

- Among foreigners and their Chinese hosts, the advances that China has made is an excellent topic, and mention of them is much appreciated.

- The Chinese are fond of talking about food, and they enjoy joking and teasing each other while eating.

GIFT GIVING

- The most popular occasions for gift giving are birthdays, visiting the sick, spring and midautumn, moon or harvest festivals, and New Year's celebrations. Weddings, meals with previously unknown persons, and returns from long journeys also require gifts.

- The Chinese tend not to celebrate any birthdays except those that are multiples of ten. The higher the age of the person, the more significant the birthday.

- On some occasions, U.S. currency is a very appropriate and desirable gift for children; it is presented wrapped in red paper. Toys for the younger children are also welcome.

- Gifts are often given to thank institutions and individuals for services or hospitality received during a visit. Items bearing the institution's logo or name are popular.

? 💡 Problem/Solution

PROBLEM

My Chinese students often burst into laughter for no apparent reason during class. They giggle, but they don't let me in on the joke. How can I stop this from happening?

SOLUTION

There probably is no joke. Laughter in the classroom is frequently a cultural response to a topic that is embarrassing or inappropriate. Find out what the most uncomfortable topics are so that you can avoid them in class discussions or in providing examples. Don't call attention to the students who are laughing; they are already embarrassed as it is.

PROBLEM

My Chinese students take voluminous notes, and they do well on tests, but I have a hard time trying to get them to participate in class. How can I increase their level of participation?

SOLUTION

Chinese students are accustomed to a formal, structured environment in which the teacher provides all information, which the students copy verbatim. The responses or opinions of the students carry little value in the Chinese culture, and your students may feel that the major issues of the times have already been addressed and judged on the public stage. A lesson on teaching styles and learning styles around the world, with emphasis on appropriate behavior in the host culture's classroom, may help them to feel more comfortable with responding and contributing.

PROBLEM

I recently discovered that my Chinese students were copying right out of the encyclopedia for their assignments, without attribution. How can I stop this?

SOLUTION

There is no such thing as plagiarism in China. Using the words of experts is an acceptable way of completing an assignment and getting a good grade. Students feel that there is no better source than the author. You might explain how the opinions and findings of experts is acknowledged in the English-speaking world, giving particular emphasis to methods of quoting, paraphrasing, and citing.

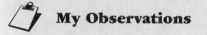 **My Observations**

Poland

 Focus on Poland

Capital: Warsaw

Population: 38,626,023

Size: 120,725 sq. mi. (312,677 sq. km.)

Location: north-central Europe, directly east of Germany

Climate: moderate to severe, with high humidity and very cold winters

Monetary Unit: zloty

Urban/Rural Life: 40 cities of over 100,000 people; primarily industrial

Religion: primarily Roman Catholic

Languages: Polish (official), including a large number of dialects

Ethnicity: 98% ethnic Poles

Government: parliamentary republic

 Personal Snapshot

Ela tells the story of shopping in the United States with her husband. He enjoyed going from one store to another when hunting for the best deal. One day, after visiting several stores in search of a particular item, he made a purchase in a computer specialty shop that guaranteed the lowest price in town. The store promised to refund the difference if the customer were to find a better deal and were to provide proof. While basically satisfied with his purchase, Ela's husband continued his quest, and in a department store nearby, he found the same item at 60 percent of what he had paid in the specialty shop. He gleefully returned to the first store with an advertisement from the second as proof of the price difference. The clerk cheerfully gave him 50 percent of his original price back, with an additional five dollars just for the trouble of the return trip. Ela was stunned and said: "But that is too much money! You should only give back the difference!" When the clerk explained that the retailer wanted the customer's goodwill and business in the future, Ela said: "Now I know I am in the United States! In Poland, they would have told me to go ahead and buy it cheaper in the other place if I wanted to." In Poland, Ela explained, the sales ethic is to raise the price to get more money, not to lower the price to get more customers.

⤙ Cultural Closeup

- Many years of foreign rule, partition, war, and Communism have produced a people who are fiercely independent and patriotic. Despite many years of foreign rule, the Poles have maintained their own cultural and religious ways. The strength of this unique identity may be seen in the fact that large ethnic Polish communities have developed outside Poland, particularly in the United States.

- The Roman Catholic Church is the dominant force in Polish life. Families dress for church and go to church together every week all over the country. It is an enormous point of national pride that Pope John Paul II was Polish.

- The Polish people maintain the self-image of the hard worker. There appears to be a national consensus that life is not easy and that nothing good comes easily.

- The Poles take great enjoyment from the arts and music and are proud that many prominent artists and composers are of Polish ancestry.

- Polish cuisine is considered somewhat opportunistic, because it has borrowed from the traditions of a variety of invading and conquering nations. In many ways, it is also a product of the practices of the Catholic Church. For example, the requirement for strict fasting created a response in the form of subsequent feasting, so religious celebrations and eating have combined to become a force for creativity and abundance in Polish cuisine.

⊚ A Closer Look

POLICY

- Education has historically been a priority in Poland, and the country's current literacy rate of 100 percent reflects the national interest in education. From the days of Communist rule to the present, the new, elected governments of Poland have continued to focus great effort on their preferences in the formation of both young people and adults. In fact, one of the more recent reforms in Poland has been to expand continuing education opportunities for adults.

- The Polish education system has become strained since the establishment of democracy. It is particularly stressed by the need to meet the demand for specially trained and educated personnel. In addition, Poland must address the serious issue of *brain drain,* the flight of accomplished individuals from Poland to areas where better economic situations prevail.

Educational Panorama

POLAND

Level/Age	Hours/Calendar	Curriculum	Required	Class Size	Exams	Grades	Classroom Setup	Homework
Preschool, ages 3–5	Varies	Individual development	No	Varies	None	None	Generally four students/table	None
Kindergarten, age 6	Includes day care and depends on parents' needs	General development, reading skills, basic mathematics	Yes	Varies according to time of day, because some children attend a few hours whereas others attend all day	None	None	Same as above	None
Primary, ages 7–15 or 7–17	Early Sept.–Christmas holidays and early Jan.–mid-June; 45-min. class periods 8:00 A.M.–2:00 P.M.	First half: reading, writing, arithmetic, memorization; second half: the preceding plus social sciences, languages, physical sciences, music, art, physical education	Yes, through age 14	23	National standardized tests every semester, along with partial and periodical exams; entrance exams to secondary schools	1 (bad)–6 (excellent). Other marks are given for behavior.	Pairs of children share large desks.	Many hours of homework are done in the afternoons, because school hours have been cut back for economic reasons.
Postprimary (includes vocational schools), ages 15–19	Same as above	Various vocational courses, college preparatory courses	No	30	National standardized tests every semester, along with partial and periodical exams; exams for admission to higher education	Same as above	Same as above	Same as above
University, ages 19–24; graduate school, age 24+	Same as above; 40 hours/week	No bachelor's degree. Students earn a master's after 4–5 years of university schooling and must have a master's to enter a doctorate program.	No	40	Oral or written exams, varying by class and professor	Practices vary widely	Auditoriums for most classes	Many hours of homework, made more difficult by the shortage of textbooks and the necessity of sharing the few that exist
Other schools, adults	Varies, including evening and correspondence schedules	Varies from equivalency courses to specialty areas needed for professional advancement	No	Varies widely	Wide variation depending on program, purpose of course, and type of school	Wide variation depending on program, purpose of course, and type of school	Wide variation depending on program, purpose of course, and type of school. Many classes are by correspondence.	Wide variation depending on program, purpose of course, and type of school

- Poland's Act on Education guarantees all people the right to receive a free education up to 17 years of age and also allows nongovernmental entities to operate and maintain educational institutions in Poland.

TEACHING STYLE

- The teacher-fronted, teacher-oriented classroom is the norm in much of Poland. Students are not expected to ask questions in class, nor are they encouraged to engage in argumentative interaction with professors. There is great respect for the teacher, who, even at the secondary level, is addressed as "Professor."

- Since the advent of democracy, teachers have a great deal more choice in terms of teaching style, materials, and so on. This era of greater pedagogical freedom and experimentation has led to the existence of considerable variation from one classroom to another and from one school to another.

- Students do not evaluate their teachers at any level of education.

LEARNING STYLE

- Students are generally very respectful, sometimes rising when called on to recite in class or when the teacher enters the room.

- Students work alone, in pairs, or in groups, depending on the subject, the type of project, and the teacher. This represents a change from the dominance of individual work in predemocracy days. Group work is becoming more popular, and teachers are encouraged to create ample opportunity for interaction.

INSTRUCTIONAL SETTING

- The Polish educational system follows the German model. Students are not given abundant amounts of latitude, if any, regarding behavior and workload, and the pressure of exams is great, especially in regard to entrance exams, which must be taken to pass from elementary school to middle school to high school.

- Poland suffers from a shortage of textbooks and other teaching materials. In some cases, one or two textbooks may have to be shared by an entire 25-person university class, working in two-hour shifts. Audiovisual equipment is in short supply in the public schools.

- Seventy percent of general, college-preparatory secondary schools have computers, compared with only 23 percent of Poland's vocational secondary schools. Computers are a relative rarity in primary schools.

- Many schools are on shift systems: half the students study in a morning shift, and a second group arrives for instruction in the afternoon.

- Many schools do not have gymnasiums, workrooms, conference rooms, or auditoriums.

- One teacher teaches all subjects for the first three grades of primary school.

- Transportation to school is not provided, nor is public transportation free to students.
- Children change from street shoes to slippers to protect the wooden floors of their classrooms. They are also given smocks with their school numbers on them to wear during the day.

ACTIVITIES

- After-class clubs and classes may include the study of foreign languages and music, performing arts groups, sports, and other recreational activities.
- School hours are short, and because most parents work until the evening hours, many students stay after class to study, take music lessons, and engage in various arts and crafts. There are also extra classes for students who want to do extra schoolwork.
- Individual schools often hold an annual scholastic competition, leading some students to devote a significant amount of time to preparing for the event. A good performance in the competition increases a student's chances of being admitted to a good school at the next level.
- School children enjoy a variety of field trips to sites of historic, natural, or artistic interest, and some excursions may last several days.

DISCIPLINE AND CLASS MANAGEMENT

- Rules and consequences for breaking them are clearly written and posted. The students are highly disciplined and get points for good behavior; they lose points for bad behavior.
- A student who has misbehaved may get detention or may be expelled from school, but the practice of suspending a student from school for a given period of time is not used.
- No corporal punishment is permitted.

TEACHER-STUDENT RELATIONSHIP

- Teachers are expected to be role models but are not expected to interact with students outside of school.
- Teachers are normally in charge of clubs, sports, and other after-school activities.

STUDENT-STUDENT RELATIONSHIP

- Students form strong friendships while in school. However, students must compete with one another for entry into the better schools, and the pressure to overtake others can create jealousy or ill will and can even force some students into cheating.
- Due to the shortage of educational supplies, including textbooks and computers, students learn to share early and often.

Protocol

IMAGES

- Bookstores are often crowded, and English books, in particular, sell briskly. English is seen as the language of opportunity, and it is eagerly studied by many in Poland.

- Christian holidays present a variety of images. On Christmas Eve, a blessed unleavened wafer is brought home after midnight Mass and shared by everyone around the table, starting with the eldest person present. After an exchange of Christmas wishes, the family breaks its day-long fast by enjoying a number of special meals. Easter food, including brightly dyed eggs, is brought to the early Mass and blessed. At home, the blessed food is passed around the table, with the eldest person being the first to eat.

- It is traditional for the entire family to dress in their "Sunday best" and walk to church together.

- The image of the rugged individualist is admired, appreciated, and often emulated in Poland. The country's cultural heroes, which include the World War II soldiers, Solidarity leader Lech Walensa and his followers, and even Pope John Paul II, are brave, tough-minded individuals who came together with others for important causes.

FORMS OF ADDRESS

- First names are used only by family and close friends. Generally, an individual's title is most often invoked.

- The female and male polite forms *pani* (madam) and *pan* (sir) may be used alone or placed before a first name (e.g., *Pani Maya*), a last name (e.g., *Pani Nowicki*), or both (e.g., *Pani Maya Nowicki*).

DRESS

- Students do not wear school uniforms, but they sometimes wear smocks over their street clothes.

- Teenagers especially like to wear the latest fashions from Europe and the United States.

- Most people dress in standard European clothing. Native or traditional dress can be seen on festival occasions and in country weddings.

POLITE/IMPOLITE TOPICS AND BEHAVIORS

- The art of argument is widely practiced and admired in Poland. People who take issue with the statements of others and stand up for their beliefs are seen in a very positive light.

- It is inappropriate and unusual for a person in a professional position to drop in on another person. An appointment is absolutely necessary. Moreover, most people are strictly punctual.

- Visitors to Polish homes will find that the cultural history of Poland, life in the host country, and family are all welcome topics of conversation. It is inappropriate to talk about items that Poles cannot afford. Reference to General Kosciuszko (a Polish/American general and U.S. Revolutionary War hero) will impress a visitor's host.

- Topics with sexual overtones are avoided, as are criticisms of the Catholic Church or clergy, both of which are held in great esteem.

- Jokes about the Polish people are considered extremely rude.

GIFT GIVING

- An odd number of unwrapped flowers (but not red roses, which imply romance) is welcome when invited to a Polish home. Chocolate and alcoholic beverages are also appropriate gifts.

? Problem/Solution

PROBLEM

I've got a couple of Polish students in my class, and they seem particularly adept at cheating. They're very bright kids, so I'm surprised by this behavior. How should I address this problem?

SOLUTION

In Poland, students may be taking up to 13 subjects at once. Competition to get into the better schools is fierce. Cheating used to be an accepted and expected means of survival under Communism, and the practice has to some extent lived on as a kind of tradition. Coming down hard on your students about cheating will not necessarily eliminate the behavior. They are already aware that cheating is wrong, but they feel there may be no other choice if they want to succeed and be at the head of the class. An alternative is to offer as much extra help as you can practically give your students. Also arrange your classroom physically during tests so that cheating is less easily accomplished.

PROBLEM

My Polish students will spend huge amounts of class time arguing a point. Consequently, the class is constantly pulled off topic by these friendly, but endless, discussions. How might I make the best of this situation?

SOLUTION

Arguing is a basic Polish social activity and is considered an art. It is an excellent way for your students to improve their speaking and rhetorical skills. Assign interesting topics and set up regular debates in your class, with specific ground rules and roles for each student.

PROBLEM

Although my students will spend hours arguing about nearly everything, getting them to ask questions of me, their teacher, is like pulling teeth. Can I do anything to encourage them?

SOLUTION

Although classroom protocol in Poland has loosened up considerably in recent years, questioning the teacher is not yet the norm. However, Polish students are used to getting points for good behavior, with the winner receiving a prize. Let your students know that asking questions is a good way for everyone to learn and is not disrespectful. Set up a point system for the behaviors you are trying to encourage in them as English speakers, including asking pertinent questions, and give a few awards at the end of your semester.

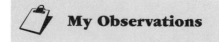 **My Observations**

Russia

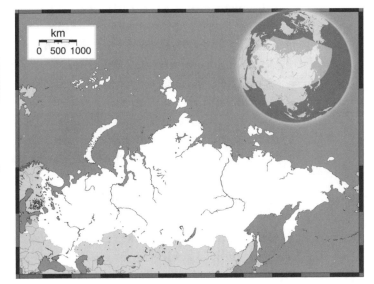

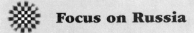

Focus on Russia

Capital: Moscow

Population: 147,500,000

Size: 6,592,745 sq. mi. (17,075,200 sq. km.)

Location: northern Asia, bordering the Arctic Ocean, between Europe and the North Pacific Ocean

Climate: ranges from subarctic in Siberia to tundra in the polar north, steppes in the south, and humid continental in much of the east

Monetary Unit: ruble

Urban/Rural Life: 78% urban, 22% rural

Religion: Russian Orthodox, Islam, Judaism, Protestantism, Roman Catholicism, other

Languages: Russian (official), more than 140 other languages and dialects

Ethnicity: 82% Russian; 4% Tatar; 3% Ukrainian; 1% Chuvash; almost 3% Bashkir, Byelorussian, and Moldavian, 8% other

Government: multiparty republic

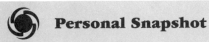

Personal Snapshot

I miss Russia sometimes. My home city is St. Petersburg. It is a very beautiful city, but there you have very many poor people, and things in life can be uncertain. Fortunately, our education system is not so bad. I mean that we seem to study and learn a lot more than the American kids I've met in school. For example, in high school, we already are doing calculus, and we know a lot about history and literature. In the United States, you have nicer buildings with air conditioning, heating, computers. Sometimes we have this, too, but then it either doesn't always work or is very old. So, I think education in Russia and in the United States is both good and bad.

119

✦ Cultural Closeup

- The history of what is today Russia dates back to the country's ancestors, the Slavic people, who settled in the steppes of European Russia in the sixth century. The czars, who were the rulers of Russia, expanded the Russian Empire from the Baltic region of Europe to central and northeastern Asia. The aristocracy owned most of the land. After the Russian defeat in World War I, the Communists seized power. Russia became part of the Union of Soviet Socialist Republics (USSR). The Soviet economy stagnated during the following decades. In the 1980s, the USSR, through its general secretary, Mikhail Gorbachev, underwent some changes under policies of *glasnost* (openness) and *perestroika* (restructuring). Gorbachev's efforts led to the fragmentation of the Soviet Union into 15 independent republics in 1991.

- The transition to a market economy has been very difficult. Russia is still struggling to achieve strong economic growth and to modernize its infrastructure. Under the Communist regime, all workers in Russia were guaranteed employment; today, there is tremendous unemployment, and both men and women need to work to survive. One thing that has not changed is Russia's fame for its achievements in mathematics, science, and engineering.

- As for home life, most Russian families are small. Couples often have only one child. However, due to tradition as well as a severe housing shortage, the extended family is still common. Grandparents normally live with their children, and the *babushka,* or grandmother, normally cares for the grandchildren. Families in the cities often live in very small apartments.

- Russians are people of deep feelings and emotions. When a Russian opens his or her heart, the listener must be prepared for a long conversation filled with opinions, philosophies, literary quotations, personal revelations, and so forth.

🎓 Educational Panorama

- Education plays an important role in this country. Even with the challenge that Russia faces today, the government makes sure that education reaches even remote areas of the country.

👁 A Closer Look

POLICY

- The education system in Russia is undergoing profound changes at all levels to keep pace with the transition to a democracy and to a market economy. The 1992 Law on Education set the foundation for all the changes taking place in education in Russia. With this law, the state no

RUSSIA

Level/Age	Hours/Calendar	Curriculum	Required	Class Size	Exams	Grades	Classroom Setup	Homework
Preschool, ages 3–6	Sept.–May, 8:00 A.M.–5:00 P.M.; Mon.–Fri.; breaks for Christmas, Easter, and national holidays	Profound changes underway; focus on development of cognitive abilities and motivation, collective games and activities, role play, drawing, creative design; ample free time for play	No	10–20	None	None	Small tables and chairs	None
Elementary primary, grades 1–3, ages 6–7	Sept.–May, 8:00 A.M.–12:00 P.M.; Mon.–Fri.; breaks for Christmas, Easter, and national holidays	Considered the first level of secondary education; focus on development of basic reading, writing, and counting skills and other academic abilities; emphasis on fundamentals of personal hygiene and healthy lifestyle; subjects include Russian language, literature, arts, social sciences, mathematics, physical training, technology	Yes	20–25	Tests and quizzes throughout the academic terms	Each institution chooses its own grading system.	2 students/desk, with desks in rows of five (usually three rows). Students generally sit where they choose.	Daily assignments in history, literature, and math
Basic secondary, grades 4–9, ages 11–16	Sept.–May, 8:00 A.M.–2:00 P.M.; breaks for Christmas, Easter, and national holidays	Last phase of compulsory schooling; focus on development of the individual as a well-integrated member of society; subjects include Russian language and literature, foreign language, arts, social studies, natural sciences, mathematics, physical training, technology, electives	Yes	20–25	Pop quizzes based on homework are often given. At the end of grade 9, students sit for major written exams in specific subjects.	Same as above	Same as above	Ample amounts of homework in Russian, English, mathematics, history, geography, and science; many exercises each day for mathematics
Complete secondary, grades 10–12, ages 16–18; initial vocational, grades 10–13, ages 16–19	Same as above	Study of a specific field or profession. After completion, students may attend secondary vocational education for advanced study of selected field.	No	20–25	Oral and written exams. At the end of grade 11, students sit for final exams in algebra and fundamentals of analysis plus 3 other subjects of their choice. Students' homework preparation shows here, as students are sometimes given esoteric questions from general readings in which they must be conversant and prepared to both supply information and demonstrate clear thinking.	Variance between systems, but generally number grades are given, 1 (lowest)–5 (highest).	Same as above	Same as above
University, ages 18+	Varies according to institution	Bachelor's, master's, and doctoral degrees in arts and sciences, humanities, medicine, teaching, etc.	No	30–100	There is extreme pressure on students to perform well on final exams. Content normally is derived from lectures and textbooks, as well as resources not directly addressed in class.	Same as above	Individual desks or lecture hall seating	Copious amounts of homework, especially reading

longer has a monopoly on education. Domestic and foreign institutions or individuals can establish schools. In 1993, a new curriculum was introduced for primary education. The system was changed from one comprised of separate subjects to one comprised of educational areas.

- Since 1991, some private schools have opened in Russia, but there are still very few. Russia has in place a system of special education for children and teenagers, but it is in need of improvement. The programs normally lack the appropriate equipment and qualified personnel to function. Almost half of preschool-aged children in Russia have functional health impairments due to pollution and the difficult social conditions under which they live.

- The Ministry for General and Professional Education administers the education system in Russia. The 1992 Federal Program on the Development of Education in Russia deals with the establishment of plans and coordinates activities. It also interprets the national education policy for the country.

- The system of higher education in Russia is undergoing profound changes. Since 1992, the system has been offering free higher professional education on a competitive basis. There are also private, social, and religious institutions of higher education with three levels: incomplete higher professional (two years), higher professional (no less than four years and leading to a bachelor's degree or specialist degree), and higher professional training (no less than six years and leading to a master's degree or doctorate). To enroll in higher education, students must have a secondary school-leaving certificate or a diploma of secondary professional education and must pass an entrance examination.

- Russia's literacy rate is 98 percent, and school attendance is outstanding. At the level of higher education alone, there are 48 universities and 519 vocational, technical, and professional schools, with some three million students in attendance. Russia's focus on education, especially in the sciences and in technology, has produced world-class Russian contributions in the fields of space research, medicine, mathematics, physics, chemistry, and education. There are proportionately far more physicians in Russia than in the United States.

TEACHING STYLE

- In the past, lessons emphasized political ideology, but teachers are now beginning to use books that were once prohibited.

- Teachers tend to lecture, and classes tend to be teacher-fronted. With the new curriculum, teaching style is changing, as new books reflect new methodologies. However, there is a shortage of books, so changes are occurring slowly.

- The level of formality in Russian schools is very high, and teachers tend to be strict with their students.

- Teachers often require students to prepare and make oral presentations.

LEARNING STYLE

- In the past, students were accustomed to rote learning, but with the changes to the overall system, this tradition has begun to change.

- Students are traditionally not encouraged to question their teachers, but this tradition is changing.

- There is an emphasis on oral production. Students are expected to sit for oral exams at some point in their studies.

- There is occasional group work.

INSTRUCTIONAL SETTING

- In the former system, the typical classroom was marked by formality. Both teachers and parents put a great deal of pressure on children to perform well in school. Students were not encouraged to speak their minds, and creative self-expression was viewed as somewhat risky. Rote memorization formed the basis of Soviet education. Today, however, the Russian classroom embraces more innovation and experimentation. It is less rigid and more open to addressing the affective dimension of the individual student.

ACTIVITIES

- Students whose schools are located in or close to a large city may attend events in music, dance, and visual arts, as well as museums and local points of interest.

DISCIPLINE AND CLASS MANAGEMENT

- Students are highly respectful of their teachers and stand when the teacher enters the classroom.

- Students are expected to raise their hands if they have questions. They may not talk while the teacher is talking.

TEACHER-STUDENT RELATIONSHIP

- Relationships between teachers and students are cordial but formal. Sometimes, a teacher and a student may become friends, but in such a case, the student is still supposed to address the teacher by his or her first and middle names, to show respect.

- Teachers are greatly respected and are accorded more authority than in the United States. For example, they are given responsibility for disciplining a student. Teachers are not allowed to strike their students, but strict discipline is expected.

- With the passing of older generations, certain stylistic accommodations are becoming more frequent in teaching, with some younger teachers encouraging students to think for themselves and speak their own minds. This should not be interpreted to mean that the student-teacher relationship is informal.

STUDENT-STUDENT RELATIONSHIP

- The relationship between students is very close. Sometimes, cohorts of students will remain together throughout their school years.

Protocol

NONVERBAL BEHAVIOR

- Russians greet guests either inside or outside of their homes. It is considered bad luck to greet guests in the doorway.

IMAGES

- In both cities and the countryside, many Russians still take a weekly steam bath in a public *banya* (bath).

- The Kremlin in Moscow is an enormous government complex. Many Russian artistic and historical treasures are housed there.

- It is very common to see people playing chess, either indoors or outdoors.

- Easter is the main religious festival of the year and is celebrated with visits to church. *Shrovetide,* celebrated for three days, occurs seven weeks before Easter. People celebrate this fun time by playing tricks, by going sledding, and even by getting married. Other important holidays in Russia include International Women's Day (March 8), New Year's Day (known as the day that Father Frost—*Dyed Maros*—brings presents for the children), Russian Orthodox Christmas (January 7), and Independence Day (June 12).

- A traditional meal in Russia begins with cold appetizers, or *zakuski.* This part of the meal is followed by a special soup, meat or fish with potatoes, and bread. Vegetables are a rarity in many parts of Russia. Hot tea is carefully, and sometimes even elaborately, brewed and served at breakfast, lunch, and dinner. Some people may drink beer or vodka with their meals.

- Rich food in plentiful amounts is offered when guests come to the home of a Russian. Dinner guests are frequently treated to an elaborate feast, the best that (and sometimes better than) the host can afford.

FORMS OF ADDRESS

- Russians often use the father's first name as the child's middle name, called the *patronymic.* Thus, the child of a man with the first name *Boris* might bear the name *Ivan Borisavich* (for a son) or *Natalia Borisovna* (for a daughter). Nicknames are very common. *Ivan* becomes *Vanya, Natalia* becomes *Natasha,* and so on.

- In schools, teachers call students by first name or title plus last names. Students call teachers by first name and patronymic together.

DRESS

- Students traditionally wore uniforms, but this is no longer true across the system.

- Teachers should wear the kind of dress that coincides with the authority and respect that is imparted to the role of education. Men wear dress pants, shirts, and ties; women wear dresses, skirts, dress pants, and hose.

POLITE/IMPOLITE TOPICS AND BEHAVIORS

- Asking about Russian history and the accomplishments of the Russian people is often an excellent conversation opener, because Russians are very proud of their country and extremely knowledgeable about its social, cultural, political, and historic traditions. In addition, they tend to know a great deal about other countries and cultures and may be eager to share their knowledge and engage in animated discussion, if not debate.

- Russian hosts are famous for their many toasts (and for the vodka that accompanies them), and they may expect their guests to propose one or two toasts of their own. It is best to be prepared beforehand for such an occasion. Toasting in Russia is a special and important part of a dinner or party, and a person making a toast is expected to show his or her emotions and genuine thoughts at this time. A host would no doubt feel offended if a guest were to refuse to make a toast or to fail to make an honest attempt at one.

GIFT GIVING

- It is normal for students to bring gifts to teachers on September 1 (beginning of school year), on New Year's Day, and at graduation. Many people give presents to their relatives as well on New Year's Day.

- Men bring flowers and gifts for their mothers, wives, and sisters on International Women's Day.

- If invited to a Russian's home, it is considered polite to bring a gift. If food is brought to the home, the host will generally prepare it immediately.

? 💡 Problem/Solution

PROBLEM

Over the last few years, I have had several Russian students in my classes and am forming the opinion that they don't respect me. They breathe heavy sighs and look totally bored. What have I done to lose their esteem, and how can I regain it?

SOLUTION

Russian students face extremely high academic expectations back home. Teachers pile on the homework and demand that students come to class prepared to recite, not to express their opinions or learn from anyone other than the teacher. Moreover, they tend to view the personal and accommodating approach of many U.S. educators as permissive and even insulting. You may need to reexamine and modify some of your teaching practices (e.g., accepting late assignments, not checking or grading homework, pacing your class according to the needs of your less advanced students, assigning group or pair tasks without a clear and explicit rationale).

PROBLEM

During class discussions, my Russian students are sometimes assertive, bordering on aggressive. The other students in the class appear to be intimidated by such vigorous outward expression. What can I do?

SOLUTION

The art of discussion and debate is highly developed in Russia, even among those without a lot of formal education. Such exchanges are lively and can be loud, with the speakers talking or shouting over each other's voices. This implies not that they're angry but simply that they're enjoying the give-and-take and the challenge of argumentation and eloquence. One way to encourage discussion that is more suitable for the classroom is to structure a formal debate with clearly prescribed roles, guidelines, and useful expressions.

PROBLEM

On final exam day, one of my Russian students brought me a bouquet of flowers, which I accepted reluctantly and suspiciously. Were the flowers a bribe for a good grade on the test?

SOLUTION

It is unlikely that the flowers were a bribe. In Russia, it is common for a student to bring flowers to the teacher either on exam day or on the first day of the school year, September 1, to acknowledge the position of the teacher and, on exam day, all the work that the teacher has done to bring the student to this important moment.

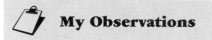 **My Observations**

Saudi Arabia

 Focus on Saudi Arabia

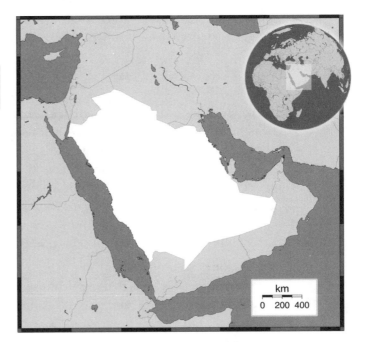

Capital: Riyadh

Population: 21,504,613

Size: 830,000 sq. mi. (2,149,690 sq. km.)

Location: Middle East, between the Red Sea and the Persian Gulf

Climate: desert hot and dry; coastal regions hot and humid in summer, cool in winter; interior temperatures up to 120 degrees Fahrenheit in summer, down to 60 degrees Fahrenheit in winter.

Monetary Unit: riyal

Urban/Rural Life: mainly urban, centered in Riyadh, Jidda, Medina, and Mecca

Religion: Islam

Languages: Arabic (official)

Ethnicity: Arab

Government: monarchy

 Personal Snapshot

When the government of Saudi Arabia introduced English into its curriculum, I was recruited by the British Council to teach English at King Abdul Aziz University. Most of the students in my class were the sons of very wealthy Arab families. (There are no coeducational schools in the Kingdom of Saudi Arabia.) There was nothing to distinguish one student from the other; they all wore very expensive clothes and jewelry and drove the best and most expensive cars. They all were bored and attached no importance to being at the university. Most forms of motivation that I tried brought no change in their attitudes, until a chance remark I made pointed the way to getting them to learn. I said to them that the ability to communicate in English could open doors to further study, which could mean opportunities for higher education and professions in medicine, engineering, and architecture and, most importantly, a chance to study in an English-speaking country. I also said that someone's level of ability to communicate in English could make a big difference in their status in the Arab community. I immediately saw a change in my students' level of interest, and I began to capitalize on their attitudes. I had found their Achilles' heel, and I encountered few problems afterward in motivating them to study.

⟶✳︎⟵ Cultural Closeup

- To understand the Saudi Arabian culture, one must understand Islam and its history. There is a seamless relationship between religion and culture, on the one hand, and the way Arabs conduct every minute of their lives, on the other. Islam prescribes the code of ethics and behavior, and the code of civil and religious law rules one's life. Mecca is the center of the Islamic world, and Saudis regard themselves as the keepers of the Great Mosque there, which holds the Kaaba, a cube-shaped stone shrine. They feel it is their duty to uphold the tenets of Islam.

- Religion is so omnipresent in the life of the Saudi that it is not unusual to hear a student who is making promises or plans say, *Insha Allah,* [God willing], or to hear a student who is beginning a test say, *Bismillah,* [in the name of God]. Arabs greet good news by saying *Ma'sha Allah* [by the will of God], to prevent others from experiencing jealousy.

- Saudis are very demonstrative and effusive, very emotional, and full of *joie de vivre.* They are also very sensitive and easily hurt. Criticizing a Saudi in public causes the criticized individual to lose face.

- Two values held dear are respect and dignity, and the degree to which these guide daily activities is very clear. Trust, forbearance, patience, and understanding are qualities that show respect and a sense of personal dignity.

- Hospitality is very important in the scale of Saudi values. They consider it a blessing to give hospitality and protection to anyone who comes to their home. Guests come first and are given the best that the home has to offer. A host will not eat until all the guests have been served.

- Friendships develop very quickly. However, the relationship carries with it certain responsibilities. In the Saudi culture, a friend is not only someone whose company you enjoy but also someone whose duty it is to do favors and give help. Saudis think it is rude to refuse a friend's request for help.

- Saudi men and women are totally segregated outside of the home and family. Foreign men should not shake hands or speak with a Saudi woman, nor should they inquire about the female relatives of a male Saudi. Saudi men object to having the names of their female relatives mentioned in public.

- Females are not permitted to be alone with a strange man.

- In the Western world, not much is known about the status of Saudi women, and what is known is significantly negative. Islamic law provides that women can own, inherit, and bequeath property in their own name. If a Saudi woman has her own means of income, she is in no way obliged to give it to or share it with her husband. Many Saudi women are owners of businesses and are employed in jobs in banking, education, social work, medicine, and psychology.

- Women must wear the traditional *abaya* (black cloak) and *hijaab* (head scarf) on the street. This is considered a form of protection against male sexual harassment.

- The weekend days in Saudi Arabia are Thursday and Friday. *Juma* (Friday) is the day of congregational prayers. The workweek begins on Saturday.

- Saudis believe that men of learning are inheritors of the prophets. Therefore, the character of a male Saudi teacher, who is considered a man of respect and learning, must be imbued with *rabaniyeen,* which is a description of someone who acts in God's ways. (The root word *rabb* means "God.")

Educational Panorama

- English is introduced in middle school and is continued into high school. In the university, some lectures are conducted in English.

- Students who fail eight or fewer courses in a school year are allowed to take the course tests again. Students who fail more than eight courses in one year must repeat the year.

- The high school grade point average (GPA) determines the college to which students will gain entry, with a high GPA aiding entry into the more prestigious schools. Only a student with a very high GPA may enter medical school.

- Because the whole education system is based on Islamic precepts, the Koran is taught from day one. From the age of five, students are asked to do analyses of Koranic *surahs* and *ayahs* (chapters and verses). Each school possesses a special room with a mosque setting, dedicated to prayers and Koranic study. Curriculum writers do not include anti-Islamic ideas or pictures of the whole female figure in the textbooks. The curriculum does not include music or dance classes. In the penultimate year before graduating from high school, students may choose to study either science or arts.

- Since there is gender separation from the age of seven (even in the family), male students are not exposed to female teachers. For many Saudi males coming to the United States to study, having a woman as their teacher is a major cultural hurdle they must overcome. They may find having a female teacher difficult to accept, since the man is dominant in the Arab culture. It may be even more difficult for female Arab students in the United States to accept male teachers. These students may be very shy with a male teacher, because they have had no previous experience in speaking to a man who is not a relative. At home, they are not permitted to participate

SAUDI ARABIA

Level/Age	Hours/Calendar	Curriculum	Required	Class Size	Exams	Grades	Classroom Setup	Homework
Preschool, ages 2–4	4 hours/day, Sat.–Wed.	Development of social skills through play	No	10–15	None	None	Game-room setup	None
Kindergarten, ages 4–6	day care 5 hours/day or depending on parents' needs, Sat.–Wed.	Not a part of the education policy; development of basic skills, Arabic language, Koranic recitation, prayers, Islamic code of ethics	No	Varies	None	None	Game-room setup	None
Elementary, grades 1–6, ages 6–12	2 semesters Sept.–June, 7 A.M.–2 P.M. Sat.–Wed.; breaks for *Ramadan* and the *hajj*	Religious and moral education (9 hours/week); math, geography, history, science, art, physical education (12 hours/week)	No	25 or fewer	Monthly tests set by teachers, consisting of multiple-choice and essay questions; no final exams.	90–100 = excellent; 75–89 = very good; 60–74 = good; 50–59 = pass; 0–49 = fail; 50 = pass/fail.	Traditional classroom setting, two students per table arranged in rows.	As necessary; also given on weekends
Intermediate, grades 1–3, ages 12–15	Same as above	Religious education (8 hours/week); science, math, history, geography, art (19 hours/week)	Yes	25 or fewer	Monthly tests, written mid-term exams, national written exams in all courses taken in the final term	Same as above; the general secondary education certificate is presented upon successful completion.	Same as above	Same as above
Secondary, grades I, II, III, ages 15–18	Same as above	Same as above; common classes for first year, thereafter divided into science and arts for 2 years. 60% of students are required to enter the science track; others go to arts.	Yes	25 or fewer	Same as above	Same as above	Same as above	Same as above
Technical junior college, ages 15–18	Oct.–July; breaks for *Ramadan* and the *hajj*	Vocational training	No	Varies	Course exams	Secondary vocational, commercial, and agricultural school diplomas	Same as above	As necessary
Postsecondary (teacher training and university), age 18+	Same as above	2 years of English prior to entering colleges of medicine, allied sciences, or engineering. A bachelor's degree requires 4 years; a master's, 2 years; a doctorate, 3 years; a teacher's degree, 4 years.	No, but students are given a monetary incentive to attend.	20 or fewer	As is necessary for the chosen majors	1–5, with 1 highest	Same as above	As necessary

in conversations with men. Even exposing her face to a man is not acceptable behavior in a woman.

- Schools are closed during the month of *Ramadan* to accommodate fasting, and for 10 days in the month of *Dhu'l-Hijja* to accommodate the pilgrimage to Mecca. Schools are also closed in the summer.

👁 A Closer Look

POLICY

- Four main authorities are given the mandate to plan educational policy in Saudi Arabia: the Ministry of Education, the Presidency of Girls' Education, the Ministry of Higher Education, and the General Organization of Technical Education and Vocational Training. Private providers of education must abide by the laws of the policy.

- The education policy of the Kingdom of Saudi Arabia derives from Islam. The objectives are social solidarity, the right to an education, human rights, political and human relations, human history and civilization, and moral and religious education. At the elementary level, the Arabic language is studied for 9 periods per week and all other subjects for 12. At the intermediate level, Arabic is studied for 6 periods per week and all other subjects for 19.

- Emphasis on education is reflected in the policy, which states that education of all types and all stages shall be free and that the state shall not charge tuition. Instruction, books, and health services are free of charge. The state provides teacher education free of charge as well.

- In secondary education, the curriculum of the last two grades is divided into four departments: the Religious Sciences Department, the Arabic Language Department, the Administrative and Social Sciences Department, and the Applied Sciences Department. Students who complete high school may attend colleges or universities. Entrance into any of these will depend on the student's high school GPA. Students may study for their master's or doctoral degrees in any field. Schools from elementary to university levels are segregated by gender for staff and students.

- Education for all has become a necessity in dealing with the technological changes and developments in social and economic fields and also as a means of reducing Saudi Arabia's dependence on expatriate staff.

- Adult education is open to persons in the public sector who have not completed their general education in high school. Such persons are permitted to sit for examinations administered by the authorities at the end of each year.

- In the past, religious and social imperatives of gender segregation have resulted in unequal opportunities. Higher education for women is therefore seen as important, and colleges for girls now grant a bachelor of arts degree after four years of study.

- The expansion of the university system has allowed the government to decrease the overall amount of financial support spent annually for study abroad. Because of the fear of negative cultural influences from the West, English language instruction has been included in the curriculum. By providing English-medium instruction in Saudi Arabia, the government limits the number of Saudi males studying abroad each year and controls the content of their instruction.

TEACHING STYLE

- Classrooms in Saudi Arabia are teacher-oriented, and lessons are conducted in a very formal style. Teachers are expected to be fully prepared when they enter the classroom. They present their lessons in the form of a lecture with notes written on the board, and students are expected to copy the notes.

- Lesson content does not conflict with Islamic precepts.

- Students should not interrupt a teacher. Students must raise their hands to ask questions and must stand when making contributions.

- Teachers correct students' work and give oral explanations.

- In science classes, teachers may use the discovery, or experimental, method. Teaching methods also include group work, oral presentations, and worksheets prepared by teachers.

LEARNING STYLE

- Initially, learning is done by rote. Students memorize whole pages of material. This is consistent with the method necessary for the memorization of Koranic verses, which is a part of the syllabus. Students cram pages of material just before an examination. They must, however, answer comprehension questions at the end of every chapter in their textbooks.

- Students are encouraged to voice their opinions, as this is considered to be a sign of excellence in a student.

- Students may help their friends answer when the teacher asks questions.

INSTRUCTIONAL SETTING

- The students remain in one room throughout the day, while the teachers move to their respective classes.

- The use of audiovisual aids, models, maps, and class libraries help satisfy the desired objectives of elementary and high school curricula. At the university level, overhead projectors, videocassette recorders, and computers are used.

- All schools are equipped with a health clinic and include a room with a mosque setting. This special room is dedicated to prayers and also includes a library for private study.

- Textbooks are authored and prepared for distribution by the Ministry of Education to ensure that they do not contain discussions of sex or include pictures of the female form.

- Saudi schools are segregated by gender. Thus, women teachers teach girls, and boys have men as their teachers.

ACTIVITIES

- Extracurricular activities are planned to enhance the academic content of the curriculum. Schools may only take their students to visit places where there are no members of the opposite sex. Students may visit industrial sites and amusement parks. Instructional visits to the national public libraries are mandatory.

- Male students in some schools may become members of a group that is almost equivalent to the Boy Scouts. The group goes camping in the desert and learns survival skills. Other duties include performing community service and overseeing the cleanliness of school premises.

- Students are taken to visit other schools in their cities. The objective of these visits is to get the students to socialize and to share information. On such a visit, students from each school might be chosen to prepare short presentations on given topics and to deliver them to the assembled group. Students also compete in friendly matches of soccer during these visits. Interschool competitions in soccer might reach the national level.

DISCIPLINE AND CLASS MANAGEMENT

- Discipline does not present a problem in the classroom. The teacher is regarded with respect and reverence.

- The typical Saudi classroom setting is very formal. Any deviation from this formality by the teacher can result in the breakdown of discipline. In other words, as far as appropriate behavior is concerned, students take their cue from the teacher.

- If a student requires disciplinary action, he or she is sent to the principal's office. In some cases, parents may be contacted.

TEACHER-STUDENT RELATIONSHIP

- Students have deep respect for the teacher and accept the teacher's role as a source of knowledge.

- The relationship between teacher and students is very formal. A few students may invite their teachers to family functions.

- The teacher may present a student with a gift for exceptional performance.

STUDENT-STUDENT RELATIONSHIP

- Relationships between students are close and noncompetitive.

- Cheating is often regarded as sharing or helping a friend or a brother.

- When a girl forms a close friendship with another girl, her parents will investigate the family background of the friend before permitting their daughter to continue the relationship.

Protocol

NONVERBAL BEHAVIOR

- At the time of the obligatory prayers, a Muslim may suddenly leave the room to fulfill this duty.

- If you sit on the floor when visiting the home of a Saudi, tuck the soles of your feet under you. Never show the soles of your feet or shoes to someone. No Saudi person will sit with the soles of his feet or shoes pointing in the direction of another person. This is considered to be a sign of disrespect. Muslims remove their shoes upon entering a home, and guests to a Muslim's home should do the same.

- Male Saudis will hold hands in public, without feeling self-conscious. Saudi men kiss each other three times on the cheek in greeting.

- Students may show a clenched fist or clap their hands to signify approval of a student's performance.

- A female teacher or student may not enter a classroom full of boys or men. Her doing so may result in some male students' leaving the classroom. By the same token, male teachers or male students may not enter a classroom full of girls or women.

- In public, men will not stand in the same line with a woman and vice versa. Men will give up their places in the line to send the woman ahead of them.

- During *Ramadan,* students will lose normal vitality, lack motivation, and often appear sleepy. This is one of the consequences of fasting during the hours from dawn to dusk.

- Loud speech spoken in anger is considered offensive. However, in a discussion, loud speech marks the degree of seriousness given to the topic.

- The left hand is never used to give anything to or receive something from a Saudi, as the left hand is considered the unclean hand. Eating with the left hand is also forbidden.

IMAGES

- Wherever you go in Saudi Arabia, there is a total absence of idols, symbols of non-Muslim religions, or depictions of the female form.

- A closed shop, bank, office, or restaurant signifies prayer time. The establishments reopen after the prayer is finished.

- All restaurants are closed during the day in the month of *Ramadan.*

- Saudis believe that people are more important than rules. This notion is reflected in such adages as *Men are not measured by the bushel, Credit goes to the seamstress, not to the needle,* and *I am the slave of anyone who teaches me even one letter.*

FORMS OF ADDRESS

- Parents are never addressed by their first names by persons outside the family. A parent is usually addressed with *umm* (mother of) or *abu* (father of) plus the name of the eldest child; for example, the name *Abu Tariq* means "father of Tariq."

- A man addressing another man, or a woman addressing another woman, will use the first name. Men do not address women outside of their families by first name.

- In school, the female teacher is addressed with *abla* plus her first name. Thus, a teacher whose name is *Zeinaab* will be called *Abla Zeinaab.* The male teacher is addressed by *ustaath* plus first name (e.g., *Ustaath Ahmad*). University professors are addressed by *doctor* plus first name (e.g., *Doctor Yasir*).

- In politics, the word *amir* is used as a title for a man; for a woman, the title used is *amira.*

DRESS

- Casual dress is not encouraged in the classroom.

- Saudi administrators and teachers wear similar, traditional Saudi dress. This similarity in dress is a sign of equality in the eyes of God. Islam discourages the man from wearing gold or silk.

- Male Saudi students wear the traditional *thobe,* a long, loose robe with long sleeves. Female Saudi teachers and students must wear the traditional *hijaab* (head scarf) and *abaya* (black cloak), which leave only the face, the hands, and the feet uncovered. They may wear any amount of jewelry. Girls may remove the *hijaab* once they enter the school, but they must put it on again if they leave.

- Foreign male teachers wear shirt and tie and, in some instances, jackets. Foreign female teachers must conform to the traditional dress for Saudi females.

POLITE/IMPOLITE TOPICS AND BEHAVIORS

- It is impolite to refuse an offer of refreshment in the office or home of a Saudi. This offer is ritualistic and has a symbolic importance. Guests must always stay until refreshment is served. All such invitations must be returned.

- There must be no excessive or loud behavior.

- It is inappropriate to ask about the female members of a man's family.

- Religion, politics, drugs, and the state of Israel should not be discussed in public. Conversational topics must be kept simple. Pork is a taboo topic.

- If you are a foreigner, never drink alcohol in public, and do not take alcohol into the country.

- Teachers should not discuss sex in the classroom and should not show the female face and form to students.

- Good conversation is a popular form of entertainment.

GIFT GIVING

- Every gift deserves a reciprocal and equal gift. Neither party should be made to feel overly obligated.

- If a visitor to a Saudi home expresses admiration for any object, the host will feel obliged to present that object to the guest, even if he or she cannot afford to do so.

- Unsuitable gifts to present to a Muslim would be alcohol or anything connected with the pig, such as a gift made of pigskin leather.

- It is considered poor form to present a gift to the wife of your host or colleague.

? 🔆 Problem/Solution

PROBLEM

My students seem very tired and listless during the month of *Ramadan.* I don't understand why a religious holiday leaves them in such a state.

SOLUTION

These students consider it very important to follow the traditions and requirements of their faith. During *Ramadan,* they have to fast from dawn to dusk for 28 to 30 days. Your students will have been up late each night praying the compulsory prayers and up early each morning to begin fasting. In Saudi Arabia, they sleep until much later in the mornings during *Ramadan,* and many businesses are open at night to accommodate those who are fasting.

PROBLEM

My Saudi students sometimes help each other during tests. What can I do to stop this?

SOLUTION

First, you need to understand that your students do not consider this practice to be cheating *per se.* Their moral code of behavior demands that they help a fellow student in need. Explain to them that the rules in your culture do not permit students to help each other during tests. Another solution is to seat the students as far apart from each other as possible.

PROBLEM

In my class, I have three Saudi students, three Korean students, and a number of students from Latin America. The Saudis seem to want to answer all of my questions all of the time. How can I encourage them to take turns with the other students in the class?

SOLUTION

Saudi Arabia has a deeply embedded oral culture. Very often, conversations include scholarly discussions about Islam. Koranic verses are memorized and repeated. Your students are a product of this oral tradition. Explain to them the concept of turn taking, identify the cues that English speakers use to determine whose turn it is to speak, and let your students know how you, in particular, let students know when their turn has arrived.

My Observations

Taiwan

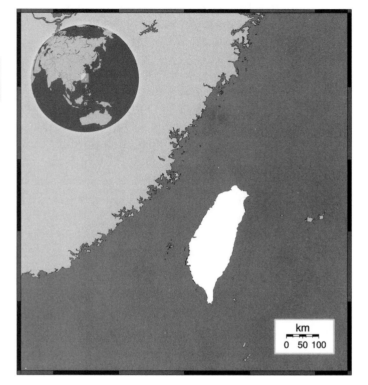

 Focus on Taiwan

Capital: Taipei

Population: 22,191,087

Size: 13,892 sq. mi. (35,980 sq. km.)

Location: island off southeast coast of People's Republic of China (mainland China)

Climate: tropical coast (70 to 90 degrees Fahrenheit), subtropical mountains (60 to 80 degrees Fahrenheit)

Monetary Unit: new Taiwan dollar

Urban/Rural Life: 90% urban, 10% agricultural and other

Religion: 93% intermixed Buddhist, Taoist, Confucian; 5% Christian; 3% other

Languages: Mandarin Chinese (official), Taiwanese (Min-Nan Hua), Hakka dialects

Ethnicity: Chinese (Han), Taiwanese, aboriginal tribes

Government: democracy with popularly elected president

 Personal Snapshot

Diverse! That's how I would describe the student population at the many English language schools in Taiwan. In my English conversation class alone, there were university students, high school students, housewives, business people, taxi drivers, and bartenders. Conversation schools are remarkably popular in Taiwan because high schools and universities do not give students many opportunities to practice their speaking skills. Moreover, Taiwanese know they need to speak English to do business with the West. Therefore, students flock to English language schools for the chance to practice their speaking skills with native English speakers. Meanwhile, students determined to attend a university in an English-speaking country attend TOEFL (Test of English as a Foreign Language) training schools, which have Chinese teachers to explain the more difficult grammar.

✦ Cultural Closeup

- Originally a Chinese province, Taiwan was ceded to Japan in 1895 following the First Sino-Japanese War. After World War II, however, Japan was forced to return the island to Chinese control. Following the Communist revolution in 1949, the Nationalists under General Chiang Kai-shek fled to Taiwan and set up a democratic government. Taiwan has been struggling to gain and maintain independence from the People's Republic of China ever since.

- Four hundred years of immigration and multiple changes in government control have contributed to the many languages and religions that influence today's culture in Taiwan. Current religions include animism (worship of nature, which comes from the indigenous people); Taoism, Buddhism, Confucianism, Matsuism, and Islam (which come from the waves of Chinese immigration); and Christianity (which was brought by the Spanish and Dutch).

- Language diversity remains as a footprint of the various cultures that have influenced Taiwan. Over 400,000 indigenous people living in the mountains of Taiwan have managed to keep their own Malay languages. Eighty-five percent of the population who are native Taiwanese speak Min-Nan and Hakka dialects brought from southern Chinese regions. Additionally, Japanese was a second language of older Taiwanese who lived on the island prior to 1945, and younger generations are able to speak Japanese because of their grandparents. When the Kuo Min Tang government arrived in 1949, Mandarin became the official language; however, it is the native language of only 13 percent of the population. Min-Nan Hua is the most widely spoken dialect on Taiwan, and despite 50 years of rule by those fleeing the Communist revolution in the People's Republic of China, many people still do not speak Mandarin Chinese well. Efforts to promote the use and spread of Mandarin eased during Taiwan's transition to democracy, and Min-Nan Hua is now widely respected. If a politician, for example, wants to win an election, he or she must be able to speak Min-Nan Hua. There is a story of a former Nationalist Party officer, not born in Taiwan, who could not speak Min-Nan Hua. For the election, he hired a tutor and mastered the language. He won the election and became a very important figure in Taiwanese politics.

- The Taiwanese people practice many of the customs associated with the People's Republic of China, such as *tai chi chuan,* and they honor the teachings of Confucius and may adhere to Chinese religions, such as Buddhism and Taoism. However, their political situation has led them to gravitate more toward Western values than have their counterparts in the People's Republic of China.

- A hierarchical attitude based in Confucianism influences government, teachers, and employers and may go some distance toward explaining why Taiwanese students are sometimes reluctant to put their own ideas forward in the classroom. All relations, hierarchical or not, are reciprocal, and this is believed to be essential to maintaining good order in the society.

- A new saying in Taiwan is *Taiwan is filthy rich.* Economic development, in other words, has been achieved at the expense of the environment. The by-products of various industries that have taken advantage of Taiwan's favorable economic climate have had a devastating effect on the air, land, and water. Although the island is only a little larger than the state of Maryland in the United States, it is home to more than 90,000 factories. Space is at a premium on Taiwan, making the price of everything from a parking space to an apartment sky-high. Although many wealthy Taiwanese can now afford the cost, they must tolerate the polluted air and water as part of the price of success.

- The concept of *filial piety,* devotion to family, is a universal virtue influencing all aspects of Taiwanese society. It originates in Confucian teaching and is the outward representation of a deeper belief in the unity of heaven and human, which gives each individual the ability to joyfully and peacefully accept his or her heaven-ordained position in life without feelings of resentment. Through filial love, Taiwanese respect and care for their parents not only until the death of the parents but also beyond, through the offering of sacrifices to ancestors during many major festivals. The American concept of retirement homes and nursing homes is not found in Taiwan. Because of filial piety, children take care of their parents in old age.

- Formal education is highly valued both for economic improvement and family honor, and because of filial piety, parents will sacrifice family resources on educating sons and daughters to the highest level possible. Conversely, the children will work hard—sacrificing social activities—to bring honor and prestige to the family. Failure brings shame. Reflecting on a parent's sacrifices for education, obedience, and intergenerational honor, both backward and forward in time, drives a student's academic achievement. Students also are taught that the greater the effort, the greater the achievement. This is illustrated by the writings in the year 300 B.C. of Chinese philosopher Hsun Tzu.

  > Achievement consists of never giving up. If you start carving and then give up, you cannot even cut through a piece of rotten wood; but if you persist without stopping, you can carve or inlay metal or stone. Earthworms have no sharp claws or teeth, no strong muscles or bones, and yet above ground they feast on the mud, and below they drink at the yellow springs. This is because they keep their minds on one thing. If there is no dark and dogged will, there will be no shining accomplishment; if there is no dull and determined effort, there will be no brilliant achievement. *(Quoted in Watson 1967)*

- If one son is studying abroad, another son also wants to study overseas, and the family does not have funds to support both, the son who is living away from home will defer to his brother and return to Taiwan. Likewise, if a sister is working on the only home computer and a sibling needs to use it, she will stop what she is doing to allow her brother or sister access. There is no squabbling. This is another example of filial piety.

- Even though the tradition of only educating sons has changed, and daughters often go on to college, there are few career women in Taiwan. It remains a patriarchal society, and once married, women take a traditional role in the home. Moreover, tradition requires a bride to move to her husband's town. By living in Taiwan, she will still remain within proximity of her family. She would never consider leaving Taiwan and leaving her family to live in another country. Furthermore, a Taiwanese woman wants a husband who is obedient to his parents and who will thereby inculcate these values in her sons.

- Taiwanese students may appear shy in class, but they are very warm and friendly outside of the classroom. In addition, they are very interested in getting to know people from other cultures, so it is common for them to invite their teachers or other students to dinner or another activity. Many develop lifelong friendships and value continuing relationships.

- Harmony among family and friends is of the utmost importance, so Taiwanese often use a mediator to settle disputes. Additionally, mediators are used for the delicate negotiating of wedding plans, so that the two families do not experience hurt feelings.

- Hierarchy is very important, yet Taiwanese value group cooperation at school, work, and home. Group cooperation is not the same as group consensus reaching. Instead, group cooperation means working in harmony with no person an island unto himself or herself. Individuality is discouraged.

- When the Kou Min Tang, the Nationalist government under Chiang Kai-shek, left Communist China in 1949, they fled to Taiwan, taking with them the largest collection of Chinese art and treasures in the world. At that time, they feared the Communists would destroy the art, as they had already destroyed a number of historic Buddhist shrines. The Kou Min Tang valued the collection not only because it represented thousands of years of Chinese culture and history but also because they believed it would legitimize their government. It is currently housed in the National Palace Museum in Taipei.

👁 A Closer Look

POLICY

- Taiwan has only existed as a nation since 1949, when the republican government was forced off the mainland by Communist armies. In 1952, the population was less than 60 percent literate. In 1968, educational reforms were introduced, resulting in a 94 percent literacy rate by 1994. Education is compulsory from age 6 to age 15. Close to 90 percent of all Taiwanese continue on to high school or vocational schools, and many move on to the more than 100 institutions of higher education in Taiwan.

Educational Panorama

TAIWAN

Level/Age	Hours/Calendar	Curriculum	Required	Class Size	Exams	Grades	Classroom Setup	Homework
Preschool/ kindergarten, ages 3–6	Sept.–Jan. and Mar.–July, half-days in mornings or after-noons or (for chil-dren of working parents) full days 9:00 A.M.–4:00 P.M.	Preschool and kindergarten are basically one and the same, although preschoolers have fewer structured lessons. Subjects include nature, art, reading, math, music, physical education. Private schools may offer bilingual English-Chinese instruction.	No, but most children attend.	15–30	None	None	Students sit in chairs at individual tables. They do not share books. Computers may be available in more expensive kindergartens.	None
Elementary, grades 1–5, ages 6–12	Sept.–Jan. and Mar.–July 7:40 A.M.–4:30 P.M. Mon., Tues., Thurs., Fri., and half-days on Wed. and Sat., plus *bu xi ban,* or cram schools.	Pronunciation and meaning of tonals, math, art, social studies, life and ethics. In grades 3–5, students learn computer skills, and reading replaces pronunciation.	Yes	40–50	Hundreds throughout the year, from unit tests to national exams for the next grade or level	A = 80–100%; B = 70–79%; C = 60–69%. Students must have a grade of 70% to pass.	The teacher stands on a podium in the front of the class. Students sit in desks in 6–7 rows. Each week, the rows move over one, so that the students' eyes develop equally. Short students sit in front, and taller ones sit in back.	Homework begins in grade 1. It is assigned daily and even during vacation breaks. Parents review assignments before they are handed in.
Middle, grades 6–9, ages 12–15	Same as above	English (compulsory), history, geography, science, computers, math, ancient Chinese literature, citizenship and morality	Yes	40–50	Hundreds throughout the year, from unit tests to national exams for the next grade or level; Senior high school entrance exam	Same as above	Same as above	Homework is assigned daily and even during vacation breaks. Parents review assignments before they are handed in. There is more emphasis on preparation for entrance exams.
High, grades 10–12, ages 15–18	Same as above, with extra classes evenings and weekends	Same as above. Students have a choice to select either natural science or social science. Vocational high schools offer more practical courses.	No	40–50	Senior high school leaving certificate	Same as above	Same as above	Same as above. Students may be required to bring a newspaper article from an English language newspaper.
University, age 18+	Most bachelor's degree courses last 4 years	142 credits required to graduate	No	Varies	Universities and colleges joint entrance exam	A = 80–100%; B = 70–79%; C = 60–69%; D = 50–59%. Passing undergraduate courses requires 60% or higher; passing graduate courses requires 70% or higher.	Varies	Varies

- The Examination Yuan is one of the five branches of Taiwanese government. It oversees the testing for every aspect of life in Taiwan—educational and professional. The education system is so test-oriented that virtually all teaching is done with a particular test in mind, and a typical Taiwanese student experiences hundreds of tests during his or her academic career, followed by many more concerning employment and certification once the formal education years are complete.

- English is not a required subject before junior high school, yet many Taiwanese students study it in cram schools in advance. In high school, the focus of English study is primarily on grammar, not speaking or writing, since it is believed that the grammatical aspects of English are the most easily tested. Virtually all testing follows the multiple-choice format, perhaps because there are so many tests that there is simply no time to grade written essays or other types of more subjective testing.

TEACHING STYLE

- Teachers adhere to the content, exercises, and activities prescribed in their textbooks. Creativity in lesson planning is not necessarily expected of teachers.

- Teachers stand at a podium in front of rows of desks so they may be seen and heard. Some teachers may use a microphone to ensure that they are heard.

- Teachers will often volunteer to teach extra hours in the evening or in the summer so that their students will be prepared for exams. They may also cooperate with other teachers to help students study. For example, a math teacher may ask a physical education teacher to give up an hour or more of a student's gym time so that the student can undergo additional test preparation.

- A teacher's questions rarely probe or elicit a student's opinion. Instead, teachers may ask questions that allow learners to display their knowledge of facts.

LEARNING STYLE

- Taiwanese students prefer to learn by watching and listening to the teacher and doing written assignments from their textbooks. Often described as field-dependent and structure-oriented, children in Taiwan thrive in well-managed classrooms and quiet environments. As a result, Taiwanese students need a little longer wait-time to give answers to oral questions than do their American peers.

- Memorization is heavily relied on as a tool for learning in all grades. Since students are accustomed to rote memorization and drills, analytical thinking and creative writing may need special encouragement.

- Group work may be done only occasionally in the science laboratory, because of a limited amount of equipment.

- Students rarely challenge a teacher.

INSTRUCTIONAL SETTING

- Every morning, the students converge in a designated area to raise the flag of Taiwan. The students stand at attention and salute during this time. Afterward, each class name is announced individually, and the students march in a line back to their classes.

- Each teacher designates specific students as class supervisors. There is a class leader, a vice leader, a minister of hygiene, and a minister of order. Each of these student supervisors assigns other students to perform tasks, such as cleaning the classroom, monitoring social conversation in class, or taking lunches to the kitchen. Occasionally, students are elected to these positions or may be granted a change of role.

- Schools that are in urban areas tend to be very large, some enrolling up to 9,000 students. Urban schools typically do not have playgrounds, because of the high price of land on the densely populated island. Schools in rural areas generally have playgrounds and playground equipment, such as slides and swings.

- Taiwanese schools often have a single computer room shared by all classes. Each classroom has an overhead projector, a chalkboard, and colored chalk.

- Students are given 30 minutes to eat their lunch and 40 minutes to nap with their heads on their desks. Napping is mandatory, even in high school. There is a 20-minute midmorning break, during which children jump rope or play dodgeball.

- Students bring a lunch of rice and vegetables from home. Just before noon, certain classmates collect the students' metal lunch boxes and send them to a steam table to be reheated. Students usually drink water for lunch; milk is not popular in Asia.

ACTIVITIES

- With the tremendous importance of exams during high school, there is very little time for other kinds of activity.

- Elementary schoolchildren take field trips to farms and science centers.

- Elementary children may learn to play Chinese instruments and may play in the orchestra. If they are very good, they may even go on to play in the high school marching band.

- Girls' and boys' varsity volleyball and basketball teams compete at elementary school, middle school, and high school levels.

DISCIPLINE AND CLASS MANAGEMENT

- Because of heavy family expectations and the fear of bringing shame to the family, there are very few discipline problems in the typical Taiwanese classroom. Some teachers have noted an increase in discipline problems in recent years, however, and may blame this problem on Taiwan's rapid political and economic change and the influence of the West.

- A Department of Discipline exists at most schools. The teacher will send a student who misbehaves to this office, where a decision will be made as to the type of punishment to be given. Although it is not encouraged, corporal punishment is allowed. Additionally, a student may have to stand in the hallway with knees bent for a set amount of time.

- Some teachers may use test scores as the basis for arranging students' desks, putting students with lower scores in the front of the classroom. The idea behind this practice is that it will bring shame to the student and motivate him or her to study harder.

- To keep students from dressing improperly or eating while walking, older students are assigned as monitors to report those who violate the rules.

- One Chinese immigrant reports, "About 15 years ago, I was punished in school by getting a 'medal' that said, 'Please speak in Mandarin.' Every student who got the medal had to find another student who didn't speak Mandarin and give the medal to the victim. The last one left holding the medal was punished by the teachers."

TEACHER-STUDENT RELATIONSHIP

- Students stand and bow when the teacher enters the room.

- Complete respect for a teacher is one of the five categories of obedience taught in Confucianism.

STUDENT-STUDENT RELATIONSHIP

- Students in Taiwan have become very competitive due to the number of examinations they must take and pass. There is sometimes distrust of student supervisors as well; often, students perceive them as bullies. Some schools will group students according to their academic abilities, causing hard feelings between and among students. Making friends in the university is much easier, because it is not as competitive.

Protocol

NONVERBAL BEHAVIOR

- A student's smile might not mean the student is pleased; instead, it may represent embarrassment or confusion.

- Direct eye contact is discouraged.

- When a student delivers or receives something from a teacher, the student will extend both hands to signal respect. The teacher will use just one hand. This behavior may also be seen between a younger person and an older one.

- Both feet are to be kept flat on the floor in public. Only at home do Taiwanese cross their legs or assume other comfortable positions.

- Nervous habits, such as bouncing a bent leg, twirling a pen, fidgeting with papers, or biting nails, are frowned on and considered signs of immaturity or instability.

IMAGES

- It is not unusual to observe an entire school bus full of students all singing the same song or playing the same game. This practice reflects the concept of group. No one in the group would dare do his or her own thing, such as listening to a personal compact disc player. This kind of behavior is considered rude.

- Chopsticks, one of the more ubiquitous stereotypical symbols of Chinese culture, are used at meals of rice, vegetables, or meat. It is acceptable to hold a bowl of food up to one's mouth and guide the food into the mouth, thus avoiding spills and messes. Soup is drunk from a bowl by using both hands to cradle it from beneath. Standing chopsticks in a bowl of rice should never be done, because this gesture functions as an omen of death.

- Motorcycles and scooters can be seen everywhere in Taiwan, where they are the predominant form of transportation—there is one motorcycle or scooter for every two people on the island. Riders are able to navigate congested city streets and reach their destinations much sooner than those who drive cars or take public transportation.

FORMS OF ADDRESS

- Taiwanese use honorifics with titles. This is a carryover from both Japanese occupation and Confucianism. For example, *jiaoshi* is the word for the occupation of teacher, but a student addresses a teacher with the title *laoshi.* A student addresses an older student as "senior classmate," because the students are not considered to be of equal status.

- Some young people, particularly students of English, have begun to adopt Westernized first names. Not only does this reinforce the English-only policy of many language classrooms, but young Taiwanese often discover in interaction with English speakers that Westernized first names are easier for native speakers of English to pronounce.

- Chinese refer to a friend of either of their parents with the term *auntie* or *uncle,* as a sign of respect.

DRESS

- Uniforms are worn by most schoolchildren, in colors determined by a child's grade or school.

- Hairstyles are regulated by each school. In the most formal schools, a boy's hair must be in a crew cut, and a girl's hair must be no longer than the bottom of her ears. However, with the current changes that are rapidly taking place in Taiwan, dress and hairstyles are becoming more Westernized. Girls wear jeans and conservative tops to school and may sport longer hairstyles and different hair colors. Boys often wear printed T-shirts, sneakers, and baseball caps.

- Girls believe that light-colored skin is more beautiful; therefore, they try to avoid exposure to the sun by wearing long sleeves, long pants, and hats or by carrying umbrellas.

POLITE/IMPOLITE TOPICS AND BEHAVIORS

- It is acceptable to ask about someone's salary or the price paid for an expensive item, such as a piece of jewelry or a house.

- Turning down the offer of an alcoholic beverage may be taken as an insult. Hosts may feel that the guest is not giving them the honor of serving their guest something special.

GIFT GIVING

- If a teacher volunteers time to help students with exam preparation during evenings or summer breaks, it is customary for the parents to respond with a gift.

- At the end of the semester, the class leader will collect money from the students and purchase a small gift, such as a pen and a card, for the teacher.

- Unwrapping a gift in front of the giver is forbidden. It should be done in private.

? ☀ Problem/Solution

PROBLEM

I have a Taiwanese student who is getting average grades but seems depressed and isolates himself from the other students. How can I be supportive of him?

SOLUTION

To this student, average may not be good enough. The student may feel that anything less than excellence will bring shame to himself and to his family. Additionally, Taiwanese parents often have difficulty accepting that their child may be depressed, because Taiwanese culture sees depressed behavior as indicative of a shameful lack of motivation. It may help to talk to the student and his family about the particular difficulties newcomers typically encounter when they enter an unfamiliar culture and educational environment. Assisting the student in targeting study skills and in taking on a tutor may help as well. Parents are usually very willing to work with teachers to help their children succeed in school. The educator needs to be very sensitive and to make it clear that psychosocial problems are not shameful. Through family participation and professional direction, the problems can be solved.

PROBLEM

I like to teach using cooperative games, such as Auction, in which students have to reach a consensus to determine answers. But whenever I use such activities, my Taiwanese student becomes very quiet and passive. How can I involve this student in such activities?

SOLUTION

Chinese games are typically for individual players, not cooperative teams. *The more, the weaker,* they say. In a story that explains the need for hierarchical decision making as well as private ownership, a Buddhist monk went to a well to get some water for those in need. A second monk came along and seized the water to give to others in need, because he thought he was equal to the first monk and thus had equal rights to the water. A third monk came by and seized the water from the second monk, for the same reasons as the second. Eventually, no one got to drink the water. On days when you want to play a consensus-reaching game, find another role for the Taiwanese student. He or she could serve as the scorekeeper or the auctioneer. This approach maintains the student's involvement in the game and gives him or her listening and speaking practice.

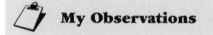 **My Observations**

Vietnam

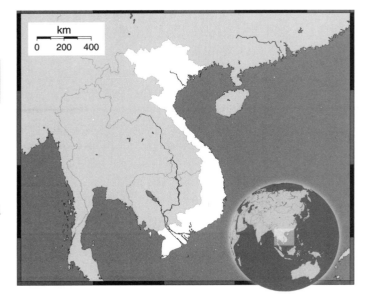

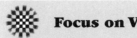

Capital: Hanoi

Population: 79,000,000

Size: 127,243 sq. mi. (329,560 sq. km.)

Location: Southeast Asia, on the eastern side of the Indochinese Peninsula; bordered by the People's Republic of China to the north, Laos and Cambodia to the west, the Gulf of Tonkin and the South China Sea to the east, and the Gulf of Thailand to the south

Climate: subtropical in the north, with cool, damp winters and hot, humid summers (average temperature 74 degrees Fahrenheit); tropical in the south, with warm, somewhat dry weather from December to May and hot, rainy weather from June to December (average temperature 81 degrees Fahrenheit); monsoons and occasional typhoons in the rainy season

Monetary Unit: Vietnamese dong

Urban/Rural Life: 79% urban, 21% rural

Religion: Buddhism (both Chinese/Mahayana and Indian/Theravada), Confucianism, Taoism, Cao Dai, Hoa Hao, animism, Christianity (mainly Roman Catholic), Islam

Languages: Vietnamese (official), some Chinese dialects, tribal languages, French, English, Russian

Ethnicity: 90% ethnic Vietnamese; 60 minorities, including Hoa (Chinese), Tay, Thai, Khmer, Cham, Muong, Nung, Hmong, and numerous mountain tribes, known as the *Montagnards* (French for "highlanders").

Government: Communist Party–dominated constitutional republic

 Personal Snapshot

Having to tell a student that he or she is just not ready to move from a preparatory writing class to a freshman English class is never a pleasant experience, especially when the student has exerted a great deal of time and effort. In my experience, most recipients of such news sigh, agree with the assessment, and resolve to pass in the coming semester. I was therefore totally unprepared for the reaction I received one semester from a Vietnamese woman in her early twenties. "I know you worked very hard this semester," I began the standard speech gently, "and your writing has shown some improvement, but you are just not ready for Freshman English yet." Her eyes filled with tears, and she lowered her head to her chest. She didn't say a word, so I continued to try to console her. I smiled and nodded encouragingly, but she still wouldn't look up. Instead, her tears increased. "You don't understand," she finally managed to say. "My parents . . . ," she began. "Would it help if I wrote your parents a note?" I interrupted. "I'll tell them what a good student you were and how hard you tried. I'll explain the system here," I offered. With this comment, the shower of tears became a downpour. "No, please, a note won't help." She shook her head firmly and explained: "Nothing will help. My parents have made great sacrifices for me, and now I have brought disrespect to my family. This is my fault."

→✳← Cultural Closeup

- The first step toward understanding Vietnam and the Vietnamese must begin with an awareness of Vietnam's long history of foreign occupation and war. One thousand years of Chinese occupation, nearly 100 years of French colonial rule (interrupted by Japanese occupation during World War II), a civil war (the Vietnam War), and border wars against Chinese-backed Khmer Rouge forces in Cambodia have made an enormous impact on the language, culture, economy, and people of the country. Throughout it all, however, Vietnam has tenaciously managed to maintain a distinct identity, and the Vietnamese people have retained a love of their country.

- One of the most dramatic changes that Vietnam has undergone in recent decades is its reunification and establishment as a Communist state. On April 25, 1976, a reunited Vietnam was renamed the Socialist Republic of Vietnam following the long and devastating Vietnam War, which saw U.S.-aided, anti-Communist South Vietnam battling against Communist North Vietnam. A foremost priority of the government at this time was to restore order to the South. Equally important, however, was the conversion of the South from a capitalist to a socialist economy and lifestyle. The Hanoi government nationalized privately owned land and property and shifted the citizens in the South to collectivized agricultural practices. Education reforms were also carried out; all religious and private schools were nationalized, textbooks were revised to conform to socialist ideology, and teachers from the North came to the South to assist in political indoctrination programs for the teachers there. Ideological reform occurred through Communist Party–sponsored study sessions required for all adults. South Vietnamese government and military officials were sent to special reeducation camps, where "rehabilitation" occurred through socialist indoctrination and "socially constructive" labor.

- Socialist ideology is present in many aspects of public life. The broadcast media are controlled by the state, as is the publishing of newspapers, magazines, and books. The content of school textbooks reflects socialist ideology, and the arts are regulated. State-sponsored literature with socialist themes is promoted, and theater actors and technical staff are considered state employees. There is general intolerance for political dissension, although strict governmental controls eased up somewhat in the 1980s. More recently, it appears that a gradual openness toward Western ideas is cautiously being demonstrated.

- Vietnam is one of the poorest countries in the world. Both the destruction caused by war and strict socialist economic policies originally hindered economic development, but in 1986, the government approved economic reforms—known as *Doi Moi,* or "renovation"—that improved the country's economic situation. Agriculture was reprivatized, and a shift was made from a centralized planned economy to a market-oriented economy emphasizing exports. Private enterprises were also allowed. As a result, Vietnam has become a major exporter of rice, the inflation rate has decreased, the standard of living has improved, and international economic relations have broadened, even though Soviet aid ceased after the collapse of the Soviet Union in 1991. Despite such gains, however, more reform will be necessary before Vietnam can compete with other nations in the region. The per capita income in Vietnam in 1999 was estimated at U.S.$1,850.

- Due to Vietnam's difficult economic situation, many Vietnamese living outside of Vietnam, who are called *Viet kieu,* feel a special obligation to assist their families or friends in their native country, and they do so by sending money through an intermediary who makes sure the funds arrive in the proper hands.

- The Vietnamese have been influenced over the centuries by the teachings of Confucianism, Buddhism, Taoism, and, more recently, Christianity, along with their earlier animistic beliefs, and many Vietnamese practice the customs of more than one religion. Under the influence of Confucianism and Taoism, children are expected to honor their parents, elders, and ancestors; demonstrate loyalty to their family; respect authority; and avoid conflict and interference in other people's lives. Buddhism contributes the values of happiness, kindness, compassion for living creatures, sacrifice for others, lack of interest in material possessions, and inner peace. Christmas is celebrated by Christians and many non-Christians alike.

- Owing to its Confucian heritage, the Vietnamese culture places a great deal of importance on the family. An individual is regarded not independently but, rather, as a functioning member of a family unit that includes not only the parents and children but the grandparents, aunts, uncles, cousins, and other relatives, all of whom have a very close relationship to one another. Family members will first seek one another's advice in times of need, and family interests are considered when making decisions, even personal ones. Family celebrations form the basis of Vietnamese social life.

- Traditional Vietnamese family roles are clear: the wife is subordinate to the husband, the children are subordinate to their parents, and younger children are subordinate to elder children. The man is the family provider; his wife ensures a smoothly run household, including managing the family finances. A wife is supposed to care for her husband's parents, who live with the family; it is not unusual to have three generations in one household. Older children are responsible for taking care of the younger children, and they do so happily.

- Related to family values is the Vietnamese practice of ancestor veneration. Vietnamese believe that everything they are and have is due to their ancestors and, further, that the spirits of the ancestors continue to influence them and to guide their lives. Most Vietnamese homes have family altars dedicated to the ancestors, and offerings are made to the altar to commemorate the anniversary of an ancestor's death, on special family occasions (e.g., weddings or funerals), or even after receiving a promotion or a good grade at school. Vietnamese consider what their ancestors would have done or wanted as they go about their daily lives, and they conduct their lives in ways they think will bring honor to their ancestors and the family name.

- Having children is important in the Vietnamese culture, because children have the duties of taking care of their aging parents and maintaining the ancestral altars and family graves. Despite government policies promoting equality of the sexes, male children still tend to be favored, especially because the wife of the first son has the duty of caring for his parents. Inequality of the sexes is also reflected in the school system. More girls drop out of school, and the number of illiterate girls is twice that of illiterate boys.

- The Vietnamese people love to sing. This comes from the oral tradition of putting literature and poetry into song to be passed down from generation to generation. In rural areas, it is common to hear groups of workers of both sexes singing as they tend the field. Even in the cities, workers tend to hum at work and make up songs. Accordingly, karaoke machines are very popular.

- In general, Vietnamese tend to be polite, reserved people known for their hard work and resourcefulness. They also tend to be trustworthy. In the countryside, for example, homes are almost never locked. Staying true to your word is yet another valued characteristic of the Vietnamese people. They consider a broken promise to be a serious social offense.

Educational Panorama

- While classes in Vietnam generally begin after the national holiday on September 2, National Independence Day, many Vietnamese students are required to report to school two weeks earlier to meet their teachers

VIETNAM

Level/Age	Hours/Calendar	Curriculum	Required	Class Size	Exams	Grades	Classroom Setup	Homework
Crèche, ages 0–3	Hours vary depending on schools and parents' needs.	Personal and environmental hygiene, physical education, movement and sensation, observation skills, language development, music, moral education; emphasis on developing intelligence, scientific curiosity, and polite behavior	No	20	None	None	Basic day-care setup; children divided into groups according to age and diet (soup or rice)	None
Kindergarten (or infant school), ages 3–6	Same as above	Same as crèche; 5–6 year olds; special focus given to education of elder group (5 year olds) who have not attended the lower levels of preschool	No, but the government is striving to have all 5 year olds attend	30	None	Good, average, poor; grades for behavior and attendance only	Chairs arranged in different groupings depending on day and activity	None
Primary grades 1–5, ages 6–11	Sept.–May or June, 28.5–29.5 hours/week Sun.–Sat. (Thurs. free)	Vietnamese language, arithmetic, nature and society; physical education and gymnastics, art, music, ethics, patriotism; manual labor and required collective activities. For economic reasons, not all schools teach the required curriculum; however, most teach at least Vietnamese, math, ethics, and nature and society.	Yes	30–40	Reading, writing, and math tests, dictations, recitations, daily oral quizzes; written midterm and final exams	8–10 = excellent; 6–7 = good; 5 = pass; 0–4 = fail.	Straight rows of tables with attached benches for 2–3 students, often with males on one side and females on the other.	Graded daily written homework: handwriting practice, reading assignments, math exercises
Junior secondary, grades 6–9, ages 11–15	Sept.–May or June, about 37 hours/week Mon.–Sat.	Vietnamese language, literature, math, physics, chemistry, history, geography, biology, art, civics, physical education/military training, foreign language, vocational orientation, patriotism. Manual labor and collective activities are required year-round.	No, due to cost	30–40	Essay tests after every unit; daily individual oral quizzes; written midterm and final exams	Same as above	Same as above	Same as above except no handwriting practice
Technical or vocational secondary, grades 10–12, ages 15–18	Sept.–May or June, Mon.–Sat. Hours vary, as do total hours of instruction/ week.	2 tracks. Technical/vocational studies lead to different levels of vocational or professional certification. Curriculum varies depending on school/level. Some programs lead to secondary school leaving certificate.	No	30–40	Essay tests, assessments of different vocational skills	Same as above	Same as above or laboratory setup	Some written homework; professional practice in various labs/facilities
Senior secondary, grades 10–12, ages 15–18	32–35 hours/week Mon.–Sat.	Preuniversity studies leading to *Bang Tot Nghiep Pho Thon Trung Hoc* (secondary school leaving certificate); collective activities and public utility or production work required year-round	No	30–40	Essay tests after every unit; daily individual oral quizzes; written midterm and final exams	Same as above	Same as above. Some schools may have single desks arranged in straight rows.	Graded daily written homework: compositions, reading assignments, math exercises, memorization of formulas
University, age 18+	Same as above. School year divided into 2 semesters.	Programs of 3–3½ years for associate bachelor's degree; degree programs of 4–6 years with general education and professional education phases; master's and doctorate degrees in limited fields. All degrees require physical education and Marxist-Leninist theory.	No	Varies	Essay tests, oral presentations of written material and research	9–10 = excellent; 7–8.99 = rather good; 5–6.99 = pass.	Lecture hall seating	Self-study and preparation; papers, reports, presentations, research

and perform cleaning and maintenance on the school. During this time, students receive military training and study lessons in patriotism that are designed to foster socialistic values and build national pride.

- Due to the economic situation in Vietnam, there is a shortage of qualified teachers, and in some districts, teachers without the desired qualifications are hired out of necessity.

- Many Vietnamese would like to go to school to learn but cannot due to the economic situation of their families. It is common to see elder children sacrifice their education and drop out of school to earn enough money for younger siblings to attend.

👁 A Closer Look

POLICY

- The Vietnamese place a great deal of importance on education and will make many sacrifices to provide a good education to their children. Historically, the value of education developed out of the Confucian emphasis on history and literature, and because education was necessary to pass the competitive national exams and enter the ruling class, or *mandarinate,* education was seen as the key to social mobility. Today, despite war and poverty, Vietnam's adult literacy rate is estimated at more than 90 percent.

- Prior to the 1950s, education was available only to a limited number of upper-class individuals. For 30 years after the establishment of North Vietnam and South Vietnam as separate countries in 1954, the Hanoi and Saigon governments separately carried out educational reforms that extended education to their peoples despite a lack of facilities and sup-plies due to the wars. While the system in the South basically followed a French model, the system in the North began to be revised to reflect the purpose and goals of the Communist government and to inculcate the values and philosophy of the government. After the reunification of Vietnam in 1976, the Hanoi government had the task of unifying the two school systems. New textbooks were introduced, and compulsory school-ing was lengthened from 10 to 12 years. Eliminating illiteracy was a primary goal. In the late 1980s, after a shift to a more market-oriented economy, further adjustments were made, and in the 1990s, the system of higher education was reorganized to address the socioeconomic goals of indus-trialization and modernization.

- Primary school in Vietnam is free, but students in secondary school must pay modest monthly fees (approximately equivalent to two to four pounds of rice per month). The fees are based on students' grades. Students who do not maintain the expected standards are required to pay higher fees than students who do. Very poor pupils, students from families who served their country exceptionally, and the children of war invalids or fallen heroes may receive a fee reduction or fee exemption, but students whose parents cannot afford the fees generally do not attend secondary school. The dropout rate at the secondary level is very high.

- As in secondary schools, students in universities are assessed different fees based on academic merit in the entrance examination, academic performance, and behavior. Candidates for admission to a university must pass an entrance exam, be in good health, and be under 32 or 35 years of age for men and 35 years of age for women. Preference may be given to students from ethnic minorities. Students whose parents worked for the U.S. military may be prevented from entering the university.

TEACHING STYLE

- In *crèche* and kindergarten, group play is emphasized. Beginning in primary school, classes are taught mostly in lecture format in teacher-fronted classrooms. The teacher talks most of the time, calling on students and asking specific questions to ensure that the students are paying attention. Students know that they can be singled out at any time; not knowing the answer causes embarrassment. Other students in the class may chime in to assist the student being questioned, particularly at the university level.

- Teachers in primary and secondary schools write almost everything on the board, and students take laborious notes. This is particularly necessary due to the lack of textbooks. Teachers in the lower levels also give dictations. Students at all levels are expected to memorize long passages of text word for word, although the government is recently encouraging teachers to replace these rote learning methods with more innovative pedagogical techniques.

LEARNING STYLE

- Students in Vietnam generally work individually; however, in the vocational and technical schools and at the university, teacher-assigned group work is common as well.

- It is rare for Vietnamese students to ask questions during class. It is more common for them to ask questions after class has finished, if at all. They often prefer to ask another student a question before asking the teacher. Understanding the material is considered the student's responsibility.

- Homework is taken very seriously. Doing it is part of a child's duty, and doing it well is part of a child's obligation to his or her family. The parents of younger students monitor their assignments; older students may form study groups.

- Having good handwriting is considered very important in Vietnam, and students spend hours practicing. Even in this area, the effects of Vietnam's difficult economic situation are noticeable. The smaller the student's handwriting, the less affluent the student. Poorer students write almost microscopically to save paper.

- Students who need extra assistance may be tutored or may attend teacher-led study sessions after school, if their families do not need them to work.

INSTRUCTIONAL SETTING

- Many schools are simple one- or two-story concrete-block buildings with large, shuttered, paneless windows and large doors. In some districts, schools may be unfurnished temporary structures of bamboo or grass. Schools are not air-conditioned, many lack running water, and many are poorly lit. A number of boarding schools were built to accommodate ethnic minority pupils in remote areas. At the time these schools were built, they were often the nicest buildings in the locality.

- There are few instructional materials apart from the chalkboard and text-books. The resources that do exist tend to be outdated, and even the outdated resources are in short supply. Textbooks are rented from the school system for a fee, and it is possible that a whole class may have only one or two textbooks at their disposal. There is also not enough paper for hand-outs, and students are expected to use their own paper for tests. Not too long ago, university students took notes on paper bags.

- Vietnamese students store their books or belongings in their desks or in school bags. There are no lockers for students.

- Vietnamese students must provide their own transportation to and from school, and most of them generally walk or ride bicycles or motorcycles. This situation can be problematic both for rural students, who may have to travel long distances, and for city dwellers, who have to fight frightening traffic conditions to get to school.

ACTIVITIES

- In primary school, collective activities are carried out by Children's Stars, teacher-designated groups of five children each. Older students are required to participate in collective activities as well, which range from organizing the school library to planting seedlings in a local park, weeding rice fields on a collective farm, doing cemetery maintenance, digging canals, or working in a seafood factory. Elite teacher-selected volunteer groups, honorifically named after Vietnamese heroes or with such names as *Good Lotus,* do community service and may take camping trips. Older students are encouraged to join and participate in the activities of the Ho Chi Minh Communist Youth League.

- Some school districts encourage competitive sports, such as soccer, table tennis, or chess.

- Field trips are rare to nonexistent, especially in rural areas. Those that are offered (e.g., visits to a coffee farm or a Buddhist temple) include a fee and may not be attended, as a consequence, by all students. Some students cannot afford to go on such trips; other students' families may need them to work.

DISCIPLINE AND CLASS MANAGEMENT

- Public school students in Vietnam begin the school week with a Monday morning assembly at which they salute the Vietnamese flag and sing. At this time, announcements for the week are made, and the class with the best-kept classroom is commended. The class with the worst-kept classroom may be reprimanded.

- In general, Vietnamese classrooms are extremely well disciplined, quiet places. Remaining silent and polite is a way for Vietnamese students to show respect for the teacher.

- Students in Vietnamese primary and secondary schools are often seated in the classroom by gender, with boys on one side of the classroom and girls on the other. Sometimes, however, a teacher will seat the students by alternating boys and girls. This seating system helps to maintain the quiet of the Vietnamese classroom. Culturally, Vietnamese youth are too shy to speak to members of the opposite sex. In fact, being seated next to a member of the opposite sex can be considered a punishment.

- Students in Vietnamese primary and secondary schools work together to maintain the classroom. Generally, a class is divided into four to six groups, which take turns at class duties on a weekly basis. Duties include cleaning the tables and benches, sweeping the floor, cleaning the board, preparing the teacher's desk (with a tablecloth and flowers), or making tea for the teacher. Some schools have classroom competitions; the rooms are inspected by a special team of honor students, and the results are announced at the weekly school assembly.

- Each class has a student monitor that is selected by the teacher based on grades and politeness. This student, the *lop truong* (literally, "top student"), takes attendance, oversees student cleaning duties, and generally ensures that the school's rules and policies are being carried out within the classroom. Given the authority this student has and his or her ability to abuse it, the *lop truong* is not necessarily the most popular student in the class.

- In secondary school, a homeroom teacher is responsible for taking attendance and monitoring the behavior and general progress of the students. The homeroom teacher consults with students' other teachers. If a student has misbehaved, he or she can expect a reprimand from the homeroom teacher. The homeroom teacher also works out any school-related difficulties a student may have.

- Attendance and punctuality are very important in Vietnam. Notes of excuse are expected for absences and sometimes for tardiness. Some teachers, however, may excuse a student who is needed to work at home.

- Disciplinary actions depend on the nature of the offending incident and the teacher. A student who has not done his homework may be embarrassed by the teacher in front of the whole class. Teachers may also hit and/or spank students; this is generally done with a ruler against the outstretched palm of a student, but it may be done on occasion with a flat hand or a bamboo reed. This type of discipline is becoming less and less common, however.

- Most Vietnamese parents are deeply involved in their children's education. Not only do they monitor homework, but they attend parents' meetings at the school two or three times per semester. At these meetings, strong students are openly praised, and poor students may be openly criticized. Individual parent-teacher interviews are not common in Vietnam, and an invitation to one will be interpreted to mean that there is a serious problem. A Vietnamese parent will not question the authority or opinion of the teacher.

TEACHER-STUDENT RELATIONSHIP

- Teachers are afforded a great deal of respect in Vietnam. They are considered to be on an equal basis with or perhaps even more highly regarded than lawyers and doctors—second only to priests. While the respect shown to teachers is historically rooted in Confucianism, students today also respect their teachers because they are aware of the economic hardships their teachers face. Teachers in Vietnam are severely underpaid, and many must take on extra jobs to survive, sometimes teaching extra classes, tutoring, or even performing menial labor, such as driving pedicabs or cleaning streets.

- Teachers in Vietnam develop extremely warm—almost parental—relationships with their students that last throughout the students' lives. In return, students cherish their teachers. Vietnam Teachers' Day (November 20) is a special day set aside to honor teachers. On this day, current and former students will travel miles to visit with their teacher at school or at the teacher's home to show their appreciation and respect. Usually, the teacher will be given a gift from the entire class. Due to the economic situation of most teachers in Vietnam, the gift is commonly food or money. This day is so important to schoolchildren that some have been killed in floods in November's rainy season while attempting to reach their teacher's house.

- Due to the parental role Vietnamese teachers assume, teachers consider themselves responsible for not only the learning but also the behavior of their students.

- A Vietnamese student generally will not openly disagree with a teacher, but a student who believes that the teacher really has made a mistake has an option: he or she will ask the teacher to check the problem or explain it again. That way, the teacher has the possibility to discover the mistake in a way that helps save face.

STUDENT-STUDENT RELATIONSHIP

- Students in Vietnam maintain warm, friendly relationships with their classmates, especially those of the same sex. Because classes of students at all levels are kept together for years at a time (five years in primary school, four years in junior secondary school, perhaps three years in senior secondary school, and perhaps several years in the university), an atmosphere of cooperation is fostered in and outside of the classroom. At the secondary school and university levels, it is common for classmates to form same-sex study groups that meet after class.

- One or two friends of a person will receive the status of *special best friend,* a person with whom innermost secrets are shared and activities are undertaken. These relationships will last a lifetime, even if the parties involved do not see each other for many years at a time.

Protocol

NONVERBAL BEHAVIOR

- Vietnamese students rise and bow when the teacher enters the classroom, and on the street and in homes, Vietnamese people bow when greeting one another. This bow may be a simple nod of the head when directed to a person of equal status; however, it is executed more formally, with crossed arms, when greeting persons in positions of greater authority and stature.

- Women do not shake hands in Vietnam, neither with women nor with men. Men may shake hands when greeting each other.

- Males and females in Vietnam have little to no physical contact with one another in public. It is rare to see a couple holding hands in public; kissing in public is virtually unheard of. However, it is quite common for members of the same sex to hug one another or to put their arms around each other's shoulders in a gesture of strong friendship. Women may also link arms as they accompany one another, and young girls may hold hands.

- In the Vietnamese culture, smiling is not necessarily an indication of happiness. Rather, a smile can be used to show a variety of emotions, including embarrassment, anger, or the acceptance of a compliment. A Vietnamese smile may further be an attempt to cover up a display of emotion, which is considered a private matter.

- Direct eye contact is often considered disrespectful and can be interpreted as a challenge. A Vietnamese speaker will generally avoid direct eye contact at the start of a conversation and perhaps ease into looking at the conversation partner as the exchange progresses.

- Touching another person's head is considered disrespectful. Only an elder may touch a child's head.

- Standing in an upright position with a raised chest and squared shoulders is considered arrogant. The Vietnamese prefer a humble posture with lowered shoulders.

- The Vietnamese consider it rude to summon a person of equal status with an upright hand or finger, a gesture used for inferiors and animals. To summon a person, the entire hand is used, with the fingers facing down.

- The Vietnamese use two hands to offer things to and accept things from a respected person. Handing something to someone with just one hand is considered extremely disrespectful.

- Excessive gesturing is considered impolite.

IMAGES

- Without a doubt, the most revered man in Vietnam is Ho Chi Minh. Born a poor farmer in 1890, he was active in revolutionary politics in Europe, and in the 1940s, he rose to organize and lead the Vietminh, an anti-French Vietnamese group, which named him president of Vietnam in 1945 and secured North Vietnam by defeating the French colonial forces in 1954. Under his leadership, North Vietnam defeated U.S.-aided South Vietnam, and the country was reunified in 1976. Today, "Uncle Ho" is the icon of the country, and his picture is displayed prominently in all public buildings. His body is entombed in a glass coffin in his mausoleum in Hanoi.

- A common sight in much of Vietnam is a three-wheeled pedicab called a *xichlo* (anglicized cyclo), which looks like a combination of a bicycle and a buggy. Passengers sit in the front and are pedaled around by a driver. This inexpensive form of transportation is available by the hour or the day. In some places, it is the only form of public transportation.

- The Vietnamese saying *Murky or clear, our pond is always better* is interpreted as an expression of encouragement for one another in hard times. It conveys the notion that however poor one's surroundings are, however humble, they are precious because they are one's own.

FORMS OF ADDRESS

- The Vietnamese have a very complex system for addressing one another, based on the age and the relationship of the people involved. Failing to use the proper form of address results in significant embarrassment for everyone involved in the conversation.

- Teachers in Vietnam are addressed by *thay* or *thay* plus given name (male) and *co* or *co* plus given name (female). Given names are preferred over family names, because there are only a few family names in Vietnam.

- At all levels of instruction, teachers in Vietnam address students by *em* or by *em* plus given name. Very small children, in *creche* or kindergarten, may be addressed by *con*.

- Students address each other by given name or by nickname. A special greeting, *may tao* (literally, "you me"), is reserved for special friends. The top student in the class is addressed using the special title *lop truong*.

- Traditionally, the family name comes first, then the middle name, with the given name last. Given names carry some meaning. Some Vietnamese living in Western cultures have reordered their names. Women tend to keep their maiden name.

DRESS

- Like many Asian cultures, the Vietnamese have a traditional style of dress. The women's traditional garment, called an *ao dai,* consists of a high-collared, long, silk tunic with front and back flaps, worn over loose trousers. It is sometimes worn with a hat called a *khan dong.* The men's traditional garment is similar to the women's. Today, these garments are worn for the New Year's celebration and at weddings and more by women than by men, who tend to be more Westernized. In some schools, female students and teachers are encouraged to wear *ao dai* to class.

- Also typical for Vietnam are *non la,* lightweight, woven conical hats made of bamboo and palm leaves. In addition to their use as a garment, the resourceful Vietnamese may use them as a bag to carry things or to collect rainwater for drinking. A somewhat fancier version of this hat, called a *non bai tho,* has sayings, poems, or designs woven into it. The poetry is thought to inspire or bring repose to the wearer.

- Older people in Vietnam may still wear an *ao ba ba.* These short silk tunics worn over trousers look somewhat like Western pajamas and are said to be very comfortable.

- Most students in Vietnam wear uniforms to school. The uniform consists of dark (navy blue or black) trousers or a dark skirt and a white shirt, often with an embroidered tag bearing the school name. Until recently, the *non la* was a required part of the uniform, and many students still wear this hat to school. However, no hats or caps of any kind are tolerated in the classroom. Girls in upper secondary school are encouraged in some school districts to wear white *ao dai* (symbolizing purity) with white or black trousers. Poorer school districts may allow their students to attend classes in street clothes; however, school uniforms are strongly encouraged, because they are believed to help form bonds between students. A girl at the postsecondary level may wear an *ao dai* in a color that depends on her school or major.

- Teachers in Vietnam dress in a variety of ways, depending on the school district and their income. While some teachers in poorer school districts may dress as casually as in a T-shirt and jeans, it is more common for men to wear a shirt and tie and trousers. Male teachers also generally have short hair and are clean-shaven. Women commonly wear dresses or *ao dai;* however, they may be permitted to wear slacks in some school districts.

POLITE/IMPOLITE TOPICS AND BEHAVIORS

- In Vietnamese society, it is very important to give people their due amount of respect based on their status, for example, by bowing, using proper speech, and addressing others with polite forms of address. Status in Vietnam is acquired through age and education, not wealth.

- It is important to avoid conflict in Vietnamese culture. Consequently, disagreement may not be expressed. Silence is preferable to saying something negative. Allowing a person to save face is more important than telling the truth.

- In general, speaking to anyone in a loud voice is considered rude, especially when accompanied by exaggerated gestures and particularly when done by a woman. People in positions of respect expect to be addressed in a low, soft, reserved voice.

- Personal information is considered public information in the Vietnamese culture, and questions about a person's salary, marital status, age, or weight are not considered impolite.

- Boasting or bragging about one's accomplishments, possessions, skills, or knowledge is considered offensive behavior. Similarly, the Vietnamese tend to shy away from praise, claiming that they do not deserve it. The Vietnamese prefer modest, humble behavior.

- The Vietnamese emphasize respect and ancestor worship, and it is considered very offensive to insult or criticize elders or ancestors.

- Very few Vietnamese women smoke or drink alcohol. It is considered disgraceful for a woman to become intoxicated.

- It is not impolite for Vietnamese to arrive late for an appointment. This is done in order not to appear too enthusiastic.

- Caution should be exercised when discussing such sensitive issues as politics and the Vietnam War. In Vietnam itself, criticizing the government in front of the wrong people can lead to trouble, and local authorities are often more severe than national policy dictates. Nevertheless, some citizens of former South Vietnam still find it difficult to accept the policies of the socialist government. Outside Vietnam, many Vietnamese refugees and immigrants may express their criticism of the new government by flying the flag of the former South Vietnam.

GIFT GIVING

- Vietnamese families typically give each other gifts for the New Year's, or Tet, celebration, for weddings, and recently, in some Westernized urban areas, for birthdays. Clothes or fabric are common birthday gifts, and money is a common gift for a wedding. At the new year, traditional foods, such as cakes, watermelon, tea, wine, or spirits, are given. Children receive from their relatives small red envelopes containing "lucky money."

- When a wrapped gift is given, it is customary to wait until the giver has departed to open it. This saves the giver any embarrassment should the recipient not be pleased.

- The Vietnamese delight in giving small gifts to colleagues and friends for little reason other than pleasing the recipient. Such gifts might be a pen, writing paper, a book, or toiletries—in other words, nothing extravagant.

- In Vietnam, invitations to social events other than family gatherings are rare. Thus, dinner invitations are not common. However, should an invitation be extended, a gift of food or drink, such as wine, fruit, or cookies, would be appreciated. Caution must be taken not to make the recipient feel obligated to return the favor at a later date.

- Sending a thank-you note after receiving a gift is not a common practice.

? 💡 **Problem/Solution**

PROBLEM

My Vietnamese students seldom ask questions in class, even when they are clearly confused, and they rarely volunteer information in class discussions. Can I encourage them to participate more in class and ask for clarification when they don't understand?

SOLUTION

Your students probably don't want to embarrass themselves in front of their classmates. Making a mistake in a public situation causes them to feel a great deal of shame, and they may feel threatened in the kind of classroom in which students speak individually rather than in chorus. Try approaching your students individually about the areas in which you feel they are having difficulty. They may feel more comfortable discussing the issue one-on-one. It may also help if you call on your Vietnamese students when you are certain they know the answer and praise them when they answer correctly. Also praise their unsolicited correct answers. This will help to build their self-esteem and may help them feel more comfortable about participating in class.

PROBLEM

I seem to have trouble assisting my Vietnamese students. When I ask them to see me after class, they sometimes don't stay. The ones who do stay seem to agree with everything I'm telling them, but I'm not convinced they understand me. They won't look at me, and they just seem to want to get the meeting over with as soon as possible. How can I communicate with them more effectively?

SOLUTION

A number of cultural influences may be affecting the behavior of your students. First, because Vietnamese prefer to avoid confrontation, a request to see the teacher after class is an intimidating and embarrassing occasion. You may want to explain at the start of your class that giving students individual help once in a while is a standard, expected instructional technique in Western countries. Your students will then feel less threatened when it is their turn. Second, Vietnamese students are more comfortable when approached individually rather than in front of the whole class. Finally, when speaking with your Vietnamese students, use a soft voice, which they will consider a sign of respect, and do not insist on direct eye contact, which is considered impolite in Vietnamese culture.

PROBLEM

The other students in my class sometimes have a very difficult time understanding my Vietnamese students' speech. How can I improve my Vietnamese students' pronunciation?

SOLUTION

Pronunciation is a special challenge for native speakers of Vietnamese. To begin with, the Vietnamese language lacks several phonemes common to the English language, among them voiced *th* (as in *bathe*) and voiceless *th* (as in *bath*), *p* in the initial position (as in *paint*), and *dj* (as in *John*). Terminal *s* and *z* (as in *bus* and *buzz*) also do not exist in Vietnamese, which is a particular problem when expressing the third-person singular (as in *she goes*), plurality (as in the word *lists*), or possession (as in *the student's*). There are also no consonant clusters, such as *sk* (as in *ski*) or *st* (as in *star*), in Vietnamese. Your students will need a lot of practice learning to hear and pronounce these sounds. Using exercises that contain voiced and voiceless minimal pairs (e.g., *bus/buzz, go/goes, see/ski*) may help.

My Observations

Language

ă	rat	ō	home
ā	race	ô	draw
ä	father	ōē	noise
b	boy	ū	goose
ch	church	û	took
d	day	ŭ	cut
ĕ	pet	ou	now
ē	Pete	p	perfect
f	fun	r	right
g	good	s	sin
h	hope	sh	shin
ĭ	in	t	tin
ī	ice	th	(voiced) bathe
j	judge	th	(voiceless) bath
k	kick	v	voice
kh	(German) *ich* rockhard	w	wide
l	lake	y	yawn
m	make	z	zebra
n	none	zh	pleasure
ng	ring	ə	about (schwa)

Pronunciation Key

Arabic

Arabic is a Semitic language and is spoken by more than 400 million people around the world. Classical Arabic, the language of the Koran (the holy book of Muslims), has remained the written language of Arabic-speaking peoples since the seventh century A.D. Modern standard Arabic has evolved from classical Arabic. The language has undergone very few changes, with the basic grammatical and phonological systems remaining the same. Muslims accept that the Koran has remained in its pure state from the time of its revelation. It follows, therefore, that the pride that Arabs take in their holy book is in equal proportion to that with which they regard their language. Arabic is an important part of the culture of the Arabs. It is the medium of communication for the government, business, law, and media. Colloquial Arabic, which differs from formal spoken Arabic, includes many dialects.

SOUND SYSTEM

Arabic has 32 consonants and 8 vowels and diphthongs. Short vowels are allophonic (sounding virtually the same to the untrained ear) and rarely carry any meaning. Hence, Arabic learners of English often have difficulty distinguishing between such words as *bit, bat,* and *bet.* The sounds *p* and *b* are not distinct phonemes (sounds) in Arabic, so Arabic speakers have trouble distinguishing between such English words as *park* and *bark.*

Glottal stops, such as the sound of the first syllable in *uh-oh,* are inserted before most vowels and strongly articulated consonants, giving Arabic a staccato cadence and meter.

The sound *r* is pronounced as a flap, similar to the trilled Spanish *r* in *gracias* or the transformation of the double *t* in the American English pronunciation of the word *butter.*

The sounds *v* and *f* are both pronounced as *f.* Thus, *save* and *safe* would both be pronounced as *safe* by a speaker of Arabic.

The sounds *g* and *k* are allophonic in most dialects of Arabic; there is no change in meaning when one or the other is used. Arabic speakers will therefore have difficulty distinguishing between English *log* and *lock.*

Consonant clusters appear in Arabic with much less frequency and range than in English. To compensate in English, Arabic speakers typically will insert vowels between the consonants of a consonant cluster. Hence, *traffic* is often pronounced as *tǝ-rǎ-fĭk.*

Word stress in Arabic is highly regular and timed. Thus, the shift in both stress and meaning of some English words, such as the verbs *prócess* (to treat or manage something) and *procéss* (to march as in a parade), can be confusing to Arabic speakers.

WRITING SYSTEM

Arabic script bears no physical resemblance to Roman script, although there is a distant relationship between some of the names of sounds, such as Arabic *alif* for Greek *alpha,* the source of the Roman letter *a.*

Since paintings and statues are forbidden in places of worship, decorative calligraphy is the highest artistic expression of the culture of the Arab peoples. The flowing curves of the letters can be beautifully translated into elaborate and very intricate designs.

Each letter has three forms, depending on whether it is word-initial, word-final, or word-medial.

Arabic is written and read, as are all Semitic languages, from right to left.

Arabic is phonetically written. The way it is spelled is exactly the way it is pronounced. The complexities that exist between English spelling and pronunciation create considerable difficulty for Arabic learners of English.

Arabic is written in a cursive system and has no uppercase or lowercase distinctions. Many of the letters have similar shapes, with diacritical marks to differentiate among them. The letters are grouped into sun and moon letters.

Only consonants and long vowels are written. The vowels are placed over the consonants to which they relate in the syllabic arrangement of the word.

GRAMMAR

The basis of Arabic grammar is the three-consonant root. Most grammatical and lexical changes take place by means of changing the order of the root components and the insertion of vowels. For example, *k, t,* and *b* combine to suggest writing. A *kattaab* is a writer; a *maktoob* is a letter.

More than 50 patterns combine with prefixes and suffixes to form the essential basis of Arabic grammar.

Written Arabic places the verb before the subject, although this is not always done in spoken Arabic.

The verb *be* does not exist as a grammatical entity in Arabic.

The perfective tenses in Arabic are more or less parallel to those in English. However, there is no form for future tense. There are no modals, but there are particles that, placed before the verb, approximate *shall* and *will*.

RHETORICAL ORGANIZATION

Because of changes in word order and placement of adjectives and adverbs, literal translations of Arabic can sound scrambled to English speakers. Likewise, Arabic-speaking English learners can produce writing samples with rather strange organization. One must remember that these learners are using a new script and that their language has no relation to English.

The rhetorical style of Arabic tends to favor rich expression over concise, logical construction, at least from the point of view of English speakers. Lower-level Arabic-speaking students will often produce run-on sentences and run-on paragraphs that do not seem to be heading to a definitive conclusion.

There is a considerable disjuncture between classical Arabic and the various vernacular dialects in terms of manner and register of expression.

The rhetoric used in Arabic is very circular, allowing writers to display their command of the language. The flowing metaphors and figurative language facilitate an oratorical style that does not lend itself to the linear arrangement of English prose. However, it must not be assumed that clarity is sacrificed to style. Because students sometimes have to commit to memory large sections of the Koran and other texts, their style of writing largely comes from one that is less creative than learned.

Written Arabic makes full use of parallelism and coordination, rather than subordination. Coordinated elements are joined together by the word *wa* (and). In the Koran, a period is used only after each *ayah* (verse), and there are no commas or other punctuation marks. In ordinary writing, sentences are punctuated by the use of commas, semicolons, and colons.

USEFUL EXPRESSIONS FOR THE CLASSROOM: ARABIC

English		Arabic	Pronunciation
good morning		صباح الخير	să-bä-ăl-khīr
good afternoon		مساء الخير	mă-sä-ăl-khīr
thank you		شكراً	shook-răn
you're welcome		أهلا وسهلا	äh-lăn wä säh-lăn
peace be unto you		السلام عليكم	ăs-ä-lă-mū ă-lī-kūm
and to you be peace (reply)		وعليكم السلام	wä-lī-kūm-sä-läm
How are you?		كيف حالك	kĕf-ă-hăluk
praise be to God (same reply)		الحمد لله	ăl-hăm-dū-lēl-lä
I'm well		أنا بخير	anä bā-kīr
God willing		ان شاء الله	ĭn-shă-ăl-lä
Do you understand?		هل تفهم	hăl tăf-hăm
please		لو سمحت	lă-ū să-mäht
good-bye (go with God)		مع السلامة	mä-ēs-sä-lăm-ä
please sit down		اجلس من فضلك	ēj-lūs mēn făd-lăk
please listen		اسمع من فضلك	ēs-mă mēn făd-lăk
good		جيد	jă-ēd
yes		نعم	nă-ăm
no		لا	lä
teacher	(male)	مدرس	mū-drĕs
	(female)	مدرسة	mū-drĕs-ä
let's go		لنذهب	lä năth-hăb

Chinese (Mandarin)

The standard, official version of Chinese in government and education, both in the People's Republic of China and in the Republic of China (Taiwan) is Mandarin, although there are many other dialects in use. The People's Republic of China promotes a simplified Mandarin character system, Baihua, and the Mandarin of Beijing as the national spoken language, Putonghua (literally, "common language"). On Taiwan, the Taiwanese dialect exists alongside Mandarin, with the former remaining the social and informal language of choice.

SOUND SYSTEM

The sounds *p, t,* and *k* at the end of words may not be pronounced at all or may be almost inaudible. In addition, the sounds *p, t,* and *k* at the end of words may not be distinguishable from *b, d,* and *g* in the same position.

The voiced sounds *v, z, th* (as in *then*), *j* (as in *jelly*) and *zh* (as in *garage*) do not exist in Mandarin Chinese and may be mispronounced. Often, their voiceless counterparts *f, s, th* (as in *think*), and *ch* may be substituted for them.

The word-final nasal sounds *n, m,* and *ng* may be dropped or used interchangeably. *Fun* may become *fŭ, fŭm,* or *fŭng.*

The sound *w* may be substituted for *l,* as in *fou* for *fall.*

The sound *r* may be substituted for *l* and *w,* so *lake* may become *rake,* and *whack* may turn into *rack.*

The sound *w* may be substituted for *v,* as in *wail* for *veil.*

The sound *d* may be substituted for *th* (as in *then*), making *loathe* sound like *load.* Both *t* and *f* may be substituted for *th* (as in *both*), so that *with* may become either *wit* or *whiff.*

There is no distinction between tense and lax vowels in Mandarin as there is in English. Examples of English tense/lax pairs include *bet* versus *bait, kin* versus *keen, full* versus *fool,* and *boat* versus *bought.* Speakers of Mandarin may not hear the differences between such words, nor might they produce the differences.

The vowel sound in the English word *band* does not occur in Mandarin and will frequently be replaced by the vowel sound in *bond.*

There is no *z* sound in most Chinese dialects, so this will often be replaced with *s*. Thus, *fuzzy* becomes *fussy*.

The vowel sound found in the first syllable of the English word *wonder* does not exist in Chinese and may be replaced with the vowel found in the first syllable of *wander*.

WRITING SYSTEM

Despite the almost limitless number of variations of Mandarin, the writing system is uniform across dialects.

The symbols of written Chinese are pictographs, one for each word.

The Pinyin writing system was designed for foreign use. It uses the Roman alphabet, rather than pictographs, to transcribe the sounds of Mandarin.

GRAMMAR

Parts of speech are not formally distinguished in Chinese, so Chinese speakers will use such English words as *difficult* and *difficulty* interchangeably.

Since Chinese words do not change to show number, gender, person, and so forth, use of the different forms of the verbs *be* and *have* in English may be problematic in a variety of ways. Learners of English may say, "Everybody are here," or "She have a dog named Ginger."

Tense and time are expressed differently in Mandarin than they are in English, giving learners difficulty in handling tenses and aspects. Common mistakes are reflected in the examples: "John has been here yesterday" and "She goes to the movies by the time you arrive home."

The absence of auxiliaries in the construction of questions or negatives in Chinese results in errors or complete omission in English. For example, Chinese speakers might produce "I do not remembered how to get there" or "How many years you study Chinese?"

Chinese uses tags as English does, as in "You like hamburgers, don't you?" But all tags may be converted to *is it?* or *isn't it?* as in "We should leave for the airport now, isn't it?"

There are no articles in Chinese, either definite or indefinite. Their appearance in a Chinese speaker's English is therefore fitful and unpredictable, as in "Today, I mow grass, and you paint the dog house."

In Chinese, word order is the same in questions (and indirect questions) as in declarative statements. A Chinese speaker might be heard to say, "You graduated from college when?" or, "She wondered what said the teacher," or, "To the store he went a fish to buy."

Plurality is not expressed in Chinese, so it is common to hear such statements as "Over the summer I read a lot of book and saw a few movie." In addition, there is no countable/uncountable distinction, so such plurals as *luggages* or *ice creams* may occur.

In the use of possessive pronouns, Chinese speakers often have difficulty grasping the difference between the adjectival (*my, your, his, her, our, their*) and the nominal (*I, you, he, she, we, they*), which results in such statements as "That is he car" and "May I borrow you pencil?"

Transitive English verbs, such as *discuss, tell, take,* and *give,* require an object in English but not always in Chinese. This grammtical difference produces errors, as in "We discussed all evening," "He told to her to hurry," and "She took with a friend to the movies."

Passives may be overgenerated in certain syntactic contexts by Chinese speakers of English, "This book is fun to be read."

Subjects and objects may be dropped by some learners, as in "After ate dinner, Susan went to a movie" or "Pick the one you want, and buy."

RHETORICAL ORGANIZATION

A linear rhetorical organization has long been taught in Anglo-American culture, to the point that there are jokes about the formula "An I, three Es, and a C"—referring to the rhetorical formula of an introduction, three examples, and a conclusion. This organization has also long been thought to be in conflict with Asian rhetorical practices, which have been likened to a spiral or a circle rather than a straight line. One should be vigilant not to perceive the norms of Anglo-American academic English as a yardstick for all composition. Should students need to learn linear rhetorical style for the purposes of conducting academic or commercial business in the West, this can be taught without giving it a higher value than styles previously learned by Chinese-speaking students.

Chinese students may diverge from the norm of English rhetoric in various ways, including regular returns to the main point before moving on, inductive expression of ideas, digression, and repetition of stock phrases.

Chinese do not consider using the words of others without giving credit to be plagiarism, and the art of proper citation will probably have to be explained to Chinese students.

USEFUL EXPRESSIONS FOR THE CLASSROOM: CHINESE (MANDARIN)

English	Chinese	Chinese Pin Yin	Pronunciation
please	请	qing	chē-ēng
thank you	谢谢	xie-xie	shē-ĕh shē-ĕh
you're welcome	你是受欢迎	bo ke qi	bū kǔ chē
hello	你好	ni hao	nyē hou
good-bye	再见	zai jian	tsī jē-ĕn
Do you understand?	你了解吗	ni dong le ma	nyē dūng lā mä
How are you?	你好吗	ni hao ma	nyē hou mä
(very) good	(非常) 好	(hen) hoa	(hĕn) hou
please sit down	请坐	qing zou	chē-ēng tsū-ä
please listen	请听	qing ting hao	chē-ēng tēng hou
Are you okay?	是你美好	ni hao ma	nyē hou mä
yes	是	shi	shĭ
no	不是	bu shi	bū shĭ
correct	正确	xheng que	tsūng chē-ĕ
homework	家庭作业	zou yie	zō yē-ĕ
teacher	老师	lao shi	lä-ō shĭ
let's go	我们走吧	women zou ba	wō-mĕn zō bä

French

SOUND SYSTEM

Because French has had an enormous influence on the development of the English language, there are many similarities between the two languages. In fact, they share many of the same words. However, the pronunciation of seemingly identical words does differ, particularly with regard to stress. The last syllable of a French word usually receives the stress: for example, *prō·nūn·sē·ă·sē·ōn′, prō·blĕm′, dē·fār·ôns′*.

Neither the voiceless *th* (as in *bath*) nor its voiced equivalent (as in *bathe*) exists in French, and French learners of English often resort to using *s* or *f* for voiceless substitutes and *z* or *v* for voiced substitutes. Thus, *myth* may become *miss* or *miff*, and *that* may become *zat* or *vat*.

The letter *h* is not pronounced in French. French learners of English will thus often say *ard* instead of *hard*. In overcompensating, they may also pronounce the *h* sound in English words containing a silent *h* (e.g., *hour*).

WRITING SYSTEM

French uses the same writing system as the other Western European languages, including English.

Accent marks, such as the acute accent (´) or the grave accent (`) may appear over certain French vowels, particularly *e*. An *i* or *o* may be capped with a circumflex (^), and a *c* may have a cedilla (̧) underneath. These symbols change the pronunciation of the letter sounds.

In French writing, one does not capitalize days of the week, months of the year, names of languages, or names of nationalities.

GRAMMAR

The French definite article is used with both singular and noncount nouns when making a generalization, as in "In life, the love is everything!"

There is no present progressive tense in French. Thus, "I sing" may mean "I sing for a living" or "I am singing now."

Certain nouns that are noncount nouns in English (e.g., *hair, furniture, luggage*) are count nouns in French (*hairs, furnitures, luggages*).

There is no distinction in French between the relative pronouns *who* and *which* when referring to human or nonhuman entities. Thus, French learners of English may produce such statements as "That's the guy which stole my watch."

French requires the verb to precede the noun in dependent clauses containing a noun subject, which results in such English statments as "Don't tell her what told you the doctor."

In French, it is possible to use an adverb between the verb and the object, as in "He climbed very quietly the stairs."

RHETORICAL ORGANIZATION

Writing in French usually requires the writer to use the formal pronoun *vous* (rather than its informal equivalent *tu*) and its accompanying second-person-plural verb conjugation. Formality, in general, is valued in French writing.

Formal French writing contains an abundance of special expressions that convey the writer's command of the language as well as his or her respect for the reader. It is not uncommon, for example, for a French letter writer to write, "I have the honor to inform you that I received your letter dated September 12," or, "I would be obliged if you could be so kind as to let me know." A typical French way to close a business letter is to write, "Thanking you for the confidence that you have shown me, I beg you to accept, Sir, the assurance of my most distinguished consideration."

Students trained in the French style of writing are not taught to use the familiar English formula "Tell them what you will say, say what you mean to say, and summarize what you have just said" (i.e., introduction, body, conclusion). In fact, this English rhetorical style is often viewed as rather mechanical, childish, and unsophisticated. A French writer would more likely allow a paragraph to meander, approach the topic lightly, then circle all the way back to address the topic. The French writer's intent is not to reach the core of the topic but, rather, to explore everything that is involved in getting to it.

The idea of a topic sentence may appear odd to a French speaker writing in English. Providing a topic sentence is seen as too obvious a technique for introducing a subject and even as insulting to the reader, who is assumed to have developed skill in reading between the lines.

The traditional subject-verb-object word order in writing is generally avoided by good writers of French. Instead, they prefer complex constructions, which prove the writer's familiarity with proper style.

Academic French writing is intended to be clear, precise, and logical. Literary French writing, however, attempts to display a variety of presentation styles. French writers strive to create surprise, irony, and suspense more than do English writers, and French writers are more concerned with color and harmony in their writing.

It is common for writers of French to conclude an essay with the introduction of another, related topic, to show that they actually know more about their topic than what they have written.

USEFUL EXPRESSIONS FOR THE CLASSROOM: FRENCH

English	*French*	*Pronunciation*
please	s'il te plaît	sē-tə-plā
thank you	merci	mār-sē
you're welcome	de rien	də-rē-ĕn
hello	bonjour	bōn-zhūr
good-bye	au revoir	ō-vwär
Do you understand?	tu comprends	tyū kōm-prän
How are you?	comment ça va	kô-män sə-vä
(very) good	(très) bien	(trā) bē-ĕn
please sit down	assieds-toi	ä-syĕ-twä
please listen	ecoutes, s'il te plaît	ā-kūt-sē-tə-plā
Are you okay?	ça va	sä vä
yes	oui	wē
no	non	nō
correct	c'est juste	sā zhyūst
homework	devoir	dĕ-vwär
teacher	professeur/professeuse	prō-fĕ-sər/prō-fĕ-sœz
let's go	on y va	ōn ē vä

Haitian Creole, or Kreyòl

SOUND SYSTEM

Haitian Creole (henceforth Kreyòl) consists of 19 to 22 consonant phonemes and 12 vowel phonemes, 5 of which are nasals and 3 of which are semivowels. Disagreement among linguists about the exact number of consonant phonemes is due to regional variations.

Word stress usually falls on the last syllable.

The American English pronunciation of the vowel sound in the word *last* becomes more like *läst* in Kreyòl.

The nasal ending of such English words as *long* and *sang* change to *lôn* and *sãn*. The nasal sound *m* at the end of a word is not pronounced in Kreyòl so much in the mouth as in the nose. Imagine that you are poised to say the word *home* but get interrupted after the vowel.

The sound *ch* in English becomes *sh* in Kreyòl; thus, *march* becomes *marsh*.

Kreyòl has no short *i* sound. *Fit* would be pronounced as *feet*.

Kreyòl speakers do not use the *j* sound as in *judge*. Thus, learners of English will transform a word like *ledger* into *lĕzhər*.

The initial-position *r* in Kreyòl has no English equivalent. It is pronounced as if the sound *h* precedes it. To some English speakers, the Kreyòl *r* may sound like a *w*.

The *th* sound does not exist in Kreyòl. Hence, such English words as *bath* or *think* may be mispronounced as *bat* and *tink*.

WRITING SYSTEM

Although Kreyòl has been spoken in Haiti since the 18th century when the French brought slaves to the island to work in the fields of sugar cane, it did not become a written language until the late 1970s.

A slightly modified Roman alphabet is used. Kreyòl does not have the letters *b, q, u,* and *x*.

Two vowels, *e* and *o*, can be marked with a grave accent and written as *è* and *ò*, thereby shortening the vowel sounds as in *pet* and *draw*.

Grammar

Kreyòl developed in the 17th to 18th centuries out of a need for African slaves to communicate with their French plantation owners and with one another. Kreyòl lexicon and phonology are primarily French, but the syntax and morphology are mainly from West African languages that do not use the verb and noun inflections of French.

The word order of Kreyòl for affirmative and negative statements and for yes-no questions is the same as in English: subject-verb-object.

Kreyòl nouns have no gender. Definite articles follow nouns, and indefinite articles precede nouns.

Plural forms of nouns in Kreyòl are not inflected by adding *s,* yet number may be expressed by adding specific words before the noun.

There are no verb inflections. All forms of the verbs are in the infinitive, but tense and aspect are expressed through the use of separate particles before the verb. For example, *monte* (ride) becomes *ap monte* (is riding). The simple present and simple past have exactly the same forms, so context is important to understand the time.

The verb *se* (to be), can be omitted between a noun and an adjective. For example, *malad* (sick) becomes *m malad* (I sick).

Possessive, object, and subject pronouns in Kreyòl all use the same form. For example, *mwen* is used for *my, me,* and *I.*

Rhetorical Organization

Because French was the official language used for government purposes and also the language taught to the elite, the writing style on the island is strongly influenced by French rhetoric. Essay introductions are often broad-based, flowery, and philosophical in tone.

Proverbs are plentiful, and it is estimated that during any serious conversation, the speaker uses one proverb to illustrate a point for every five or six sentences.

USEFUL EXPRESSIONS FOR THE CLASSROOM: HAITIAN CREOLE, OR KREYÒL

English	Kreyòl	Pronunciation
please	souple	sū-plā
thank you	mèsi	mĕ-sē
you're welcome	pa gen pàn	pä gān pän(g)
hello	bonjou	bôn(g)-zhū
good-bye	orevwa	ōhrĕvwä
Do you understand?	ou konpran	ū kôn(g)-prän
How are you?	ki jan ou ye	kē zhän ū yĕ
(very) good	(trè) byen	(twĕ) byān
please sit down	chita, souple	shē-tä sū-plā
please listen	koute, souple	kū-tä sū-plā
Are you okay?	ki jan ou ye	kē zhän ū yĕ
yes	wi	wē
no	non	nō
correct	kòrek	kô-rĕk
homework	devwa	dā-vwä
teacher	pwofesè	pwō-fā-sĕ
let's go	annou ale	ä-nū ä-lā

Japanese

SOUND SYSTEM

Japanese children learn to read by memorizing hundreds of *kanji,* characters that give no pronunciation clues.

There is no *ô* sound in Japanese; thus, *taught* becomes *tote.*

The English vowel in *cab* does not exist in Japanese, nor does the *ə,* or schwa sound (as in *cub*). Therefore, both *cab* and *cub* become *kăb.*

The lips are not rounded when pronouncing a *u* sound in Japanese. *Fool* may sound more like *full.*

The consonant *b* may be substituted for the consonant *v* because the latter does not exist in Japanese. *Very* may become *berry.*

The substitution of *l* for *r* does not change the meaning of the word as it would in English (*lice* versus *rice*). Instead, the distinction in Japanese between these two sounds is closer to the distinction in English between the *p* in *spit* and the *p* in *pit,* the latter being accompanied by a heavier puff of air. Just as both articulations of *p* may sound the same to native English speakers, the *l* and *r* in Japanese are almost indistinguishable.

Consonant clusters, such as *pr, st,* or *kl,* are rare in Japanese. Instead, the sound system of the language is basically sequenced in a consonant-vowel-consonant-vowel pattern. Therefore, Japanese speakers may insert a vowel between sounds in an English consonant cluster. *Cream* may become *kū-rēm-ū.*

Japanese words may not end in any consonant except *n.*

The sound *th,* whether voiced or voiceless (*either* versus *ether*) does not exist in Japanese and will likely be replaced by *s, z, f, or v;* thus, *think* becomes *sink* or *fink,* and *then* becomes *zĕn* or *vĕn.*

WRITING SYSTEM

Japanese is the most complex writing system used among the developed nations of the world. However, there is no evidence that an indigenous writing system was ever developed exclusively for Japanese; rather, all Japanese writing has always been done by borrowing and/or adapting Chinese characters.

Japanese is usually printed or written in vertical columns, from top to bottom and from right to left. However, certain reference works and scientific publications, as well as magazine or newspaper headings, may appear in horizontal lines.

Japanese uses four main punctuation marks: (1) periods, for the ends of sentences; (2) commas, used arbitrarily to show how words break in a sentence; (3) *middle-dots,* used when nouns are written in a row and for abbreviated dates, hours, and so on or when separating foreign names or initials transcribed in Japanese; and (4) quotation marks. Question marks and exclamation points are not commonly used.

Japanese words are typically written in *kanji.* These are ideographs; that is, they do not represent the sounds of given words as letters do in English. Rather, a single *kanji* may represent a single concept, such as "tree" or "middle," or may consist of a combination of elements. The *kanji* for the word *ai,* meaning "love," consists of four elements; those meaning "claws," "roof," "heart," and "move slowly." Minimal basic literacy requires the mastery of at least 1,850 *kanji.*

In addition to the *kanji,* the Japanese use a simpler set of characters called *kana. Kana* are phonetic symbols that were created in Japan by altering parts of *kanji.* They are used to express interjections and conjunctions, as well as inflectional endings for tense, plurality, and so forth. Thus, *kaku* (to write) plus *mashita* (the past tense ending) equals *kakimashita* (I wrote). The *kana* are further divided into two sets, or syllabaries: *katakana* and *hiragana. Katakana* are derived from parts of Chinese characters and are angular; *hiragana* are a set of more rounded characters derived from Chinese cursive writing.

For writing by hand, there are three different styles: *kaisho* (square style), *gyosho* (running style), and *sosho* ("grass-writing" style).

GRAMMAR

Word order in Japanese is not critical, since word endings often provide an explanation for such things as subject, object, and tense. Relative age, status, and role, mutual familiarity, and gender influence word choice and grammatical endings. There are four different levels of politeness. Japanese women do not always use the same forms as do men.

Verbs in Japanese may contain both the subject pronoun and object pronoun, so learners of English tend to drop these, rendering "I like these" as simply "like."

Most Japanese nouns are not marked for plurality, because the context provides sufficient information concerning number. "Tokyo has four daily newspaper" would not be an uncommon rendering.

Articles do not exist in Japanese, so learners of English will often supply them in a seemingly haphazard way, as in "I went to the Boston University to study some international politics."

RHETORICAL ORGANIZATION

According to the respected authority John Hinds, composition *(sakuban)* is not taught beyond the sixth grade in Japan. Despite the lack of formal composition classes, preferred writing styles exist. The following are four major styles that influence the organization of Japanese compositions.

Jo-ha-kyuu

This style is a literary tradition developed from the No drama. The characters in *jo-ha-kyuu* may be interpreted as introduction, development, and climax. This style, which proceeds in a fairly direct line to the climax, or conclusion, is similar to the standard English rhetorical style.

Ki-shoo-ten-ketsu

This style, also a literary tradition, developed from classical Chinese poetry and can be found throughout modern prose. The characters in *ki-shoo-ten-ketsu* can be explained as follows: first, begin the argument (*ki*); next, develop the argument (*shoo*); *ten* (at the point where the development is finished, turn the idea to a subtheme with a connection, but not a directly connected association, to the major theme (*ten*); and last, bring all of this together and reach a conclusion (*ketsu*). Three aspects of this style are particularly interesting when compared to standard English rhetoric. First, the *ki,* while roughly equivalent to an introduction in that the topic of the composition is introduced, does not generally contain the thesis. Second, the *ten* provides a twist, an abrupt shift, which examines the topic from a completely different angle that may seem unrelated at first. The *ten* may confuse English readers, who generally do not expect digressive or un- related material to appear suddenly in rhetorical writing. Third, the *ketsu* is the conclusion in which the different ideas are drawn together, but this is not necessarily done in a Western fashion. In fact, Japanese writers may here introduce new ideas only loosely connected to the rest of the essay, to stimulate thought. The Japanese *ketsu* need not be decisive; it may ask a question or indicate a doubt. Nonetheless, the *ketsu* frequently contains the thesis, perhaps the result of a Japanese writer's reluctance to assert an opinion.

Fish Fried in Batter

As the name of this primarily journalistic style expresses, Japanese news articles frequently cover the main contents of the story (the "fish") with layers of details (the "batter"). Whereas English news articles begin with a lead (the main information) in the first sentence, Japanese news stories begin with the details, concealing the lead until as much as three-fourths of the way into the article.

Return to the Baseline Theme

In this writing style, before the author can progress to a new perspective, he or she must overtly return to the theme he or she has selected. Unlike English rhetoric, in which each paragraph contains a dominant topic sentence and proceeds with subordinate supporting sentences, the main theme must be partially repeated each time a new subtopic is introduced. With regard to paragraph structure, each paragraph has one logical subject, identified by the particle *wa* in the first sentence. After that, the subject is implied rather than stated, because the reader knows from the first sentence what the subject is.

USEFUL EXPRESSIONS FOR THE CLASSROOM: JAPANESE

English	*Japanese*	*Japanese Pronunciation*
please (asking a favor)	お願いします	ō-nä-gä-shē-mä-sū
thank you	ありがとう	ä-rē-gä-tō
you're welcome	どういたしまして	dō-ē-tä-shē-mä-shē-tä
hello	こんにちは	kōn-nē-chē-wä
good-bye	さようなら	sī-yō-nä-rä
Do you understand?	わかりましたか	wä-kä-rē-mä-shē-tä-kä
How are you?	元気ですか	gĕn-kē dĕ-sū-kä
(very) good (good job)	（とても）よくできました	(tō-tä-mō) yō-kū-dä-kē-mä-shē-tä
please sit down	座ってください	sü-wä-tä kū-dä-sī
please listen	聞いてください	kē-ē-tä kū-dä-sī
Are you okay?	大丈夫ですか	dī-yō-bū dĕ-sū-kä
yes	はい	hä-ē
no	いいえ	ē-ē-ĕ
correct	正解です	sä-ē-kī dĕ-sū
homework	宿題	shū-kū-dī
teacher	先生 / 教師	sĕn-sä/kyō-ēn
let's go	行きましょう	ē-kē-mä-shō

Korean

SOUND SYSTEM

While the origin of Korean remains unknown, theories link the language to the Altaic languages of Manchu, Mongolian, Turkish, and Japanese.

The Korean sound system comprises 10 basic vowels and 14 simple consonants, which expand to 21 vowels (including 13 diphthongs), and 19 consonants, for a total of 40 symbols.

The sounds *p* and *b* may be substituted for *f* and *v*, respectively, because the latter do not exist in Korean. This may result in *pan* for *fan* and in *TB* for *TV.*

Korean has one sound that is similar to both *l* and *r* in English. Its pronunciation is determined by its position. In English, the *l* is most often substituted for *r* in initial positions, resulting in *light* for *right.* The sound *r* may be substituted for *l* between vowels; *filing* would be pronounced as *firing.*

The *th* sound does not exist in Korean. Speakers may substitute aspirated *t* or *d.* Thus, *thin* becomes *tin,* and *those* becomes *doze.* Other possible substitutions include *s* for *th* (resulting in *sing* for *thing)* or *z* for *th* (resulting in *zə* for *the*).

The English sound *z* does not exist in Korean. Speakers might say *jest* for *zest.*

Korean has no word-initial consonant clusters. As a result, Korean speakers tend to insert a short *uh* (ŭ) sound between the consonants and to pronounce the cluster as two syllables: *stop* would become *sŭ-täp.*

Korean has a limited number of middle and final consonant clusters. In Korean, *n* becomes *l* when followed by *l;* thus, *womanly* might be pronounced *wū-məlē.* The phrase *sunlight* might be pronounced as *sŭ-līt.*

Vowel length may be used contrastively in Korean to indicate meaning. For example, *bam* can mean "night" or "chestnut," and *nun* can mean "snow" or "eye," depending on the length of the vowel.

Korean speakers tend to have difficulty distinguishing the vowel sound in *met* from the vowel sound in *mat.*

There is no distinction between tense and lax vowels in Korean. In English, the vowel in *beet* is tense, and the vowel in *bit* is lax. Similarly, the lax equivalent of *bait* is *bet,* and that of *fool* is *full.* Thus, Korean speakers of English may produce a tense vowel, rather than a lax vowel, and vice versa, when speaking. These pronunciation differences change the meaning of words, of course.

WRITING SYSTEM

The Korean alphabetic script, *hangu,* was invented in the 15th century. Prior to that, the Korean writing system adapted Chinese characters, sounds and glosses. Chinese characters introduced into Korean have, however, been completely adapted to Korean use.

Hangu is a phonemic writing system. Dots, straight lines, and circles form the letters, which are combined and written as syllabic blocks rather than in a linear order. Symbols are written from top to bottom and from left to right.

Korean does not have capital letters; thus, there is no differentiation in writing for proper versus common nouns.

In Korean, a syllable is the smallest unit of pronunciation that contains at least one vowel. There are six types of syllables possible in written form (v = vowel, c = consonant): v, c-v, c-v-c, c-v-c-c, v-c, and v-c-c. However, in spoken form, there are only two: c-v-c and v-c.

Korean is most often Romanized according to the McCune-Reischauer System developed in 1939 and used mainly in the United States and other Western countries. Korea revised its own Romanization system in 1984, and the two systems are basically one and the same. In 2000, the system was again revised, to allow for more variations. *Busan* and *Pusan* are both acceptable forms, for example. In these systems, individual Korean phonemes (individual sounds) may be represented by more than one Latin letter.

GRAMMAR

Korean is an agglutinative language, which means that suffixes bind to noun and verb stems one after the other. These affixes may indicate speech styles, mark cases or sentence types, denote honorifics, or express moods and aspects.

Korean uses four levels of speech: higher honorific, simple honorific, simple familiar, and lower familiar. Honorifics show respect or intimacy between the speakers based on age and social superiority. Special honorific particles are added to the subject and inserted into the verb when speaking to parents, the elderly, or teachers. Korean uses six speech styles, which vary according to the age of the person being spoken to.

Korean sentence structure is typically subject-object-verb. Subjects precede the verbs; adverbs precede the verbs or adjectives they modify. Because nouns are marked for case, some free word order is possible. The following variations of "Mary saw John yesterday" are all possible in Korean: "Yesterday Mary John saw," "Mary John yesterday saw," "Yesterday John Mary saw," and "John yesterday Mary saw."

Korean allows sentences without pronouns. Possible answers to the question "Did John see Mary yesterday?" include "Yes, saw her" and "Yes, saw."

Verbs contain the root, tense markers, and sentence-type suffixes. Plural markers may be added for emphasis. Sentence endings indicate whether the sentence is declarative, interrogative, imperative, or propositive. Thus, a verb in the past tense could be constructed as follows: stem–subjective honorific–preterit marker–honorific for hearer–period and indicative mood marker.

The articles *a, an,* and *the* exist in Korean but are typically omitted and are generally used only when emphasis is desired.

There is no gender distinction (masculine, feminine, neuter) in Korean.

Every Korean noun may be used as a countable noun. It would not be uncommon for a Korean speaker to say, "I read many news." It may be difficult for a Korean speaker to distinguish whether the word *chicken* means the animal or the meat of the animal.

Although the expletives *it* and *there* occur in Korean, they are often omitted. For example, "It is raining" may become "is raining."

In Korean, negative questions are answered according to whether what the speaker has said is correct. For example, the question "Didn't you write the essay?" may elicit the response "Yes, I didn't write it." In such a case, saying "yes" means that what the speaker has said is correct, that is, that the essay was not written; saying "no" would mean that what the speaker said is incorrect, that is, that the essay was indeed written.

Korean does not have relative pronouns or relative clauses. Clauses will precede the nouns they modify, no matter the length, as in "The used-to-live-next-door-to-my-family-in-Seoul-before-we-moved man sent us a letter."

Requests in Korean use the imperative (command) form and typically do not include such words as *please,* which are instead embedded in the honorifics used. As a result, a direct English translation of a request by a Korean speaker may sound rude or demanding when, in fact, it is not.

RHETORICAL ORGANIZATION

Popular genres include poetry, short novels, and expository essays. Modern poetry evolved from two types: *shijo,* three or four lines of approximately 15 syllables per line; and *kasa,* longer verse whose content is essaylike.

Short novels, comparable in length to English short stories, are often published as serials in newspapers.

Expository essays are viewed as writings produced by the experts in the field. Essays are typically organized from specific to general and do not contain a directly stated thesis. The thesis, unstated, is often found in the conclusion of the work.

Writers of expository essays devote large amounts of time to organizing their thoughts before putting them on paper and thus do very little in the way of revising or rewriting their work.

It is believed to be the reader's responsibility to interpret written works, and writing may often show what something is not, rather than what it is. It is common for criticisms to be hidden in metaphors.

USEFUL EXPRESSIONS FOR THE CLASSROOM: KOREAN

English	Korean	Korean Pronunciation
please	Usually embedded in honorifics	
thank you	고맙습니다	kō-mäp-sūm-nē-dä
	고마워요	kō-mäh-wōh-yōh
you're welcome	Not said in Korean.	
hello	안녕하세요	än-nyūng-hä-sĕ-yō
good-bye	안녕히 가세요 to departing guest	än-nyūng-hē-kä-sĕ-yō
	안녕히 계세요 to host	än-nyūng-hē-kyā-sĕ-yō
Do you understand?	이해가 되십니까	yē-hī-gä-dō-shēm-nē-kä
	이해가 되요	yē-hī-gä-dë-yō
How are you?	안녕 하세요	ōä-tō-kĕ-chē-nī-shēm-nē-kä
(very) good	(아주) 좋아요	(ä-jü) jō-ä-yō
please sit down	앉으세요	än-chū-sĕ-yō
please listen	잘 들어보세요	chäl-drōä-bô-sĕ-yō
Are you okay?	괜찮아요	kūän-chän-ä-yō
yes	예 / 네	yā/nā
no	아니요	ä-nē-yō
correct	맞았습니다	mä-jä-sūm-nē-dä
homework	숙제	sūk-jä
teacher	선생님	sāōn-sääng-nēm
let's go (hurry up)	같이 가요	gä-chē gä yō

Polish

SOUND SYSTEM

Even among experts, there are disagreements about how many consonant and vowel sounds there are in Polish. Estimates range between 25 and 35 consonant sounds (including four forms of *z*) and 7 or 8 vowel sounds.

Many Polish sounds are either difficult or impossible to approximate in spoken English. The most notable are the nasalized vowels and palatal consonants. One area of particular difficulty for Polish speakers learning English is segmental phonemes, such as diphthongs and consonant clusters.

WRITING SYSTEM

Polish uses a standard Western, or Latin-based, orthography. However, several letters, notably *z,* are supplemented with diacritical marks. The letters *q, v,* and *x* do not exist in Polish and are used only in mathematical formulas.

GRAMMAR

Many Polish speakers feel that because of its declensions and seven grammatical cases, the Polish language is better suited than English for the eloquent expression of mathematical, scientific, and logical concepts.

Polish has grammatical gender, which is expressed through the word endings of adjectives and nouns.

There are no set rules for word order, although there are preferred patterns. The pattern subject-verb-object is common.

Polish has no articles, definite or indefinite. Reference is generated through suffixes and prefixes.

RHETORICAL ORGANIZATION

The Slavic—and therefore Polish—approach to rhetoric is to attack a subtle point from a variety of perspectives, a method known as *circumvoluted discourse,* culminating in the proposition of a thesis somewhere near the very end of the written piece. What an English speaker may perceive as wandering off topic is to Polish speakers simply approaching the problem from different points of view. At the same time, these twists and turns have the superficial appearance of logical deduction. While the sciences have come to adopt the more Western, linear approach, the humanities have yet to embrace this concept. Speakers of Polish who are learning English must be taught this concept—for academic or professional purposes—along with the English language itself.

Native Polish speakers frequently have a culturally rooted distrust of government and hierarchy, which may manifest itself in a refusal to quote experts or statistics. To cite them would invite skepticism and ridicule from their peers. Writers may prefer to compare and contrast various ideas or to define and redefine ideas rather than to refer to the work of others. They do not provide concrete proof, because they are not required to do so.

Polish rhetorical form requires a constant restatement of the same idea, which will necessarily lengthen any written work well beyond what most English writers and teachers are accustomed to.

USEFUL EXPRESSIONS FOR THE CLASSROOM: POLISH

English	Polish	Pronunciation
please	proszę	prô-shĕ
thank you	dziękuję	jĕŋ-kū-yĕ
you're welcome	niema za co	nyĕ-mə zə tsō
hello	dzień dobry	zhān dô-brĭ
good-bye	do widzenia	dô vē-jĕn-ē-ə
Do you understand?	czy Pan razumie	chē pän rä-zūm-ĕ
How are you?	jak się Pan ma	yäk sā pän mä
(very) good	(dobrzę) dziękuję	(dôb-zhĕ) jĕn-kū-yĕ
please sit down	niech Pan siada	nĕkh sä-dä pän
please listen	proszę niech pan stucha	nĕkh pän swū-khä prô-shĕ
Are you okay?	czy Pan jest w porządku	chē pän yĕst fpô-zhōnt-kū
yes	tak	täk
no	nie	nē-ĕ
correct	prawda	präv-də
homework	pracy domowe	prä-chē dô-mô-vĕ
teacher	naucyzciel (male)	nä-ū-chē-chəl
	naucyzcielka (female)	nä-ū-chē-chəl-ka
let's go	pójdziemy	pô-yē-jĕ-mē

Portuguese (Brazilian)

SOUND SYSTEM

Syllable stress of Brazilian Portuguese is different from that of European Portuguese in that the latter has stressed and unstressed syllables, like English, whereas the former has the same stress on all syllables that are not marked. Therefore, Brazilian Portuguese speakers may have trouble comprehending long words that have a stressed syllable in the middle.

Placing stress on words that should not be stressed in an English sentence can also cause problems of intended meaning for Portuguese speakers. The stressing of auxiliary verbs, prepositions, pronouns, and articles may cause the speaker to sound aggressive.

English word endings that have unstressed vowels may sound as if they have been swallowed: for example, *city* becomes *sĭt,* and *office* becomes *ôfs.*

There are fewer consonant clusters in Portuguese than in English, so speakers will often insert vowels where they do not belong: for example, *clothes* becomes *klō·thĭs,* and *park* becomes *pär·kĭ.*

When the letter *c* has a cedilla under it (*ç*) or when it follows the letters *a, o,* and *u,* it is pronounced *s.* It would not be surprising for a Brazilian learner of English to see the word *pace* and pronounce it *pāsh.*

Dialect differs between Rio de Janeiro and the rest of Brazil. For example, in Rio, the *s* is pronounced *sh* at the end of words or before a consonant: for example, *ingles,* the Portuguese word meaing "English," is pronounced *ēn-glāsh,* and *ěsta* ("is") is pronounced *esh-tä.* Also, *t* is pronounced *ch,* and *d* is pronounced *j* before the sounds *i* or *e* when they occur in the last syllable. Thus, *poverty* could become *pä·vār-chē,* and *mundane* could become *mən-jān.*

WRITING SYSTEM

Portuguese is spelled exactly as it is heard, so pronunciation errors will likely manifest themselves as spelling errors in writing, such as *poliched* for *polished* and *bin* for *been.*

The Portuguese alphabet has 23 letters (18 consonants and 5 vowels). The letters *k, w,* and *y* do not belong to the Portuguese alphabet, but they can be used in names, such as *William,* or international terms, such as *kilogram.*

The following accent marks are used in Portuguese writing to indicate modifications in pronunciation: acute ('), grave (`), circumflex (^), tilde (~), umlaut (¨), and cedilla (¸).

Months, days of the week, and nationalities are written using lowercase letters.

Punctuation marks are the same as those used in English.

GRAMMAR

Portuguese verbs exist in the following forms: active and passive; past, present, and future tenses; perfect and progressive aspects; and auxiliary and modal. The present perfect is used for recent actions and events, unlike the North American English use of rendering duration in, for example, "I haven't eaten beef since 1995."

Questions are formed by a rise in intonation at the end of a statement, not by word order. Negation occurs by placing *não* before the verb. Personal pronouns may be placed before or after the verb, and the verb follows the question word in indirect speech, as in "I don't know what is the time."

Adjectives usually follow nouns, and an adjective must agree with the noun in number and gender.

Diminutives are often used in Brazil, either to refer to a small version of something or, especially with children, as a form of affection. The diminutive forms *-inho* or *-inha* are attached as suffixes. Thus, *cavalo* (horse) becomes *cavalinho* (small horse).

About 20,000 words come from the indigenous languages that were widely spoken before the arrival of the Portuguese, and many others come from African languages that were spoken by the slaves from 1530 to 1850.

RHETORICAL ORGANIZATION

Discourse that uses persuasive devices, such as reminding the reader that a particular notion or action will benefit everyone, is often mistrusted and viewed as an attempt to exploit others.

Unrestrained details often result in digression from the topic and loss of focus.

Written texts, especially those that call for an opinion, tend to demonstrate more interaction with the reader by using the pronouns *you* and *I* routinely. Additionally, interaction with a reference allows the writer to evade stating a direct opinion.

Formal or academic writing makes use of longer sentences with more subordination, prepositions, infinitives, and repeated use of key nouns.

Common genres include poetry and folktales, both of which use extensive symbolism with metaphor and allegory. The use of realism in poetry and novels is used to epitomize the suffering, hardships, and social injustices of the proletariat.

USEFUL EXPRESSIONS FOR THE CLASSROOM:
PORTUGUESE (BRAZILIAN)

English	Portuguese	Pronunciation
please	por favor	pōr fä-vôr
thank you	obrigado/obrigada	ō-brĕ-gä-dū/ō-brĕ-gä-dä
you're welcome	de nada	dĭ nädä
hello (good day)	olá	ō-lä
good-bye	tchau	chou
Do you understand?	está entendendo	ĕsh-tä ĭn-tän-dän-dū
How are you?	como vai	kō-mū vī
(very) good	(muito) bem	(mū-ē-tū) bām
please sit down	por favor, sente-se	pōr fä-vôr sĭn-tä-sā
please listen	por favor, escute	pōr fä-vôr ĭ-skū-tä
Are you okay?	você está bem	vō-sä ĕsh-tä bām
yes	sim	sēm
no	não	nou
correct	correto	kô-rĕ-tū
homework	lição de casa	lē-sou dĭ kä-zä
teacher	professor/professora	prō-fĕ-sōr/prō-fĕ-sōr-ä
let's go	vamos	vä-mōzh

Russian

SOUND SYSTEM

Generally speaking, Russian is a more phonetic language than English, which means that the pronunciation of Russian words is usually apparent from their spelling. In other words, sound-symbol correspondence is simpler in Russian than in English, so one can pronounce Russian words correctly without understanding what is being said.

The Russian vowels are *ä, ĕ, yĕ, yō, ĭ, ē, ō, ū, yū,* and *yä*. Most Russian vowels are very close in pronunciation to their English counterparts. In fact, since Russian is an Indo-European language, as is English, there are many similarities in vocabulary and pronunciation. One particular Russian vowel, however, Ы (*yĭ·rē*), does not have a corresponding sound in English. It can be described as a combination of the vowel sound in *look* and the vowel sound in *see*.

There are no diphthongs in Russian, neither does the distinction between long and short vowels exist.

Most Russian consonants are also close in pronunciation to their English counterparts. The remaining ones—*kh, ts, ch, sh, shch,* and *zh*—only occur in English as combinations of consonants. For example, you can hear the sound of the Russian consonant *ts* in the end of the English word *bits*. The consonant *shch* occurs when certain English words are produced sequentially, as in the phrase *cash checks*. The consonant *r* is trilled in Russian.

The English sounds *th* (as in *bath* and *bathe*), *ng,* and *w* do not occur in Russian, so Russian learners of English often encounter problems with their pronunciation.

WRITING SYSTEM

Russian uses the Cyrillic alphabet, named after Saint Cyril, its creator: Аа Бб Вв Гг Дд Ёё Жж Зз Ии Йй Кк Лл Мм Нн Оо Пп Рр Сс Тт Уу Фф Хх Цц Чч Шш Щщ Ъъ Ыы Ьь Ээ Юю Яя. Although the Cyrillic alphabet at first glance appears daunting, it is actually quite easy to learn. Approximately half of the Cyrillic alphabet is the same as the alphabet used by English speakers.

Some letters in the Cyrillic alphabet—Ъъ, Ыы, Ьь—have no sound. They are normally symbols that affect the pronunciation of previous sounds.

The Russian and English punctuation systems share most of the same features. However, Russian writers use commas to offset a dependent clause. They may thus write, "I know, how to play the piano." Russian quotation marks are also somewhat different, appearing, for example, as follows: „I live in Florida."

GRAMMAR

Russian is a synthetic language, meaning that instead of word order indicating grammatical meaning, the endings of nouns and adjectives carry grammatical meaning. Words may be placed virtually anywhere in a Russian sentence. Nouns and adjectives *decline,* or change, according to case—nominative, genitive, dative, accusative, instrumental, and prepositional. The Russian word meaning "boat," for example, has a variety of endings depending on whether one wants to say "of the boat," "to the boat," "in the boat," and so forth. Declension is much like conjugation. A user of the Russian language declines nouns and adjectives but conjugates verbs.

The endings of Russian verbs change according to person—first-, second-, or third-person singular and plural.

Russian nouns may have one of three genders: masculine, feminine, and neuter. Pronouns, likewise, vary according to case, number, and gender. In English, *I, me, my,* and *mine* refer to the self. In Russian, there are many words to refer to the self. A sampling includes *yä, mēnyä, mnyě, mnōē, mōē, mäyěvō, mäyěmū, mäyēm,* and *mäyōm.*

Russian has no articles. "Cat sat on mat" would be a perfectly good sentence in Russian. Auxiliary verbs, such as *have, do,* and *will* also do not occur in Russian.

Neither perfect nor progressive tenses exist in Russian.

There is no *there is* (or *there are*) in Russian, so learners of English may write, "I hope that lots of presents under the tree."

Russian does not distinguish between *this* and *that* or *these* and *those.*

Russian discourse often includes a long series of adjectives before the noun.

RHETORICAL ORGANIZATION

Native Russian-speaking academics often joke that even they have difficulty reading scholarly texts in Russian. This is due to the deliberate complexity of academic Russian discourse. Long paragraphs may consist of a single sentence. Scholars, editors, and other professional writers show their command of language and convey the importance of their thoughts through use of subordination, multiple parallel constructions, parenthetical commentary, and technical terminology (often undefined). A similar pattern may be observed not only within a given paragraph but within an extended composition; that is, despite several long digressions within a paragraph or essay, writers tend to return to what English teachers would call the *topic sentence* or *thesis statement.*

Russian writers have long been admired, and their works have long been analyzed. The culture has a stellar literary tradition that encompasses both novels and poetry. Some of Russia's most famous writers include Dostoevsky, Tolstoy, Chekov, Yevtushenko, Pushkin, Gogol, Turgenev, Pasternak, and Solzhenitsyn.

USEFUL EXPRESSIONS FOR THE CLASSROOM: RUSSIAN

English	Russian	Pronunciation
please	пожалуйста	pə-zhäl-stə
thank you	спасибо	spä-sē-bə
you're welcome	пожалуйста	pə-zhäl-stə
hello	привет	prē-vyĕt
good-bye	до свидания	də-svē-dän-yə
Do you understand?	понимаешь	pə-nē-mī-ĕsh
How are you?	как поживаешь	käk pə-zhē-vä-ĕsh
(very) good	(очень) хорошо	(ō-chĕn) khô-rô-shō
please sit down	садитесь пожалуйста	sä-dē-tyĕs pə-zhäl-stə
please listen	слущай пожалуйста	slū-shī pə-zhäl-stə
Are you okay?	ты хорошо	tə̄ khô-rô-shō
yes	да	dä
no	нет	nyĕt
correct	правильно	prä-vēl-nə
homework	домашнйи задание	də-mäzh-nē-yĕ zə-dän-yə
teacher	учитель (male)	ū-chē-tyĕl
	учительница (female)	ū-chē-tyĕl-nēt-sə
let's go	пойдём	pä-ē-dyōm

Spanish

SOUND SYSTEM

Spanish has five vowels and five diphthongs. Since vowel length is not a distinctive feature of Spanish, learners may have problems distinguishing between the English vowels ĭ (as in *sit*) and ē (as in *seat*) or between ĕ (as in *bet*) and ā (as in *bait*).

Some learners may have problems differentiating between ä (as in *cot*), ă (as in *cat*), and ŭ (as in *cut*).

The *u* (as in *pull*) and ū (as in *pool*) are often both pronounced ū by Spanish speakers.

The English schwa, as in the last (unaccented) syllable of the word *circus,* has no correspondence in Spanish; learners may substitute the sound of the vowel as if it were accented. For example, *circus* becomes *sīr-kūs, symbol* becomes *sīm-bōl, edible* becomes *ĕd-ē-būl,* and *element* becomes *ā-lā-mānt.*

Diphthongs are generally not difficult for Spanish speakers.

Most English consonants are not problematic for Spanish speakers. In English, *p, t,* and *k,* when they occur in initial position, are *plosives,* meaning they require aspiration, or a puff of air. In Spanish, this is not the case. Word-final voiced plosives are very rare in Spanish, and learners will use *t* for final *d* (*hid* becomes *hit*), *k* for final *g* (*wig* becomes *wick*), and *p* for final *b* (*tab* becomes *tap*).

The English *z* has no correspondence in Spanish, and learners may use *s* instead. Thus, *lose* becomes *loose.*

In Spanish, the difference between *v* and *b* is minimal and does not change the meaning of the word as it would in English: *very* is different from *berry* in more than just pronunciation. Spanish speakers may not be able to hear the difference, and they are likely to make no distinction between *b* and *v* in speech.

Spanish speakers often have problems pronouncing *y* as in *yes.* They may use the sound *j* instead.

Since there is close correspondence in Spanish between spelling and pronunciation, some speakers may pronounce English words letter by letter. The word *varied,* for example, may be pronounced *vĕ-rē-ĕd.* In addition, Spanish does not emphasize pitch; instead, speakers may use extra length.

WRITING SYSTEM

Because of the close correspondence between pronunciation and spelling in Spanish, the spelling of English can be difficult for learners. Double letters in English may be reduced to one (e.g., *professor* to *profesor*), and the pattern of writing two vowels and one consonant (as in *read*) or one vowel and two consonants (as in phi*loso*phy) is often confusing for writers.

Punctuation conventions in Spanish are similar to those in English.

GRAMMAR

Spanish has a highly inflected verb system, and most of its tenses can be found in English. In Spanish, there are no modal auxiliaries, such as *can, would,* and *might,* so learners may find this concept difficult.

In Spanish, it is common to use *have* plus a noun (e.g., "to have hunger") to express what English would express with *be* plus an adjective (e.g., "to be hungry"). Spanish speakers also say, for example, "I have thirty years," instead of saying "I am thirty years old."

The endings *-ing* and *-ed* do not have active or passive meanings in Spanish as they do in English (e.g., "The professor is boring me," "I'm bored by the professor"). In Spanish, there are no *-ing* nouns, or gerunds, such as in "Playing tennis is my favorite pastime." Instead, the infinitive is used as a noun, as in "To play tennis is my favorite pastime."

In Spanish, the infinitive can be used as an abstract noun, (as in "To see is to believe"), and learners can find it difficult to understand the use of a gerund acting as the subject in a sentence, as in "Seeing is believing."

When generalizing, the definite article is often used in front of mass and plural nouns, as in "The love makes the world go round" or "The Colombians are South Americans."

Word order is much freer in Spanish than in English. The order subject-verb and the order verb-subject do not generally correspond to statement and question, respectively, as they often do in English. The position of the emphasized word is normally placed last, as in "Is big my family." Adjectives are normally placed after the nouns they modify, as in "Birthday happy," and adverbs can be placed in several positions in a sentence, as in "Carefully choose your words," "Choose carefully your words," "Your words carefully choose," and "Choose your words carefully." Word order for questions is very flexible in Spanish, and there are no auxiliaries.

Adjectives and nouns show gender and number. The ending *-s* is used in Spanish to show plural number in adjectives, articles, possessives, and nouns, as in "Mis amigos venezolanos son los mejores en el mundo" [*My Venezuelan friends are the best in the world*].

Double negatives are commonly used in Spanish. Thus, "No tengo ningun problema" is literally translated as "I don't have no problem."

It is possible in Spanish to drop the subject pronoun because the ending of the verb indicates person and number. "Tienes chicle en tu cabello" translates as "Have gum in your hair." Spanish-speaking learners of English may omit the subject pronoun.

There is no apostrophe to show possession in Spanish. Possession is indicated with *of* plus a possessive pronoun. "This is Camila's bed" is rendered as "This is the bed of Camila."

There is no distinction between personal and nonpersonal relative pronouns, such as *who* and *that* in English. In Spanish, both *who* and *that* are expressed with the word *que*. The relative pronoun can never be reduced in Spanish as it can in English, as in "This is the cat ~~that~~ I found." This is a difficult concept for learners to grasp.

Some English prepositions are troublesome for learners. For example, *in, on,* and *into* are expressed in Spanish with the same word, *en.* Also, *to, at,* and *in* are expressed with the single Spanish word *a,* and *as* and *like* are rendered in Spanish with *como.* Thus, Spanish learners of English may produce such erroneous constructions as "The cat is lying in the table," "She left in four o'clock," and "I'm as tired like I can be."

RHETORICAL ORGANIZATION

Spanish speakers may encounter difficulties when writing in English due to differences in writing style. It is not common in Spanish to organize compositions using connectors or transition words like those taught to students of English composition. Instead, a Spanish speaker may first write the main idea and later add more ideas related to it. English writing patterns tend to be more formal and to follow a stricter pattern.

It is not uncommon for Spanish speakers to deviate from the main idea when writing. These deviations are accepted in Spanish as long as the writer returns to the original point being made.

Spanish speakers writing in English may have difficulty guiding the reader through the text. In English, writers use all kinds of metatextual elements, such as connectors (e.g., "first … second …"), previews (e.g., "in this paper, I propose …"), reviews (e.g., "up to this point, I have shown …"), action markers (e.g., "to sum up, …"), and the like. In Spanish, however, writers use these elements less often.

USEFUL EXPRESSIONS FOR THE CLASSROOM: SPANISH

English	Spanish	Pronunciation
please	por favor	pōr fä-vōr
thank you	gracias	grä-sē-äs
you're welcome	de nada	dā nä-thə
hello	hola	ō-lä
Do you understand?	comprendes	kōm-prĕn-dĕs
How are you?	cómo estás	kō-mō ĕs-täs
(very) good	(muy) bien	mū-ē bē-ĕn
please sit down	por favor siéntense	pōr fä-vōr sē-ĕn-tĕn-sā
please listen	por favor escuchen	pōr fä-vōr ĕs-kū-chān
Are you okay?	estás bien	ĕs-täs bē-ĕn
yes	sí	sē
no	no	nō
correct	correcto	kō-rĕk-tō
homework	tarea	tä-rā-ə
teacher	maestro (male)	mä-ā-strō
	maestra (female)	mä-ā-strə
let's go	vámonos	vä-mə-nōs

Vietnamese

SOUND SYSTEM

Vietnamese is a monosyllabic, tonal language. It differentiates between six different tones: level, high-rising, low, low-falling, high-falling-rising, and low-falling-rising. Changing the tone of a syllable changes the meaning of the syllable; accordingly, each syllable can have six different meanings, depending on how it is pronounced. The standard example to demonstrate this aspect of the language is the word *ma,* which carries the meanings "ghost," "mother," "that," "horse," "tomb," and "burgeon" among others.

Due to the monosyllabic nature of Vietnamese, there is no linking of sounds from one word to the next in a sentence. Vietnamese is pronounced in a somewhat choppy fashion, with just a hint of a pause between each distinctly pronounced syllable. Final stops *p, t,* and *k* tend to be unreleased; that is, the usual puff of air is not produced.

Most letters in the Vietnamese alphabet are pronounced similar to their pronunciation in French, due to the Romanization of the written language by French missionaries. The letters *f, j, w,* and *z* are not used at all, and the letter *p* is used only at the ends of words or in combination with *h* to produce an *f*-like sound. The *z* sound is represented in Vietnamese by the letter *d,* the letter *r,* and the combination *gi;* the *d* sound is represented by the crossed letter *đ.* The letter *x* represents the *s* sound.

In Vietnamese, there is no *th,* either voiced (*bathe*) or voiceless (*bath*), no initial *p,* no *j,* and no final *s* or *z.* The last two phonemes present a particular difficulty due to their grammatical necessity in English when expressing the third-person singular, plurality, or possession.

The Vietnamese language lacks consonant clusters, such as *st, sk, ks, str, lt,* and *nt.* Depending on where the cluster falls in a word, the Vietnamese speaker may leave part or all of the cluster out. This also accounts for the tendency of Vietnamese speakers to prefer separated negations to contractions. For example, *did not* is preferred to *didn't.*

Vietnamese vowels are represented in the Roman alphabet by modifying some vowel characters with diacritics: *ă, â, ê, ô, o',* and *u'.*

WRITING SYSTEM

Vietnamese was first written using Chinese characters, beginning around the 9th century. This system, called *chu nho,* was used in the schools and for all official documents and government transactions, artistic literature, and correspondence. Around the 13th century, a new writing system, called *chu nom,* became popular. In *chu nom,* Chinese characters were modified and/or combined to represent Vietnamese words. Used mostly in literature, *chu nom* never became the official writing system of Vietnam. The current writing system, *quoc ngu,* originated in the 17th century. At that time, Catholic missionaries Romanized the writing system to facilitate the spread of Christianity. *Quoc ngu* slowly gained popularity, particularly during the French domination of Vietnam, and it became the official writing system in the early 20th century.

Clause and sentence punctuation in Vietnamese is very similar to punctuation in English or French, making use of the period, comma, colon, semicolon, parenthesis, question mark, and exclamation point. A few exceptions are the use of a question mark after an indirect question (as in "I asked if she wanted to eat now or later?"), the lack of a final comma after an embedded element in a sentence (as in "My father, arriving home well after dark did not wake me up"), and the marking of certain quotations with dashes (-), or quotation marks borrowed from French (« »). Vietnamese capitalization is also very similar to English, with only a few departures.

The six tones in Vietnamese are written using tone marks over or under the vocalic portion of a syllable. The marks are ´ (high-rising), ` (low), . (low-falling), ? (high-falling-rising), and ~(low-falling-rising). A level tone carries no mark.

Having good handwriting is considered very important in Vietnam, a remnant of the rigid pre-Communist school system, which required adherence to "an identifiable handwriting model." As a result, many Vietnamese have absolutely beautiful handwriting.

GRAMMAR

The Vietnamese language does not have definite or indefinite articles. It specifies nouns using a system of classifiers and categoricals. Classifiers identify the general type of object or concept and specify the number (e.g., a set, a flat rectangular object, a couple, an individual item, a sudden violent state). Categoricals are more specific in reference to the type of object or concept but may or may not refer to a single entity (examples are a person rating highest respect, a portion of a day, a place, a box). Nouns are added to classifiers and categoricals to make specific references. For example, *chuoi* means "banana," *cay chuoi* literally means "tree banana," and *trai chuoi* means "fruit banana." Vietnamese students generally have difficulty determining when to use articles and may overuse classifiers in English.

Vietnamese words are invariable in form. They take no prefixes or suffixes. Consequently, Vietnamese students may encounter difficulty with English verbs, with indicating plurality or possession, and with forming the comparative and the superlative, as well as with recognizing and using correct word forms (e.g., distinguishing between *excellent* and *excellence* or between *obstruct, obstruction,* and *obstructive*).

Verbs are not inflected for person or tense in Vietnamese; they have only one form. The tense in a Vietnamese sentence is understood from the type of verb (momentary action or extended state), the context, and time markers, and tense is not marked unless necessary. Vietnamese verbs are also basically neither active nor passive; there is an extra marker for voice. Consequently, learning the complex system of tenses in English can be quite a challenge for the Vietnamese learner.

The verb *to be* in English represents another challenge for speakers of Vietnamese. In Vietnamese, the word *la* corresponds to all forms of *be*. Since Vietnamese verbs are not inflected, there is only one form for all persons, and this form does not change tense. To further complicate the issue, *la* is used only with nouns, not with adjectives or with adverbs indicating place. Consequently, speakers of Vietnamese will form such sentences as "It wonderful" or "she not here."

Unlike most Western languages, Vietnamese makes almost no use of person; that is, it is not important to indicate whether the speaker is referring to himself or herself, to the listener, or to a third party. The status of the persons involved, however, must always be indicated, and there are many words in Vietnamese that denote kinship, profession, education, and so on. As a result, much Vietnamese discourse occurs in the third person, as in "Does older sister want to come?" and "Where is mother's brother's wife?"

RHETORICAL ORGANIZATION

From the 2d century B.C. to the 10th century A.D., Vietnam was occupied by China. As a result, Vietnamese writing, from its earliest beginnings up to the 18th century, strongly reflects Chinese cultural influence (although a rich tradition of Vietnamese popular narrative exists). Beginning in the 19th century, Vietnam, like much of Asia, developed a desire for Western philosophy and culture. Vietnamese intellectuals, influenced by Chinese writers undergoing a similar transformation, introduced Vietnam to short stories, novels, and plays along Western lines. Further contact with French prose and poetry under the period of French domination introduced a critical, analytical approach to writing. The end of the 19th century saw a proliferation of prose works on every topic available, from translations of Chinese novels to French school texts to Western scientific literature.

Vietnam has a long and distinguished history of both oral and written poetry. For Vietnamese from all walks of life, whether scholars, farmers, shopkeepers, or craftspeople, making poetry is seen as an accepted and expected way to deal with life experiences. Hearing, reading, singing, and writing poetry is considered a natural part of life.

As a high art form, early written Vietnamese poetry followed the Chinese classics. Later poems were written in *chu nom* (a Vietnamese adaptation of Chinese) and finally in Vietnamese itself. Written Vietnamese poetry can be extremely complex in its tonal prosody and rhyme schemes.

Vietnamese students are introduced to the writing of compositions as early as primary school and are expected to produce lengthier compositions in junior secondary and secondary school. Due to the influence of the French on the school system, Vietnamese students are familiar and comfortable with the basic rhetorical structures of a Western essay (introduction, body, conclusion). In execution, however, the form and purpose of these basic parts in a Vietnamese composition may vary considerably from the standard Anglo model.

USEFUL EXPRESSIONS FOR THE CLASSROOM: VIETNAMESE

English	Vietnamese	Pronunciation
please	làm ơn	läm ŭng
thank you	cám ơn em	käm ŭng ĕm
you're welcome	không có gì em	khŭng kô zē ĕm
hello	chào em	chou ĕm
good-bye	tạm biệt em	täm bēĕt ĕm
Do you understand?	em hiêủ không	ĕm hē-ū khŭng
How are you?	em khỏe không	ĕm kwhä-ŭ khŭng
good	đúng	dûng
very good	giỏi	zē-ô-ē
please sit down	mòi em ngồi	mŭ-ē ĕm ngō-ē
please listen	xin lắng nghe	sēn läng ngā-ŭ
Are you okay?	em có sao không	ĕm kô sou khŭng
yes	có	kô
no	không	khŭng
correct	đúng	dûng
homework	băi tập về nhà	bä-ē täp vä ngyă
teacher	thầy (male)	tä-ē
	cô (female)	kō
let's go	đi	dē

Bibliography

Ahmad, F. *The Making of Modern Turkey.* New York: Routledge, 1993.

Akatsuka, N., ed. *Japanese/Korean Linguistics.* Stanford: Center for the Study of Language and Information Publications, 1994.

Allendoerfer, C. "Creating 'Vietnamerican' Discourse: Ethnic Identity in the ESL Classroom." Paper presented at the annual meeting of the American Educational Research Association, Montreal, Canada, April 4, 1999. Dialog, ERIC, ED428578.

Armbrust, W. *Mass Culture and Modernism in Egypt.* Cambridge: Cambridge University Press, 1996.

Avery, P., and S. Ehrlich. *Teaching American English Pronunciation.* Oxford: Oxford University Press, 1992.

Axtell, R. E., ed. *Do's and Taboos around the World.* 3d ed. New York: John Wiley and Sons, 1993.

Axtell, R. E., ed. *Do's and Taboos around the World.* 4th ed. New York: John Wiley and Sons, 1995.

Axtell, R. E., ed., *Gestures: Do's and Taboos of Body Language around the World.* New York: John Wiley and Sons, 1991.

Bahgat, G. "Education in the Gulf Monarchies." *International Review of Education* 45 (1999): 127–36.

Birkenmayer, S. S. *Introduction to the Polish Language.* New York: Kosciusuko Foundation, 1978.

Bosco, J. "*China Teaching Workbook: Taiwan and Hong Kong.*" East Asian Institute, Columbia University, 1996. Retrieved May 3, 2001, from <http://www.easc. columbia.edu/itc/easp/webcourse/chinaworkbook/taiwan.intro.htm>.

"Brazil." Retrieved May 3, 2001, from <http://cwr.utoronto.ca/cultural/english/ brazil/index.html>.

"Brazil: A Country Study." Retrieved April 28, 2001, from <http://lcweb2.loc.gov/ frd/cs/ brtoc.html>.

"Brazil: Education System." Retrieved May 15, 2001, from <http://www.unesco.org/ iau/whed-2000.html>.

Cadet, J.-R. *Restavec: From Haitian Slave Child to Middle-Class American.* Austin: University of Texas Press, 1998.

Carter, R. D. "Teaching the Process Approach in Poland." Paper presented at the annual meeting of the Conference on College Composition and Communication, New Orleans, March 13–15, 1986. Dialog, ERIC, ED268531.

Chaplin, H., and S. Martin. *A Manual of Japanese Writing.* New Haven: Yale University Press, 1967.

"China: A Teaching Workbook." Retrieved May 3, 2001, from <http://afe.easia. columbia.edu/teachingaids/china/chinaworkbook/intro.htm>.

Chu, H. "Linguistic Perspective on the Education of Korean-American Students." In *Asian-American Education: Prospects and Challenges,* ed. C. Park and M. Chi, 71–86. Westport, CT: Bergin and Garvey, 1999.

Civan, M. "The Haitians: Their History and Culture." 1994. Retrieved May 5, 2001, from <http://www.cal.org/rsc/haiti/htoc.html>.

"Colombia." Retrieved January 9, 2001, from <http://www.odci.gov/cia/publications/factbook/co.html>.

"Colombia at a Glance." Retrieved June 7, 2001, from <http://www.worldbank.org/data/countrydata/aag/col_aag.pdf>.

"Colombia: Education System." Retrieved May 15, 2001, from <http://www.unesco.org/iau/ whed-2000.html>.

Corbett, B. "Haiti." Retrieved May 15, 2001, from <http://www.webster.edu/~corbetre/ haiti/haiti.html>.

"Côte d'Ivoire." Microsoft Encarta '98 Encyclopedia, 1993–1997 [CD-ROM]. Microsoft Corporation, 1998.

"Côte d'Ivoire." Microsoft Encarta Virtual Globe, 1995–1997 [CD-ROM]. Microsoft Corporation, 1998.

"Côte d'Ivoire." Retrieved June 6, 1999, from <http://www.odci.gov/cia/publications/factbook/iv.html>.

"Cuba: Consular Information Sheet." Retrieved May 27, 2001, from <http://www.travel.state.gov/cuba.html>.

"Cuba: Cultural Profiles Project." Retrieved May 18, 2001, from <http://cwr.utoronto.ca/cultural/ english/cuba/index.html>.

"Cuba: Education System." Retrieved May 18, 2001, from <http://www.unesco.org/iau/whed-2000.html>.

"Cubafacts." Retrieved May 26, 2001, from <http://www.cubafacts.com>.

"Cubans: Their History and Culture." Retrieved June 1, 2001, from <http://www.cal.org/rsc/cubans/CONT.htm>.

Durand, M. M., and N. T. Huan. *An Introduction to Vietnamese Literature.* Translated from French by D.M. Hawke. New York: Columbia University Press, 1985.

"Egypt." Microsoft Encarta '98 Encyclopedia, 1993–1997 [CD-ROM]. Microsoft Corporation, 1998.

"Egypt." Retrieved June 29, 1999, from <http://home.moe.edu/index.html>.

"Egypt." Retrieved January 7, 2000, from <http://www.ibe.unesco.org/Inf_Doc/Nat_reps>.

"Egypt." Retrieved May 5, 2000, from <http://memory.loc.gov/cgi-bin/query/r?frd/cstdy: @field(DOCID+eg0073>.

"Egypt." Retrieved May 8, 2000, from <http://infoplease.lycos.com/ida/A0107484. html>.

"Egypt." Retrieved April 14, 2001, from <http://cwr.utoronto.ca/cultural/english/egypt>.

Fisiak, J. "Polish-English Contrastive Project." In *Zagreb Conference on English Contrastive Projects,* ed. R. Filipovi, 87–96. Zagreb: Institute of Linguistics, 1971.

Gomes de Matos, F., and A. Pinto. "English Language Education in Brazil: Progress and Partnerships." *ESL Magazine,* November/December 2000, 26–28.

Grabe, W., and R. Kaplan. "Writing across Cultures." In *Theory and Practice of Writing,* ed. C. Candlin, 176–201. New York: Longman, 1996.

Gussmann, E. *Studies in Abstract Phonology.* Cambridge: MIT Press, 1980.

Hac, P. M. *Vietnam's Education: The Current Position and Future Prospects.* Hanoi: Gioi Publishers, 1998.

"Haiti." Retrieved April 27, 2001, from <http://www.odci.gov/cia/publications/factbook/geos/ha.html>.

"Haiti." Retrieved May 3, 2001, from <http://cwr.utoronto.ca/cultural/english/haiti/index. html>.

"Haiti." Retrieved May 3, 2001, from <http://www.usaid.gov/htm>.

"Haiti: A Country Study." Retrieved April 28, 2001, from <http://lcweb2.loc.gov/frd/cs/httoc.html>.

"Haiti: Education System." Retrieved May 15, 2001, from <http://www.unesco.org/iau/whed-2000.html>.

Hall, E. *The Hidden Dimension.* New York: Anchor Books, 1990.

Handbook of Korea, A. Seoul: Samhwa Printing, 1990.

"Hankuko: Ki-bon dan-o" (Hankuko: Basic words). Retrieved April 14, 2001, from <http://www.travlang.com/languages/cgi-bin/langchoic/cgi>.

Hinds, J. "Inductive, Deductive, Quasi-Inductive: Expository Writing in Japanese, Korean, Chinese, and Thai." In *Coherence in Writing: Research and Pedagogical Perspectives,* ed. U. Conner and A. Johns, 87–109. Alexandria, VA: TESOL Publications, 1990.

Hinds, J. "Linguistics and Written Discourse in English and Japanese: A Contrastive Study (1978–1982)." *Annual Review of Applied Linguistics* 3 (1982): 78–84.

Houtsonen, J. "Traditional Qur'anic Education in a Southern Moroccan Village." *International Journal of Middle East Studies* 26 (August 1994): 489–500.

Huang, G. "Beyond Culture: Communicating with Asian American Children and Families." *ERIC Clearinghouse on Urban Education,* ED366673, December 1993. Retrieved May 3, 2001, from <http://eric-web.tc.Columbia.edu/digests/dig94. html>.

Hutchison, W. R., C. A. Poznanski, and L. Todt-Stockman. *Living in Colombia: A Guide for Foreigners.* Yarmouth, ME: Intercultural Press, 1987.

Huynh, T. S., ed. *An Anthology of Vietnamese Poems: From the 11th through the 20th Centuries.* New Haven: Yale University Press, 1996.

Hyde, M. "The Teaching of English in Morocco: The Place of Culture." *ELT Journal* 48 (October 1994): 295–305.

International Grade Conversions. New York: World Education Services, 2000.

"Ivory Coast." Retrieved September 22, 1999, from <http://lcweb2.loc.gov>.

Javier-Brozo, M. "Learning in Morocco." Retrieved March 13, 2001, from <http://cwr.utoronto.ca/cultural/english/morocco/learning.html>.

Jimenez, E., and M. E. Lockheed. *Public and Private Secondary Education in Developing Countries: A Comparative Study.* Washington, DC: World Bank, 1991.

John, P. B. "A Guide to Teaching English in Vietnam: The Vietnamese Learner." Retrieved June 28, 2001, from <http://www.vietnam-notes.com/guide/guide04.html>.

John, P. B. "The Vietnamese Language." Retrieved June 28, 2001, from <http://www.vietnam-notes.com/language.html>.

Kataoka, H. C., and T. Kusumoto. *Japanese Cultural Encounters and How to Handle Them*. Lincoln, IL: Passport Books, 1994.

Kim-Renaud, Y. *Theoretical Issues in Korean Linguistics*. Stanford: Center for the Study of Language and Information Publications, 1994.

"Korea." Retrieved March 12, 2001, from <http://www.ibe.unesco.org/International/Databanks/Wde/wde.htm>.

Korean Language, The. Seoul: Si-sa-yong-o-sa Publications, 1983.

"Learn about Vietnam." Retrieved July 10, 2001, from <http://www.vietnamembassy-usa.org>.

LeCorde, P. "Kreyol." Retrieved May 8, 2001, from <http://www.angelfire.com/ky/LeCorde/kreyol.html>.

Lee, C., and R. Scarcella. "Building upon Korean Writing Practices: Genres, Values, and Beliefs." In *Cross-Cultural Literacy: Global Perspectives on Reading and Writing*, ed. F. Dubin and N. Kuhlman, 143–61. Englewood Cliffs, NJ: Prentice Hall, 1992.

Lutjens, S. L. "La Politica Educativa en Cuba Socialista: Las Lecciones de Cuarenta Años de Reforma." In *Cuba: Construyendo Futuro*, ed. M. Pérez, M. Riera, and J. V. Paz, 287–330. Barcelona, Spain: El Viejo Topo and Fundación de Investigaciones Marxistas, 2000.

Marett, R. *Mexico*. New York: Walker and Company, 1971.

"Maria-Brazil: Brazilian Culture on the Web." Retrieved May 17, 2001, from <www.maria-brazil.org>.

Matsuda, P. "Contrastive Rhetoric in Context: A Dynamic Model of L2 Writing." *Journal of Second Language Writing* 6 (January 1997): 45–60.

Mazur, B. W. *Colloquial Polish*. London: Routledge, 1983.

McGregor, J., and M. Nydell. *Update Saudi Arabia*. Yarmouth, ME: Intercultural Press, 1990.

"Mexico." Retrieved February 8, 2001, from <http://www.sep.gob.mx>.

"Mexico." Retrieved February 22, 2001, from <http://cwr.utoronto.ca/cultural/english/mexico/html>.

"Mexico." Retrieved February 22, 2001, from <http://www.odci.gov.cia/publications/factbook/ve.html>.

"Mexico." Retrieved March 11, 2001, from <http://memory.loc.gov/cgi-bin/query/r?frd/cstdy:@field(DOCID+mx0049)>.

"Mexico." Retrieved March 11, 2001, from <http:www.inegi.gob.mx/difusion/espanol/acercamexico/facermex.html>.

"Mexico." Retrieved March 13, 2001, from <http://www.ibe.unesco.org/international/Databanks/Dossiers/mainfram.htm>.

Mitchell, D. "A Review of Spanish Writing Preferences." Department of Languages and Linguistics, University of South Florida, 1998. Photocopy.

"Morocco." Retrieved June 22, 2000, from <http://www.odci.gov/cia/ publications/factbook/ mo.html>.

"Morocco: Education." Retrieved May 13, 1999, from <http://www.mincom.gov.ma/ english/ generalities/e_genera.html>.

"Morocco: Education System." Retrieved May 15, 2001, from <http://www.unesco.org/ iau/whed-2000.html>.

Morrison, T., W. A. Conaway, and G. A. Borden. *Kiss, Bow, or Shake Hands: How to Do Business in 60 Countries.* Yarmouth, ME: Intercultural Press, 1994.

Muller, K. "Life in Vietnam." *Hitchhiking Vietnam: Letters from the Trail.* Retrieved June 29, 2001, from <http://www.pbs.org/hitchhikingvietnam/life>.

Nguyen, D. H. *Vietnamese Phrase Book.* Rutland, VT: Charles E. Tuttle Company, 1976.

Nguyen, T. T., and B. Weigl. *Poems from Captured Documents.* Amherst: University of Massachusetts Press, 1994.

Nolasco, R., and L. Arthur. "You Try Doing It with a Class of Forty!" *ELT Journal* 40 (April 1986): 100–106.

Nydell, M. K. *A Guide for Understanding Arabs.* Yarmouth, ME: Intercultural Press, 1996.

Ocana, D. "Study, Work, Rifle: Cuba's Educational System Presses Revolutionary Message along with ABC's." *Miami Herald,* August 6, 2000. Retrieved May 26, 2001, from <http://www.canf.org/English/Humanrights/study.htm>.

O'Grady, W. *Categories and Case: The Sentence Structure of Korean.* Amsterdam and Philadelphia: John Benjamins Publishing.

Oster, P. *The Mexicans: A Personal Portrait of People.* New York: William Morrow and Company, 1989.

Park, C. C., and M. M. Chi, eds. *Asian-American Education: Prospects and Challenges.* Westport, CT: Bergin and Garvey, 1999.

Parker, O. "Cultural Clues to the Middle Eastern Student." *International Educational and Cultural Exchange* 12 (summer 1976): 12–18.

"People's Republic of China." Retrieved March 1, 2000, from <http://www. ibe.unesco.org/ InfDoc/Natreps/profilee.htm>.

Picus, M. "The Writing Strategies of Vietnamese Students." Master's Thesis, University of Houston, 1983.

Pogonowski, I. *Polish-English, English-Polish Hippocrene Standard Dictionary.* New York: Hippocrene Books, 1993.

Psacharopoulos, G., C. Rojas, and E. Velez. "Achievement Evaluation of Colombia's Escuela Nueva: Is Multigrade the Answer?" *Comparative Education Review* 37 (August 1993): 263–76.

Richmond, Y., and P. Gestrin. *Into Africa: Intercultural Insights.* Yarmouth, ME: Intercultural Press, 1998.

Rodd, L. *Japan at a Glance.* Tokyo: Kodansha International, 1997.

"Russia." Retrieved April 13, 2001, from <http://cwr.utoronto.ca/cultural/english/ russia>.

"Russia." Retrieved April 13, 2001, from <http://icweb2.loc.gov/frd/cs/cshome.html>.

"Russia." Retrieved April 13, 2001, from <http://www.departments.bucknell.edu/russian/russian.html>.

"Russia." Retrieved April 13, 2001, from <http://www.ibe.unesco.org/international/databanks/wde.htm>.

"Russia." Retrieved April 15, 2001, from <http://www.odci.gov.cia/publications/factbook/ve.html>.

"Russian Language with Alexei Ivanov." Retrieved March 15, 2001, from <http://russian.about.com/homework/russian/mbody.htm>.

Savain, R. "Haitian Students in the United States." *ESL Magazine,* July/August 1998, 28–30.

Shen, W., and M. Weimin. "Reaching Out to Their Cultures: Building Communication with Asian-American Families." Retrieved May 3, 2001, from <http://eric-web.tc.columbia.edu/pathways/asian_pacific/cultures.html>.

Silva, V., C. Boyd, and R. Porter. "Teaching English to Brazilian Students." *ESL Magazine,* September/October 1999, 26–28.

Sloper, D., and L. T. Can, eds. *Higher Education in Vietnam: Change and Response.* New York: St. Martin's Press, 1995.

Smirnitsky, A. I. *Russian-English Dictionary.* New York: E. P. Dutton and Company, 1973.

"Socialist Republic of Vietnam." Retrieved June 28, 2001, from <http://www.apcc.com.tw/Vietnam.html>.

Sullivan, P. N. "Sociocultural Influences on Classroom Interactional Styles." *TESOL Journal* 6 (fall 1996): 32–34.

Swan, M., and B. Smith. *Learner English: A Teacher's Guide to Interference and Other Problems.* Cambridge: Cambridge University Press, 1987.

Szwedek, A. J. *Word Order, Sentence Stress, and Reference in English and Polish.* Edmonton, Alberta, Canada: Linguistic Research, 1976.

"Taiwan." Retrieved April 28, 2001, from <http://www.odci.gov/cia/publications/factbook/geos/tw.html>.

"Taiwan." Retrieved May 3, 2001, from <http://cwr.utoronto.ca/cultural/english/taiwan/index.html>.

"Taiwan: Education System." Retrieved May 3, 2001, from <http://www.unesco.org/iau/whed-2000.html>.

Taiwanese Student Association, University of Southern California. "About Taiwan." Retrieved October 5, 2001, from <http://www.usc.edu/dept/TSA/tsa.html>.

Thompson, L. C. *A Vietnamese Grammar.* Seattle: University of Washington Press, 1965.

Tillyer, A. Personal posting to TESL-L list server. Retrieved October 14, 1996, from <http://hunter.cuny.edu/~tesl-l>.

Townsend, C. E., and L. A. Janda. *Common and Comparative Slavic.* Columbus, OH: Slavica Publishers, 1996.

Tran, H. A. "Revisiting Vietnam." (unpublished manuscript)

Valdman, A. "Creole: The National Language of Haiti." Retrieved May 6, 2001, from <http://www.indiana.edu/~creole/creolenatllangofhaiti.html>.

"Venezuela." Retrieved January 7, 2000, from <http://icweb2.loc.gov/frd/cs/cshome.html>.

"Venezuela." Retrieved May 8, 2000, from <http://www.odci.gov.cia/publications/factbook/ve.html>.

"Venezuela." Retrieved February 12, 2001, from <http://www.ibe.unesco.org/international/databanks/wde.htm>.

"Venezuela." Retrieved April 13, 2001, from <http://cwr.utoronto.ca/cultural/english/venezuela>.

"Vietnam: A Country Study." Retrieved June 28, 2001, from <http://memory.loc.gov/frd/cs/vntoc.html>.

"Vietnam: Background Notes." Retrieved July 9, 2001, from <http://www.state.gov/www/background_notes/vietnam_0900_bgn.html>.

"Vietnam: Cultural Profiles Project." Retrieved May 18, 2001, from <http://cwr.utoronto.ca/cultural/english2/Vietnam/vietnamENG.htm>.

"Vietnam: Education System." Retrieved May 18, 2001, from <http://www.unesco.org/iau/whed-2000.html>.

"Vietnam Traditions." Retrieved July 10, 2001, from <http://www.vietnampeople.net/vntraditions>.

Wagner, D. A. "Reading and Believing: Beliefs, Attributions, and Reading Achievement in Moroccan Schoolchildren." *Journal of Educational Psychology* 81 (September 1989): 283-93.

Watson, B., ed. *Basic Writings of Mao Tzu, Hsün Tzu, and Han Fei Tzu.* New York: Columbia University Press, 1967.

Wenzhong, H., and C. Grove. *Encountering the Chinese.* Yarmouth, ME: Intercultural Press, 1999.

Yasin, M. "Arabs Communicating: A Sociolinguistic Approach." *Incorporated Linguist* 20 (summer 1981): 96-99.

Zhang, S., and A. Carrasquillo. "Chinese Parents' Influence on Academic Performance." *New York State Association for Bilingual Education Journal* 1 (summer 1995): 46-53. Retrieved May 3, 2001, from <http://www.ncbe.gwu.edu/miscpubs/nysabe/vol10/nysabe106.htm>.

Zich, A. "Taiwan: The Other China Changes Course." *National Geographic* 184 (November 1993): 2-32.